DIVIDED SPACES

DIVIDED SPACES
Discourse on Social Exclusion and Women in India

Editor
Durga P. Chhetri

GYAN

ISBN : 978-81-212-1225-0
Price : ₹ 750

First Published 2014

Published by

Gyan Publishing House
23, Main Ansari Road, Darya Ganj
New Delhi-110002
Ph. : 23242060, 23261060
Fax : 011-23285914
E-mail: books@gyanbooks.com
Website : www.gyanbooks.com

Laser Typesetting : Rudra Computer Graphics, Delhi
Printed at : G. Print Process, Delhi

Cataloging in Publication Data—DK
Courtesy: D.K. Agencies (P) Ltd. <docinfo@dkagencies.com>

Divided spaces : discourse on social exclusion and women in India / editor, Durga P. Chhetri.
p. cm.
Includes bibliographical references and index.
ISBN 9788121212250

1. Marginality, Social—India—Congresses. 2. Women—India—Social conditions—Congresses. 3. Women in development—India—Congresses. I. Chhetri, Durga P.

DDC 305.560954 23

Contents

Preface

The concept of social exclusion became popular during the 1970s and 1980s and since then it has become central to policy and academic discourse in both western and eastern parts of the globe. With the spread of concept beyond France, where it was first developed, the meanings attached to the concept adapted to reflect prevailing political and cultural contexts. In other words, the understanding of social exclusion and its manifestations varied according to the socio-economic environment and value system. Ruth Levitas has rightly observed that 'The language of social exclusion is no longer the preserve of a temporary specialist unit. It has become commonplace in public discourse, and pervades government policy'. The spread of concept from North to South or from developed to developing nations has been linked to the rise of neo-liberal ideology and individualism from the 1970s. This apart, the concept of exclusion is perceived as less threatening than the concept of poverty and hence is readily acceptable to a range of political positions across the globe. Some scholars are also of the view that the growing popularity of the concept of social exclusion is mainly due to the fact that it has the potential to provide novel insights into the nature, causes and consequences of poverty, deprivation and discrimination and give new direction to remedial policies.

The exclusion discourse in India is closely linked with a wide range of socio-economic inequality. The existence of social pattern based on caste hierarchy systematically excluded the large groups and kept them outside the gamut of social life.

Caste is the most elaborate form of social stratification in Indian society and is also the most exhaustive and obnoxious of all exclusionary systems. Hence, in India, the most rigorous form of exclusion is practiced by the institution of caste, followed by religion, ethnicity and gender. Social exclusion also operate by means of cultural norms that are transmitted through social interactions at the community level and allow the exclusion of those who do not speak, dress or behave in certain ways. Alternatively, exclusion may operate through informal networks that provide or deny access to job and educational opportunities. The contours of the exclusion perpetuated by these variables constantly change with the context, time and space according to a given society's social and cultural norms, customs and rules.

Many social groups in India have been experiencing some form of inequality or social exclusion. The scheduled castes and scheduled tribes, who together make up about a quarter of the population of India are perhaps the most excluded social groups. Their exclusion is reflected in a lack of access to political institutions, to public services, to public places and to income-earning assets, among many others. Across social groups, women face exclusion and discrimination in many areas of life, though their status varies significantly according to their social and ethnic backgrounds. The history of civilisation shows that women were excluded from the public sphere. There are separate spaces for women and men. By tradition also, the public sphere is male domain and women have been confined to their homes (private sphere) and relegated to the background. The persistence and reproduction of women's exclusion is also supported by social norms and religious values. In many communities, traditional barriers still prevent women from going out of their homes to work. Their primary or sole responsibility is confined to household duties, including childcare, cooking food, fetching water, etc. and they have generally been restricted to the roles inside the house, those of wife and mother. This divided spaces based on traditional gender roles led to the further exclusion of women. Hence, the society based on social constructs of proper gender roles and separate spheres marginalised women from participating in activities within the public sector. Though reforms in governance have generated a profusion of new spaces for citizen engagement but men continue to dominate that sphere especially at the top levels of government, business, social institutions and religion.

Divided Spaces: Discourse on Social Exclusion and Women in India makes a unique contribution to the literature on social exclusion and inclusion. Based on the results of UGC-sponsored National Seminar held at Southfield College, Darjeeling, West Bengal, the book explores several forms of social exclusion in the context of India. The book brings together leading scholars from several of the disciplines that have developed concepts of exclusion and various dimensions of exclusion/inclusion. The contributions by different authors show that the social exclusion of any form affects the overall well-being of both individual and the society as a whole. The book will be useful for students and scholars of political science, sociology, geography, anthropology, social psychology and the history. Further, it is hoped that this volume contributes to our understanding of the complexities of social exclusion and provide policymakers with guidance for corrective policies and social inclusion to combat the different forms of social exclusion.

Durga P. Chhetri

Acknowledgements

This book emerged from the UGC-sponsored National Seminar organised by Southfield College in collaboration with the Centre for Women's Studies, North Bengal University; we must therefore thank first the University Grants Commission, ERO (Kolkata) for providing financial support. The Seminar would not have been possible without the generous assistance of a grant by the UGC. We would also like to express our appreciation to the staffs of the Southfield College and Centre for Women's Studies for making available their facilities and for their work in easing the task of organising and running the Seminar.

In the process of editing and in translating from a collection of papers to a book, we have been forced to leave out some of the papers presented in the Seminar and hence this volume includes only the twelve selected papers. The editor would like to take the opportunity to thank all the contributors for their diligent efforts to respond to our suggestions for revision, submission of their papers on time and most importantly for providing chapters which truly cast new light on issues of social exclusion/inclusion in varied contexts and with new perspectives.

We also wish to acknowledge with much appreciation the many friends and colleagues for their support and encouragement. Last but not the least our special thanks are due to Gyan Publishing House for bringing out the book in its present form.

Abbreviations

BJP	:	Bharatiya Janta Party
BPL	:	Below Poverty Line
CEO	:	Chief Executive Officer
CII	:	Confederation of Indian Industries
DRC	:	Democratic Republic of Congo
DFID	:	Department for International Development
EEVFAM	:	Extrajudicial Execution Victims Family Association Manipur
EC	:	European Commission
EU	:	European Union
GAD	:	Gender and Development
GEM	:	Gender Empowerment Measure
GDI	:	Gender Development Index
GII	:	Gender Inequality Index
GoI	:	Government of India
GP	:	Gram Panchayat
GVSA	:	Gun Victims' Survivors Association
HDI	:	Human Development Index
HIV	:	Human Immunodeficiency Virus
HRLN	:	Human Rights Law Network
HSRB	:	High Risk Sexual Behavior
ICDS	:	Integrated Child Development Service
IDS	:	Institute of Development Studies
IILS	:	International Institute for Labour Studies
ILO	:	International Labour Organisation
IP	:	Intermediate Panchayat
IRDSO	:	Integrated Rural Development Social Organisation

KDF	: Kerala Dalit Federation
KDMF	: Kerala Dalit Mahila Federation
MGNREGS	: Mahatma Gandhi National Rural Employment Guarantee Scheme
MGSN	: Manipur Gun Survivors Network
MHA	: Ministry of Home Affairs
NCEUS	: National Commission for Enterprises in the Unorganised Sector
NGO	: Non-Governmental Organisation
NRHM	: National Rural Health Mission
NRI	: Non Resident Indian
NSS	: National Sample Survey
NSSO	: National Sample Survey Organisation
ODPM	: Office of the Deputy Prime Minister
OECD	: Organisation for Economic Cooperation and Development
PRI	: Panchayati Raj Institution
PSU	: Public Sector Unit
RIMS	: Regional Institute of Medical Sciences
RMK	: Rashtriya Mahila Kosh
RSS	: Rashtriya Sewyamsevak Sangh
SATP	: South Asia Terrorism Portal
SC	: Scheduled Caste
SEP	: Socio-Economic Programme
SGSY	: Swarnajayanti Gram SwarozgarYojana
SHG	: Self-Help Group
ST	: Scheduled Tribes
STEP	: Supporting to Training and Employment for Women
UGC	: University Grants Commission
UK	: United Kingdom
UN	: United Nations
UNDP	: United Nations Development Programme
UNESCO	: United Nations Educational, Scientific and Cultural Organisation
US	: United States
VHP	: Vishwa Hindu Parishad
WEP	: Women's Economic Programme
WHO	: World Health Organisation
WID	: Women in Development
ZP	: Zilla Panchayat

List of Tables

List of Tables

List of Figures

List of Contributors

Anil Rajak is an Assistant Professor in Political Science at Kaliyaganj College, West Bengal.

Deepika Rose Alex is a Research Scholar at Tata Institute of Social Sciences, Mumbai, India.

Gangotri Chakraborty is a Professor and Head of Department of Law at University of North Bengal, Siliguri, West Bengal.

Kaustav Chakraborty is an Assistant Professor in the Department of English at Southfield College, Darjeeling, West Bengal

Pallav Mukhopadhyay is an Assistant Professor of Journalism and Mass Communication at the West Bengal State University, Barasat, West Bengal.

Pawan Gurung is an Assistant Professor in Political Science at Southfield College, Darjeeling, West Bengal.

Priyanka Nandi is a researcher at Pratichi Institute, Pratichi Trust, India.

Raghunath Ghosh is presently a Professor of Philosophy and Ex-Dean, Faculty of Arts, Commerce and Law, University of North Bengal at University of North Bengal, Siliguri, West Bengal.

Samrat Sinha is an Assistant Professor and Assistant Director, Centre for Study of Political Violence, Jindal School of International Affairs, O.P. Jindal Global University, Sonipat, Haryana

Sandip Kumar Ghatak is Associate Professor in Political Science at Asonsol Girls' College, Burdwan, West Bengal.

Shelly Parul Bhadwal is a Research Scholar in the Department of English and Cultural Studies at Punjab University, Chandigarh.

Upasana Mahanta is an Assistant Professor and Assistant Director, Centre for Women, Law and Social Change, Jindal Global Law School, O.P. Jindal Global University, Sonipat, Haryana.

1

Introduction

Durga P. Chhetri

Social exclusion has become one of the important themes in contemporary social policy debates in both the developed and developing countries. It has become central to policy and academic discourse in Western Europe and increasingly in other parts of the globe. As far as the use of the term social exclusion is concerned, it arose in Europe and more particularly in France, in the wake of prolonged and large-scale unemployment and the failure of the welfare state. Silver (1994) is of the opinion that economic restructuring in North American and European countries since the mid-1970s has given rise to such terms as 'social exclusion', 'new poverty' and the 'underclass' to describe the consequent negative effects on the more vulnerable populations in these countries. The coining of the term 'social exclusion' is however attributed to Rene Lenoir who was then Secretary of State for Social Action in the Chirac Government in France. Lenoir in his 1974 publication titled *Les Exclus, un Francais sur Dix* (The excluded, one Frenchman in ten) estimated that 'the excluded' made up one-tenth of the French population; the mentally and the physically handicapped, suicidal people, aged invalids, abused children, drug addicts, delinquents, single parents, multi-problem households, marginal, asocial persons, and other 'social misfits'. When Lenoir spoke of *"Les Exclus"*, he was referring to population groups that were unable to find a place in the salary nexus and whose rights to social citizenship were thus limited or, at least, not recognised. As increasing numbers of people were unemployed and hence excluded from the salary relationship, the search for ways of compensating individuals and groups in precarious labour market conditions began. Over time this has involved the individualisation of social protection in the context of globalisation and increasing labour flexibility.

The concept of social exclusion is not a new one. The historical roots of the concept of social exclusion go back as far as Plato. Plato in his work ranks people of city-state in three specialised classes, the ruler (perfect guardians), the soldiers (auxiliaries) and the producing class (which Plato calls farmers). He insisted on a strict and exclusive division of functions – as guardian must dedicate themselves to ruling and the producers should be excluded from any role in the political life of the state -which means that most of the population are excluded from the political order. The slaves, resident aliens and women were completely excluded as they did not possess political rights nor any social rights.

The process of exclusion continued in the middle ages and between twelfth and nineteenth centuries. During this period, the socially excluded were those people considered unacceptable by the church (Allard, 1973). This group included killers, thieves, the poverty-stricken (known as paupers), certain occupations such as butchers, decorators, mercenaries, etc., women, the physically and mentally handicapped, the elderly, the prostitutes, the beggars, etc.

While the concept's historical roots can be traced back to Plato, the theoretical roots of social exclusion however lie in classical sociology. In the work of Max Weber, the idea referred to the ways in which groups can, through a process of 'social closure', secure and maintain privilege at the expense of those different from their own members (Berting and Villain-Gandossi, 2001). The underlying concern with social integration and cohesion has been identified with the theoretical stance of Emile Durkheim and Robert Merton (Levitas, 1998; Born and Jensen, 2002). Daly and Saraceno (2002) are of the view that modern usage of term social exclusion is however more political than sociological in origin. It is usually traced to France, where it was deployed in the 1970s and 1980s to refer to a range of marginalised groups who had fallen through the net of the French social insurance system (Evans, 1998).

The 'social exclusion' now became the fashionable terminology. Ruth Levitas (2005) observed 'The language of social exclusion is no longer the preserve of a temporary specialist unit. It has become commonplace in public discourse, and pervades government policy'. The idea of social exclusion has been rapidly and enthusiastically adopted across the European Union (EU), decentring discourses around poverty. European interest in social exclusion grew in large part from debates surrounding the EU's antipoverty programmes. In 1989, the Council of Ministers of Social Affairs of the then European Community passed a resolution to fight 'social exclusion' and to foster integration and a 'Europe of Solidarity'. Similarly, the European Commission's 1994 White Paper, "Growth, Competitiveness, Employment' called for fighting exclusion and 'the poverty which so degrades men and women and splits society in two'. The British government also created the cross-ministerial Social Exclusion Unit in 1998. Today, most of the European countries like France, Denmark, Germany, Italy, Portugal and Belgium have introduced new institution to take action on social exclusion (Kronaeur, 1993; EC Commission 1994, 1992, 1991; Room *et al*, 1992; Yepez del Castillo, 1993). There is also interest in the concept of social exclusion in the international arena, the documents that emerged from both the World Summit on Social Development (1995) and the Fourth World Conference on Women (1996) talk of 'inclusive' societies and the need for social 'inclusion', as distinct from the eradication of poverty. In fact, since the Social Summit in 1994, there has been increasing attention paid to the usefulness of the concept to concerns with poverty, inequality and social justice in the developing country context by, among others, the Institute of International Labour Studies, the Asian Development Bank, and the Inter-American Development Bank. The Organisation for Economic Cooperation and Development (OECD, 1997) and the World Bank have also embraced social exclusion/inclusion.

This gradual rise in popularity of the social exclusion concept has been attributed mainly to two important reasons:

firstly its political appeal and secondly of neo-liberal ideology. It has been argued that social exclusion is perceived as less threatening than poverty and its semantic flexibility allows it to be acceptable to a range of political leaderships. Furthermore, social exclusion is perceived, potentially, as a political concept of great strength and appeal, enabling 'a better understanding of the politics of growth and the fact that the politicians were using it reflected their greater sensitivity to the great changes occurring in the world' (Gore and Figueiredo, 1997).

Secondly, its emergence has also been linked to the rise of neo-liberal ideology and individualism from the 1970s. More generally, the shift from a poverty discourse to the discourse of social exclusion in the EU has been linked to the rise of neo-liberal ideology and the culture of the individual from the 1970s onwards (Veit-Wilson, 1998; Byrne, 1999; Levitas, 2005; Gough and Eisenschitz, 2006). Gough and Eisenschitz (2006) argue that within neo-liberal political economies, the notion of poverty as 'a misfortune occasioned by the vagaries of the market' has been superseded by the concept of social exclusion understood as detachment from social life in general and the labour market in particular. For these writers, this shift is linked in turn to a critique of universalist welfare state policies portrayed within neo-liberalism as: 'expensive and wasteful, as a disincentive to provide for one's self, as nationally-centrist and dictatorial and as sapping individuals' enterprise and independence and limiting their choice'.

In addition, its popularity may in part be attributable to a belief that the concept of social exclusion offers an original perspective on the social world. Understood as multi-dimensional, it has the potential to provide new insights into the nature, causes and consequences of poverty, deprivation, inequalities and discrimination and give new direction to remedial policies.

As a result of its popularity, the theory and concept of social exclusion though originated in developed countries, have been applied extensively to developing countries. The International Institute for Labour Studies has played a key role in introducing the idea of social exclusion into the developing country debate. The understandings of social exclusion and its manifestations however, varied according to the socio-economic environment, region and value system. In higher-income countries, "social exclusion" tends to be associated with processes of social disqualification and from economical and social problems that affect urban areas, many of whom have had previously better living conditions. In the definition of UK's Social Exclusion Unit, "*Social exclusion is a shorthand term for what can happen when people or areas suffer from a combination of linked problems such as unemployment, poor skills, low incomes, poor housing, high crime environments, bad health and family breakdown*" (Blair, 1998). By contrast, social exclusion south of the Equator has a significantly different setting. In most areas suffering from social exclusion, its population has never had acceptable living conditions. Therefore, in developing nations, social exclusion has to be measured from the viewpoint of considering what would be a basic standard of living (Sposati, 2000). Establishing the basic standard of life implies defining what needs are considered basic and universal according to a collective ethic of life.

Furthermore, social exclusion in developed countries is mostly directed towards minorities (the poor, immigrants) (Byrne, 2005) while in developing countries it occurs to the majority at the bottom of the social pyramid (see also Sen, 2000; Saith, 2001). Gore and Figueiredo (1997) also observe that the 'exclusion' is very much associated with long-term unemployment, the loss of rights associated with work and the welfare state in industrialised states, whereas 'social exclusion' is very much related to the process of labour market formation in developing states. He further notes that in such "fragile" societies, it is not only closely associated to social rights, but also to the enforcement of civil and political rights.

Notwithstanding its variation in understanding in the context of socio-economics and regions, the concept of social exclusion was judged in the main by the ILLS to be relevant both in developed and developing nations. The analytical potential of the concept was recognised, perhaps most significantly, in a note prepared by the IILS for the ILO's 1997 Conference on overcoming social exclusion:

'Social exclusion complements traditional poverty analyses by illuminating the multi-dimensional aspects of deprivation and their interrelationships; the dynamics of social disadvantage; the processes of impoverishment; the role of institutions and rights in generating - or alleviating - deprivation in the process of economic growth' (IILS, 1998).

There are also major questions of relevance in country contexts and regions where the great majority of a population are living in severe poverty or where there is formalised and deeply entrenched exclusion through apartheid and caste systems for instance. Moreover, at a "Policy Forum on Social Exclusion" organised by the IILS in 1996, and bringing together academics and representatives from governments and international agencies, concerns were raised about the political and ideological implications of the increasing prominence of the concept of social exclusion in development policies:

'The great danger of the deployment of the notion of social exclusion was that it was being politically used to make "real, nasty, genuine, poverty" invisible as it became hidden under the umbrella of social exclusion... in the immediate post-colonial situations exclusion had been a broad screen, a curtain, which hid problems of desperate destitution... it was important that social exclusion did not become a "blaming label", which was used to make the poor responsible for their predicament, as had happened with the term "underclass" in the USA' (Gore and Figueiredo, 1997).

However, the limitations of applying a concept developed in the industrialised nations of the northern hemisphere with well developed welfare systems, to nation states with weak governance, minimal welfare provision, largely informal economies and a majority of the population living in extreme poverty, have been pointed out. More generally, the danger that 'exclusion' may be used as a screen to hide extreme poverty and as a blaming label to make the poor responsible for their condition has also been recognised.

What is Social Exclusion?

Despite the increasing use of the term, there is no single universally acceptable definition of social exclusion and the term is used with a variety of definitions in mind. For some, social exclusion is merely a new way to refer to existing concepts such as poverty or unemployment (Levitas, 1997; Paugam, 1993). On the other hand, a number of commentators have adopted a broader definition centred on a notion of 'integration', rather than a sole concern with the distribution of resources. Hence, there is a considerable debate about the precise meaning of the term social exclusion (Evans, Paugham and Prelis, 1995; Atkinson, 1998; Klasen, 1998). The multiple, often contradictory, connotation and synonyms of exclusion transform it into an "essentially contested concept" in that the proper use of it 'inevitably involves endless disputes (Gallie, 1956). Social exclusion is a "contested idea" (Hills, 2002) and is polysemic (Silver, 1994-6; De Haan, 1997; Sen, 2000; Kabeer, 2000; Peace, 2001; Jackson, 1999; Room, 1999) in that it has many meanings. One European Union document conceded that "it is difficult to come up with a simple definition" (EU Commission, 1992). Similar conclusion has been arrived at the recent review of sociological theories of exclusion where the observers agree on only one point i.e. the impossibility of having a single, simple criterion with which to define exclusion. The numerous surveys and reports on exclusion all reveal the profound helplessness of the expert and responsible officials.

There are, therefore, many definitions of social exclusion by many social scientists. Social scientist Ruth Levitas describes the process of developing an agreed measure of social exclusion as 'an ongoing struggle'. According to Duffy (1995), social exclusion is concerned with the 'inability to participate effectively in economic, social, and cultural life and, in some characteristics, alienation and distance from mainstream society'. Room (1995) has added a new dimension to the discussion by couching the issue of social exclusion in a rights-based language when he defines social exclusion as the 'denial or non-realisation of civil, political, and social rights of citizenship'. The approach of exclusion developed by Room has great affinity with the capability approach developed by Amartya Sen which calls for efforts to ensure that people have equal access to basic capabilities such as the ability to be healthy, well-fed, housed, integrated into the community, participate in community and public life, and enjoy social bases of self-respect (Sen, 1992; 1999).

A definition of the United Nations Development Programme attempts to include social exclusion in both developed and developing countries. Social exclusion is defined as lack of recognition of basic rights, or where there is recognition, lack of access to political and legal systems necessary to realise the rights (Burchardt, *et al.*, 2002). An European Commission document, 'Observatory on National Policies to Combat Social Exclusion, Report of 1992' defined social exclusion "in relation to social rights of citizens - to a certain basic standard of living and to participation in the major social and occupational opportunities of the society" (Gore, *et al.*, 1995).

Beall and Piron (2005) offer an abbreviated working definition of social exclusion as 'a process and a state (deriving from exclusionary relationships based on power) that prevents individuals or groups from full participation in social, economic and political life and from asserting their rights'. Stewart *et al.* (2006) defines it as a concept 'used to describe a group, or groups, of people who are excluded from the normal activities of their society, in multiple ways'. Both these definitions probably derive from the EU definition of social exclusion in the mid-1990s as a 'process through which individuals or groups are wholly or partially excluded from full participation in the society in which they live' (Laderchi *et al.*, 2003). Beall and Clert (2000) point out that the reason for this wide and less than rigorous application is that "in its colloquial and political usage, the concept of social exclusion has tremendous resonance and is very compelling".

Dimensions of Exclusion

Social exclusion is a multifaceted phenomenon and is considered by many to be both an outcome and a process. It is driven by a complex interplay of demographic, economic, social and behavioural factors, which means that people from certain backgrounds and experiences are disproportionately likely to be socially excluded: 'The risks of social exclusion are not evenly shared but concentrated in the poorest individuals and communities' (ODPM, 2004). Social exclusion processes occur through the interaction of many dimensions which involve social, economic, political, cultural and spatial exclusion as well as lack of access to specific areas such as information, medical provision, housing, policing, security, etc. These dimensions are seen to interrelate and reinforce each other: overall they involve exclusion in what are seen as the 'normal' areas of participation of full citizenship (Percy-Smith, 2000). Burchardt *et al.* (1999) have identified five dimensions of social exclusion in terms of the 'normal activities' in which it is important that citizens participate. These dimensions are as follows:

1. Consumption activity: relates to traditional measures of poverty.
2. Savings activity: includes pensions, savings, home ownership.
3. Production activity: defined in terms of 'engaging in an economically or socially valued activity, such as paid work, education or training, retirement . . . or looking after a family'.
4. Political activity: defined as 'engaging in some collective effort to improve or protect the immediate or wider social or physical environment'.
5. Social activity: defined as 'engaging in significant social interaction with family, or friends, and identifying with a cultural group or community'.

Sen (2000) presents two types of exclusion that are distinguishable depending upon the nature and the context of exclusion. They are active and passive exclusion. Active exclusion, according to Sen, is the fostering of exclusion on some groups from equal opportunity through deliberate means. When, for example, immigrants or refugees are not given a usable political status, it is an active exclusion. Passive exclusion, on the other hand, is explained as the exclusion which results from a set of circumstances. When the deprivation comes about through social processes in which there is no deliberate attempt to exclude, the exclusion can be seen as a passive kind.

Percy-Smith (2000), on the other hand, identifies seven dimensions of social exclusion. These include, economic, social, political, neighbourhood, individual, spatial and group (Table 1.1).

Table 1.1: Dimensions of Social Exclusion

Dimension	*Indicators*
Economic	Long-term unemployment Casualisation and job insecurity Workless households Income poverty
Social	Breakdown of traditional households Unwanted teenage pregnancies Homelessness Crime Disaffected youth
Political	Disempowerment Lack of political rights Low registration of voters Low voter turnout Low levels of community activity Alienation/lack of confidence in political processes Social disturbance/disorder
Neighbourhood	Environmental degradation Decaying housing stock Withdrawal of local services Collapse of support networks
Individual	Mental and physical ill health Educational underachievement/low skills Loss of self-esteem/confidence
Spatial	Concentration/marginalization of vulnerable groups
Group	Concentration of above characteristics in particular groups: elderly, disabled, ethnic minorities

Source: Janie Percy-Smith, 2000.

In an economic sense, exclusion refers to the inability to be engaged in gainful employment which yields enough income to satisfy basic requirements. Hence, the economic approach to exclusion is concerned with questions of income and production and access to goods and services (or commodity bundles) from which some people are excluded and others are not. They may be excluded from income and livelihood, from employment and the labour market and from the satisfaction of such basic needs as housing/ shelter, health and education (Bhalla and Lapeyre, 1997).

Among the many indicators, employment is very important in distinguishing economic exclusion from others. Sen (1975) defined the employment concept in terms of three aspects: income, production, and recognition. It was implicitly assumed that employment is a means of alleviating poverty. The economic approach to exclusion seems to cover mainly the first two aspects. The third refers to the idea that 'employment gives a person the recognition of being engaged in something worth his while' (Sen, 1975). The economic dimension of exclusion has a number of different aspects to it that go beyond unemployment. It certainly includes length of unemployment and households in which no working-age adults are in employment, but it also includes other changes affecting the labour market such as casualisation, decreasing job security and fragile attachment to the labour market.

In a social term, exclusion is equal to denigration, the loss of respectability and dignity in one's own eyes, as well as those of others. The social dimension of social exclusion includes the breakdown of traditional households, the rise in the numbers of unwanted teenage pregnancies, homelessness, crime and disaffected youth. Other social dimensions to be considered include participation in decision-making of certain social groups as well as marginalisation of such disadvantaged categories as women and ethnic groups. Bhalla and Lapeyre (1997) outlines three main categories of the social aspects of exclusion: (i) access to social services (such as health and education); (ii) access to the labour market (precariousness of employment as distinct from low pay); and (iii) the opportunity for social participation and its effects on the social fabric (greater crime, juvenile delinquency, homelessness, and so on).

In political sense, exclusion implies a lack of access to sources of power and the inability to participate meaningfully in decision-making processes. This form of exclusion concerns more on the denial of particular human and political rights to certain groups of the population. The UNDP (1992) notes these rights as: personal security, rule of law, freedom of expression, political participation and equality of opportunity. Marshall (1964) has classified these rights into three main categories: civil (freedom of expression, rule of law, or right to justice); political (right to participate in the exercise of political power); and socio-economic (personal security and equality of opportunity, right to minimum health care and to unemployment benefits, and so on). Hence, an individual may be excluded from having either of these rights because of their immigration status or by not registering to vote or due to inertia, apathy, transience or the wish to evade officialdom. This becomes obvious that the political dimension of exclusion involves the notion that the State, which grants basic rights and civil liberties, is not a neutral agency but a vehicle of the dominant classes in a society. It may, therefore, discriminate between insiders and outsiders and may exclude some social groups and include others (see Rodgers, 1994).

Other forms of political activity include participation in community fora of various kinds such as tenants' organisations, school governing bodies, pressure groups, service user groups, and so on. All of these bodies will have some impact on decision-making and the quality of local life.

The neighbourhood dimension of social exclusion includes the indicators of environmental degradation, a decaying housing stock, the withdrawal of local services (e.g. shops, public transport), increasingly overstretched public services and the collapse of local support networks (related to the political aspects of social exclusion, namely low levels of participation in community and voluntary activities). All these indicators show that neighbourhood dimension of social exclusion is clearly related to both the social and spatial aspects.

Individual dimension of social exclusion includes the different types of problems an individual faces in a day-to-day life. For instance, the increasing levels of physical and mental ill health, educational underachievement and failure to acquire or update skills, and low self-esteem are all indicators of individual dimension of exclusion. Walton's (2000) studies on educational under achievement and low levels of skills, Moran and Simpkins' (2000) on the relationship between health status and social exclusion and Jane Mathieson' *et al.* (2008) on health inequalities are all based on the individual dimension of social exclusion.

Under the spatial dimension of exclusion, the area itself is defined as disadvantaged, irrespective of the characteristics of the individuals who live there, and becomes subject to further exclusionary process (e.g. withdrawal of local services). In this type of dimension, the large numbers of socially excluded individuals scattered throughout the rest of the population become largely invisible. However, social exclusion might also affect localities not because of the concentration of socially excluded individuals and households within the population but because of the nature of the area itself (Percy-Smith, 2000).

According to Percy-Smith (2000), certain groups are at greater risk of social exclusion either because they differ in some way from the dominant population or because of their position within society. The individuals or groups who, to some degree, do not accept the values, norms or lifestyle of mainstream society are more vulnerable if they are also affected by one or more of the other dimensions of social exclusion. Nationality, ethnicity, language and religion are obvious aspects of group difference. Secondly, due to their circumstances, some groups that are discriminated and denied the equal opportunities, are particularly vulnerable. Examples of such groups include elderly people dependent on state benefits, lone parents and young people not in education or training and without a job.

Cultural exclusion is another dimension of social exclusion. For Will Kymlicka, cultural exclusion occurs when the culture of a group, including its language, religion or traditional customs, are denigrated or suppressed by the State. Conversely, cultural inclusion refers to the public recognition, accommodation and support to the culture, language, religion, customs and life styles of a group. According to Rajeev Bhargava (2004), cultural exclusion occurs either when one group in society persistently misrecognises, denigrates, humiliates or suppresses another cultural group or when some members of a cultural group suppress, denigrate or misrecognise members of a sub-culture of their own group. Within cultural aspect of exclusion, comes the religious exclusion. By religion-related exclusion Bhargava mean to broadly cover two forms of exclusions. Firstly, the exclusion of people from the domain of religious liberty and equality which he describes as the exclusion from religion, or more simply, religious exclusion. Secondly, the exclusion of people from the wider, non-religious domain of liberty and equality (citizenship rights) which he called religion-based exclusion and it occurs when a person's religion or religious identity is seen to be sufficient ground for excluding him/her from the legal, economic and political benefits/rights available more generally.

Social Exclusion and Poverty

The term 'social exclusion' originated in the social policy of the French socialist governments of the 1980s and was used to refer to a disparate group of people living on the margins of society and, in particular, without access to the system of social insurance (Room, 1995; Jordan, 1997; Burchardt *et al.,* 1999). In social sciences literature, there is general agreement on the core features of social exclusion, its principles indicators, and the way it relates to poverty and inequality (Buvinic, 2005). Some writers have commented that the term social exclusion was preferred to the term poverty in European circles because of the difficulties on the part of some member states at that time to apply the term poverty to their own countries (see Lee and Murie, 1999). Indeed the EU poverty programmes which had been in existence since 1974 were brought to an abrupt halt in 1994 when the Council of Europe rejected a new poverty programme. Since then, social exclusion, rather than poverty, has been the main focus of EU's social policy and, furthermore, the approach to social exclusion has, in practice, reflected a more limited concern with labour market exclusion (Geyer, 1999). The concept of social exclusion is collapsed into a concept of poverty, either as social deprivations or else as social processes leading to poverty. Gore and Figueiredo (1997), for instance, in their efforts to resolve how social exclusion should be differentiated from poverty, argue that the former refers to processes of impoverishment, versus categorisations of "the poor". Similarly, Laderchi *et al.* (2003) explicitly treats social exclusion as one of four poverty approaches. Gore (1995) on the other hand clarifies that the early French debates of the 1970s and 1980s did not necessarily equate social exclusion with poverty as such, but with processes of social disintegration. The concept only became more closely equated with poverty in the early

1990s after the European Commission defined social exclusion in relation to a certain basic standard of living, among other factors. Room (1999) also notes that the multi-dimensional, dynamic and community aspects often promoted as the novelties of the social exclusion approach all existed in the "classic" studies on poverty. According to him, the more original element of social exclusion is found in its emphasis on relational issues (inadequate social participation, lack of social integration and lack of power), versus the primary emphasis of poverty on distributional issues.

Many authors however are of the view that one can conceive of social exclusion outside poverty. This was mentioned on many occasions in the summary of the IILS debate in Gore and Figueiredo (1997) and in the IDS workshop summarised in O'Brien *et al.* (1997). In both cases, it was recognised that it is possible to be poor and not socially excluded, but also to be socially excluded and not poor, with examples taken from the Indian caste system, or from classic cases of discriminated minority groups specialising in trade and commerce, such as the Chinese in South-east Asia or the Jews in Europe for many centuries. In OECD countries, Atkinson (1998) notes that poverty does not necessarily always go together with social exclusion. Levitas (2006) points out that, even in the UK, paid work may in some cases limit social "inclusion" or that "economic inactivity" does not, in itself, necessarily lead to exclusion from social relations.

Matt Barnes (2005) has attempted to draw distinctions between poverty, deprivation and social exclusion. In his schema (see Table 1.2), and in contrast to poverty and deprivation, the concept of social exclusion 'evokes a multi-dimensional notion of participation in society, involving a combination of physical, material, relational and societal needs, over a period of time' (Barnes, 2005). This approach echoes Estivill's (2003) suggestion that: 'if poverty is a photograph, exclusion is a film'.

This sharp juxtaposition of poverty and social exclusion is however criticized by many scholars. First of all, the distinction between static poverty and dynamic exclusion may be questioned. Silver (1994) argues that exclusion is not only a dynamic process, but it also points to the outcomes of historical developments. It may, therefore, very well be regarded as a

Table 1.2: Comparison of Poverty, Deprivation and Social Exclusion

Poverty	*Deprivation*	*Social Exclusion*
One-dimensional	Multi-dimensional	Multi-dimensional
Physical needs	Physical needs Material needs	Physical needs Material needs Societal participation
Distributional	Distributional	Distributional Relational
Static	Static	Dynamic
Individual Household	Individual Household	Individual Household Community

Source: Barnes (2005).

static condition, or a state, sometimes referred to as 'being socially excluded' or 'excludedness'. Poverty, on the other hand, can be regarded in a dynamic fashion, as happens in empirical research on the process of becoming poor and terminating periods of poverty (see e.g., Goodin *et al.*, 1999; Jäntti and Danziger, 2000).

Alcock (1991) also uses a wider approach of the poverty concept and tends to regard poverty as a multidimensional phenomenon. At first sight, poverty, thus conceived, may even seem to be synonymous with social exclusion. However, some authors note an essential difference: although deficiencies other than financial shortages are included in the broad definition of poverty, the reason for those deficiencies is mainly financial (see Nolan and Whelan, 1996). In the case of social exclusion, by contrast, there may be other causes than lack of financial means, such as illness, old age, neighbourhood factors, and discrimination. Thus, one might be socially excluded without being financially poor (Burchardt *et al.,* 2002; Uunk and Vrooman, 2001; Saraceno, 2001; see also Abrahamson, 1997; Room, 1997; De Koning and Mosley, 2001).

One can conclude from the above discussion that the concepts of poverty and social exclusion are not synonymous. Social exclusion encompasses more than just poverty, although poverty is frequently an inevitable characteristic of most of the socially excluded. The concept of social exclusion contributes to an understanding of the nature of poverty and helps identify the causes of poverty that may have been otherwise neglected. It also encourages deeper thinking on the subject of social policies for reducing poverty. In contrast to poverty which focuses on individuals or households, social exclusion is primarily concerned with the relationship between the individual and society, and the dynamics of that relationship. Hence, poverty is not necessarily identical to exclusion. People may suffer from deprivation, but if they are not in a position to relate their own circumstances to conditions in which other people live, there is no reason for them to feel excluded.

Referring to this more recent heritage, Levitas (2006) mentions the difficulty in distinguishing social exclusion from poverty in the UK context, which is "sometimes masked by references to 'poverty and social exclusion' as an inseparable dyad". Pantazis *et al.* (2006) also points out that the 1999 Poverty and Social Exclusion Survey for the UK proposed impoverishment as one of four dimensions for measuring social exclusion, alongside labour market exclusion, service exclusion and exclusion from social relations. Levitas (2006) adds that most of the indicators proposed by the EU Social Protection Committee in 2001 relate either to income or to labour-market position, while those that were eventually adopted widen the scope to include deprivations in education, housing and health. Notably, all these attempts at quantification include notions of poverty (income and multidimensional) in their operational definitions. In a workshop convened by the Institute of Development Studies in Sussex in 1997, de Haan thought that, despite its overlap with the concept of poverty, the concept of social exclusion could be useful because it focused on processes and because it was multidimensional in nature. However, he was doubtful whether these aspects made it different from poverty, particularly in light of recent debates on poverty that were concerned with similar types of issues. The distinction is only clear if one adopts a narrow view of poverty (cited in O'Brien *et al.*, 1997). Saith (2001) makes a similar point and, in order to avoid a relabeling of poverty studies, she emphasises the processual theme of social exclusion. Bhalla and Lapeyre (1997) argue that "social exclusion overlaps with poverty broadly defined, but goes beyond it by explicitly embracing the relational as well as distributional aspects of poverty".

Some attempts have been made to avoid explicitly associating social exclusion with poverty, although these nonetheless tend to use an idea of norms to situate exclusion within a social context. For instance, Beall and Piron (2005) offer a working definition of social exclusion as "a process and a state (deriving from exclusionary relationships based on power) that prevents individuals or groups from full participation in social, economic and political life and from asserting their rights". Stewart *et al.* (2006) define it as a concept "used to describe a group, or groups, of people who are excluded from the normal activities of their society, in multiple ways". Both these definitions are probably influenced by the EU definition of social exclusion in the mid-1990s as a "process through which individuals or groups are wholly or partially excluded from full participation in the society in which they live" (cited in Laderchi *et al.*, 2003).

Contextualising Social Exclusion in India

In India, the process of social exclusion is a not a new phenomenon and is particularly visible given that the country has traditionally been characterised as a heterogeneous society with diverse culture, religion, caste and unequal distribution of income. There are many small ethnic groups quite heterogeneous, with households of different income levels living side by side and sharing the same public space. This heterogeneity provided a social difference between individuals of different cultural and socio-economic backgrounds. The presence of various ethnic groups without stable employment or educational attainment and better opportunities for social mobility are in most disadvantageous and vulnerable position. Further, compounding the country's inequality, some social groups and individuals are more likely to remain stuck in poverty. A significant number of extremely poor people with low education levels remain at the bottom of the income distribution, largely untouched by economic development. Poverty has become increasingly concentrated among populations with specific characteristics: indigenous people; children and youth and the unemployed; people employed in agriculture or rural areas; and people employed in the informal sector. Hence, in the Indian context, exclusion revolves around institutions that discriminate, isolate, shame and deprive subordinate groups on the basis of identities like caste, religion and gender (Thorat and Newman, 2007). Unlike in West, in contemporary Indian society, four different bases of social exclusion can be identified. The first is the caste-based social exclusion under which groups, identified as 'low' caste in the hierarchy of Hindu society have been placed at disadvantaged social, economic and political position through ages. Second is the cultural and spatial isolation under which certain ethnic groups (tribes) kept away from the mainstream and thus got socially excluded from many important spheres of the modern Indian economy. Thirdly, the religious exclusion of certain groups including women who have been excluded from the domain of religious liberty and freedom. Finally, the universally observed case of gender-based discrimination and exclusion.

Caste-based Exclusion

Caste-based exclusion is a ubiquitous feature of the Indian society. The Hindu caste system in India and Nepal, as well as caste-like identities in Pakistan, "exclude lowest caste groups from ownership of land and key productive assets and assign them to various forms of labour and services which are considered to be menial, degrading and dirty" (Kabeer, 2006). Historically, the caste system has regulated the social and economic life of the people in India. A caste system is a type of social condition that divides people on the basis of inherited social status and occupation. Shah *et al.* (2006) argue that each caste had a specific place in the hierarchy of social status. The caste system, also known as the Brahmanical system, has regulated the life of the people of India over centuries, in which the organisational scheme is based on the division of people into endogamous caste groups and the civil, economic, political and religious rights of each individual caste are ascribed inequality by birth and made hereditary. This system has resulted to the forced exclusion of one caste from the rights of other castes in all sphere of life (Thorat, 2008). Furthermore, 'The caste system prevents common activity and by preventing common activity it has prevented the Hindu from becoming a society with a unified life...... The caste system is infested with the spirit of isolation, and in fact, it makes isolation of one caste from another a matter of virtue' (Ambedkar, 1936). Caste system, according to Ambedkar, denies not only the right to existential dignity to the Bahujans and relegates them a subhuman existence but also denies their right to identity. Both B.R. Ambedkar and Mahatma Jotirao Phule who launched the movement of social revolution called it the Brahmanical ideology which conceived the caste system a 'ideology of exclusion' that moulds a social order based on inequality where no two castes are equal and the divided castes are made to oppose each other.

The rigid caste system in India, therefore, is the root cause and very source of social exclusion. Social hierarchy based on caste system exhibits social discrimination and inequality. As a result, the dalits, untouchables and downtrodden communities were considered to be at the bottom of the Hindu social hierarchy and were not a part of the four-fold 'varna system' comprising Brahmin, Kshatriya, Vaishya and Shudra. They were denied equality before law, equal protection of law and equal opportunities. This apart, the practice of untouchability denied vast multitude of the population access to the very basic human life and also denied the civil and political rights and opportunities for economic mobility.

Ethnicity and Social Exclusion

Ethnicity is another form of group identity which has served as a basis of social exclusion across the world. Race and ethnicity have been identified as 'an important dimension of social cleavage along which processes of social exclusion run throughout Europe' (Cars *et al.*, 1998). In the Indian context also, social exclusion follows largely ethnic lines in the region. The indigenous ethnic group that comes closer to the dalits in terms of exclusion and deprivation are by no means homogenous. Furthermore, the basis of tribal isolation and exclusion is not caste or religion but ethnicity. They suffer from isolation, neglect and exclusion, which cause considerable deprivation and poverty among them (Thorat, 2006a). Unlike caste, the tribes are identified on the basis of certain criteria such as primitive traits, distinct culture, geographical isolation and general backwardness. However, the terms 'scheduled caste' and 'scheduled tribe' are nowhere defined in the Constitution of India. They comprise within them more than four hundred castes and tribes respectively, with large cultural heterogeneity (Singh, 1993; Singh, 1994). This group can make up significant proportions of the population in the country. As per the 2011 Census, the tribal population in India is estimated to be 104.3 million, i.e., 8.6 per cent of the total population of India, classified under 461 different communities. 'Indigenous' ethnic minorities are mostly located in hilly and forest, and difficult geographical areas. They are largely concentrated in the remote, usually upland and mountainous areas of the central and north-eastern parts of the country with poor access to services and with little infrastructure. Many of them are still nomadic or semi-nomadic in their way of life and practised jhum cultivation at high altitudes. For this reason, and also due to years of neglect and exploitation at the hands of the government and other citizens, the Human Development Indicators (HDI) of India's *Adivasi* population are much lower than the HDI of the rest of the population in terms of all parameters (literacy, infant mortality, etc). Poverty is also very high among tribal populations. Studies by Thorat (2006b) show that poverty is highest among the tribals in rural areas despite better access to agricultural land. According to Sen (2000), it is 'active and passive exclusion' affected by development policies of the states and other agents causing land alienation and displacement.

Religion and Social Exclusion

Religion is an integral part of culture. Walter Burkert (1996) opined that there has never been a society without religion. The religion has codified customs into binding source books that predate the whole concept of gender equality and have both legal and the institutional structures to enforce their principles. The different monotheistic religious (Judaism, Christianity, Islam or Hinduism) norms impose partiarchial regimes that disadvantage women. The story of gender in traditionalist cultures and religious is that of the domination of women by men, of women's exclusion from public power and of their subjection to patriachcial power within family (Raday, 2003). Women have been excluded from the hierarchies of canonical power and subjected to male domination within the family. Hence, under most of the monotheistic religious norms, women are not entitled to equality in inheritance, guardianship, custody of children, or division of matrimonial property. Further, in most of the branches of the monotheistic religions, women are not eligible for religious office, and in some, they are limited in their freedom to participate in public life, whether political and economic (Raday, 2003). Today, the use of culture and religion to deny women rights is a global phenomenon rather than specific to one religion. Women are generally excluded from several practices of their own religion. For example, Islam does not permit women to offer prayers in mosques. There are no known women archbishops, Imams or pujaris. Islam, in its most widely practiced forms, has maintained and asserted the validity of all its patriarchal religious norms, including polygamy, the recognition of the husband as the head of the family, unequal inheritance, denial of eligibility for religious office, and in many cases, restrictions of participation in public life. Muslim contexts provide a highly significant example of the power dynamics that actively disempower women because of the growing influence of political Islamists claiming that religion itself legitimizes - even demands - the disempowerment of women.

In Hinduism, there are restrictions on women participation in religious rituals at the time of menstruation. Entry to temples is similarly restricted because their very capacity to menstruate makes their bodies impure for this entire period. In medieval Christendom, ordinary, lay persons had access to God only via the Clergy. Even potentially, salvation was not, therefore, available to everyone (Bhargava, 2004). Further, some segments of Christianity have retained rules that disadvantage women, mandating obedience of a wife to her husband, denying eligibility for religious office, and prohibiting contraception and abortion. This is evident from above-mentioned facts that women's rights have been denied by using culture and religion and women find themselves disadvantaged and marginalised.

Gender based Exclusion

Gender-based exclusion and discrimination is found to be a common phenomenon across the globe. Gender is a widespread basis of social discrimination, the intersection of gender inequality and economic deprivation means that women from poor household represent a particular category of the multiple-disadvantaged. Women and girls face gender discrimination at every stage of their life, starting even before they are born. Women belonging to socially excluded groups face greater challenges. In Indian society, women experience structural exclusion in societies that perceive them as inferior and subordinate to men. Majority of women and girls are at a disadvantage to men and boys in relation to literacy, education, earnings and employment. The imposition of inhuman practices and restrictions like widow burning, enforced widowhood, child marriage has been the means by which social exclusion of women has been maintained. Social exclusion and inequalities are embedded in and structured by Brahmanism in India. Some argued that Brahmanical world view is grounded on the understanding that inequalities are a natural phenomenon. The woman who is considered naturally inferior is bound to suffer exclusion from social, political, economic and religious realms. This totalitarian exclusion relegated women to a subhuman existence (Pradgna, 2010). The brahmanical ideology imposes stringent restrictions on women because purity of women is central to Indian patriarchy, as purity of caste is contingent upon it (Nanda, 2006).

The tribal and *dalit* women suffer from endemic gender and caste discrimination, violence and exploitation and their situation constitutes an extreme case of active exclusion. Pervasive violence against tribal and *dalit* women in India is the core result of gender-based inequalities. They suffered from various forms of violence which include physical assault, verbal abuse, sexual harassment and assault, rape, sexual exploitation, forced prostitution, kidnapping and abduction, forced incarceration and medical negligence regarding female foeticide and infanticide, child sexual abuse and domestic violence from family members. This apart, a disproportionate number of women experience relative poverty in India. The unequal possession of power and ownership of resources result in a greater risk of poverty among women. Women are also more likely to have experienced poverty at some time in their lives (Payne and Pantaziz, 1997), and to suffer recurrent and longer poverty spells (Ruspini, 1998; 2001; DWP, 2003). The UNDP in its reports revealed that in both North and South, poverty all too often wears a female face (UNDP, 1995; 1997). The evidence from the EU and the US also shows that, to varying degrees and with the clearest exception of Sweden, women face a greater risk of poverty than men (Bradshaw *et al.*, 2003; Daly and Rake, 2003). Hence, the majority of women experience poverty in both developing and developed countries alike. Women are overrepresented among people living in poverty and suffer from exclusion from basic education, landownership and employment.

The incidence of poverty among women is further aggravated by the unfriendliness of Indian labour market. Women constitute almost one half of the population, but less than one-third of the workforce. Three-fourths of the women workers are in agriculture which is generally low-productivity and low income sector. Only a small percentage of women

Table 1.3: Work Participation Rates by Sex: 1991 and 2001(in per cent)

Census Year	*T/R/U*	*Female*	*Male*	*Persons*
1991	Total	22.27	51.61	37.50
	Rural	26.79	52.58	40.09
	Urban	9.19	48.92	30.16
2001	Total	25.63	51.68	39.10
	Rural	30.79	52.11	41.75
	Urban	11.88	50.60	32.25

Source: Modified from the Report of the Working Group on Empowerment of Women, Planning Commission, Government of India, 2007-2012.

workers are in better paying modern sectors of the Indian economy. In public sector, which provides secure and better paid jobs with social security benefits, only 16 per cent of its employees are women. In the organised sector as a whole - both public and private together - only 20 per cent of workers are women. Only 11 per cent of women workers as against 19 per cent of men have regular jobs (Papola and Sahu, 2012). This gender discrimination present in the labour market contributed to low economic participation of women. According to the

Table 1.4: Gender and Social Exclusion Indicators

	Gender Related Indicators		*2011*
1.	Gender Inequality Index (GII)		0.617
2.	GII Rank out of 146		129
		1996	2006
3.	Gender Related Development Index (GDI)	0.514	0.590
4.	Gender Empowerment Measure (GEM)	0.416	0.497
		2000	2010
5.	Rate of Cognizable crimes against women (per cent)	14.1	18
		2004-06	2007-09
6.	Maternal Mortality Ratio (Per 1,00,000 line births)	254	212
			2011
7.	Male Literacy rate		82.14
8.	Female Literacy rate		65.46
9.	Gender Gap in Literacy		16.68
10.	Proportion of seats held by women in Parliament (per cent)		10.7

Sources: Human Development Report 2011, UNDP (No. 1-2);

Gendering Human Development Indices: Recasting GDI and GEM for India 2009, Ministry of Women and Child Development, GoI and UNDP (No. 3-4);

Crime in India 2000 and 2010, Ministry of Home Affairs, GoI (No. 5); Special Bulletin on Maternal Mortality in India 2007-09, SRS, June 2011 (No. 6);

Census 2001 and Census 2011, Provisional Population Totals Paper 1 of 2011 India series1, Registrar General of India (No. 7-9);

Human Development Report 2011 and Human Development Report 2000, UNDP (No. 10)

estimates of Censuses and NSSO, the women's workforce participation in India is very low as compared to men.

An estimate of the 2001 Census shows that the work participation rate for women was 25.63 per cent in 2001, which is an improvement from 22.27 per cent in 1991. In 2001, work participation rate for women in rural areas was 30.79 per cent as compared to 11.88 per cent in the urban areas (see Table 1.3). In the rural areas, women are mainly involved as cultivators and agricultural labourers while in the urban areas, almost 80 per cent of women workers are working in the unorganised sectors like household industries, petty trades and services, buildings and construction. The NSSO figures, unlike the Census figures provide a more complex picture. It indicates a decline in work participation rates for women between 1993-94 and 1999-2000 from 28.6 per cent to 25.9 per cent. There was an increase again in 2004-05 to 28.7 per cent, and in recent years, there has been a marginal but steady increase in work participation (Sunny, 2007; NCEUS, 2009).

Despite the fact that women face discrimination in many areas of life, improvements is seen in gender-based human development indices, with GDI and GEM showing little improvement from 0.514 to 0.590 and 0.416 to 0.497 respectively. However, crimes committed against women have increased over time. Maternal mortality in India is reported to be 212 per 100,000 live births. This can partly be explained by the widespread poverty and limited health services available for much of the population. In addition to this, educational exclusion is most pronounced among the poorest children, and especially girls. There are large gaps in literacy rate and level of education between male and female. High drop out in school, poor quality of education, discrimination in education, are some of the educational problems faced by girl child. In 2011 (latest census year for which data are available), literacy rate of females was 65.46 per cent compared to 82.14 per cent of males. There was thus a gender gap of 16.68 per cent in literacy. Women have also been excluded from political power and participation in democracies. There are at present only 10.7 per cent of seats in Parliament that are held by women.

Overview of Chapters

This book is intended to provide a broad understanding of social exclusion/inclusion and women in India through a multidisciplinary approach. The opening chapter by Raghunath Ghosh has dealt at length the concepts of social inclusion and exclusion with special reference to women. The author provides a historical understanding of exclusion and inclusion of women in Indian society by citing the example from Manusmriti and other scriptures. Ghosh suggests that the problems of the women can be realised and solved by the women themselves if they are given an opportunity. In order to prevent the women-related evils including their exclusion from the society, women alone should come forward, initiate a leading part and restore their glorious cultural identity. It is possible if they are given constitutional powers.

In her contribution, Gangotri Chakraborty introduces jurisprudential discussion on social exclusion. The concept of social exclusion has the advantage of situating individuals in a social and relational context and the experience of exclusion due to the reasons of poverty, caste, race, gender, etc., is almost universal. According to her, the rapid social and economic changes associated with information age and globalisation have exacerbated and fostered new forms of social exclusion. That, in the society, individuals are continuously in motion either solitary or in community, is evident from the various form of unsettlement, such as geographic mobility, social mobility, economic mobility, political mobility and marital mobility. She concludes that remedies to social exclusion is to provide sufficient levels of capabilities, which in turn, is justice in transition.

Shelly Parul Bhadwal in her essay claims that patriarchal ideology always keeps the women under subjugation and domination. According to her, patriarchy has ever since used it as a tool to hegemonize women in all walks of life. Even in the instances of praise for women, it is the patriarchal order that remains the covert beneficiary. Women, though are professed to be considered as 'Devi', 'Durga', and 'Lakshmi', but their exploitation and exclusion in the name of tradition and culture continue to persist rampantly. Hence, women on the one hand are given a high pedestal within the social framework by associating them with divinity, while on the other hand, it is this very divinity through which women are exiled indoors. They are turned into objects of worship, and at the same time, the household is demarcated as their field of action. In this way, the social exclusion and inclusion of women takes place as a simultaneous event.

Upasana Mahanta and Samrat Sinha in their paper highlighted the problem of conflict induced widowhood in India with reference to the state of Manipur. Women and girls are affected by armed violence in different ways, including direct and indirect conflict violence, and lethal and non-lethal conflict violence. However, like most conflict situations, gendered violence is systematic but typically overshadowed by attention to 'harder' security matters. One of the serious fallouts of the proliferation of armed conflicts, and the high levels of military and civilian casualties, is a large increase in the number of widows in many countries. Widowhood can affect the physical safety, identity and mobility of women and children. It can also affect their access to basic goods and services necessary for survival, and their rights to inheritance, land and property, in addition to the wider impact it has on the community. The problem of conflict induced widowhood in the case of Manipur is an extremely serious one. This is primarily because of an absence of precise or reliable estimates as to the number of persons who have been widowed as a consequence of the long standing armed conflict in the state.

Sandip Ghatak in his essay portrays the situation of tribal community and their exclusion in the Bankura district of West Bengal. The tribal population in our country is excluded from the developmental process which is reflected in respect to a number of development related indicators. The incidence of poverty is very high among the tribes, majority of whom are landless, unemployed and illiterate. As a whole, ST community is excluded from the enjoyment of some of their basic human rights as a human being.

Priyanka Nandi in her paper explores the theories of social exclusion and ideas about development/social progress briefly, in the contexts of political history, variables and hierarchies of power and modernity. She also examines the attempted translation of these ideas into action in India, paying special attention to the confrontations between theory and stereotypical constructs about the developing world, and the diversity of indigenous ideologies on the ground.

Deepika Rose Alex discusses the lives and struggles of Dalit Women as the members of Dalit communities, the most excluded groups in Indian society, as per the caste hierarchy. Her paper explores the experiences of oppression a group of Dalit women activists faces in their relationship with Dalit men, in families and Dalit organisations. The paper asserts that oppressions and negotiation that happens in relationships between Dalit men and women need to be understood in the light of dominant gender ideology, and as an inevitable outcome of intersectional oppression of caste, gender and class. The paper discusses the dominant gender ideology of Kerala, division of spaces as private and public, confining women to the private sphere, which has permeated the Dalit culture gradually.

Kaustav Chakraborty in his paper tries to depict the marginalised reality along with the attempt of historicizing their exclusion in India. Taking the help of Indian Classical Literature, the author also tries to investigate the authenticity of the tag of 'western vice' that is often attached with these women of alternative orientations. The narration has also documented the Indian Queer Movement aiming at the inclusion of these subjugated women. Finally, the paper is an endeavor to retell the academic world, these lesbian tales; and listening to this voice with a difference, as Carol Gilligan believes, will transform the patriarchal world: "To have a voice is to be human".

Mainstream Hindi films cannot present women revolting against patriarchal society because of what Noam Chomsky describes as the function of media in manufacturing consent. Popular films are a consensus between the filmmaker and audience expectation, it is an agreement between people who finance a film and their expectation of recovering that money by entertaining an audience without offending their 'sensibilities'. This includes their individual understanding of the position held by women in families and extended social groupings. It is in this backdrop, Pallav Mukhopadyay in his chapter tried to investigate the portrayal of women in recent

Bollywood Hindi films and also tries to enquire the status of women in recent mainstream Hindi films in the first decade of the 21st century.

Women, though constitute half of the population, are politically marginalised world over. They are although increasingly active in community support systems, yet gender disparities persist in public positions at all levels: global, national, regional and local. Women are, therefore, continued to be under-represented in formal decision-making structures. As the full participation of women is a prerequisite for governance that is truly democratic, hence there is a need to make special provisions to include women in the democratic governance at different levels. Decentralisation and local governance are frequently presented as good and beneficial for women. It includes women in the democratic governance at different levels. Drawing on the experience of decentralisation reforms in India, which is invariably considered as an example of good practice in advancing gender equity in governance, Durga P Chhetri in his essay explores the hitherto under-researched relationship between decentralisation and social inclusion. More specifically, the author examines the impact of decentralisation reforms on, and how this relationship in turn promotes social inclusion of, women at the grass roots politics.

The chapter written by Pawan Gurung highlights some of the problems faced by the religious minorities in India. This also deals on the role of police in communal violence in the context of minority community in India. The genesis of this problem and the contemporary issues are also discussed which will help the reader to understand the problem of communalism critically in India.

The book ends with an essay by Anil Rajak on the Empowerment of Women through Inclusive Governance.

References

Abrahamson, P. (1997). Combating Poverty and Social Exclusion in Europe, in W. Beck, L. Van der Maesen and A.Walker (eds) *The Social Quality of Europe*, The Hague: Kluwer Law International.

Alcock, P. (1991). *Understanding Poverty*, London: MacMillan Press.

Allard, G.H. (1974). Aspects de la Marginalité au Moyeh Age, Montreal, Canada.

Ambedkar, B.R. (1936). Annihilation of Caste, Writings and Speeches, Vol. I, Government of Maharashtra, Bombay.

Atkinson, A. B. (1998). 'Social Exclusion, Poverty and Unemployment', in A. B. Atkinson and J. Hills (eds.) *Exclusion, Employment and Opportunity*, CASE paper 4, January, 1-24.

Barnes, M. (2005). *Social Exclusion in Great Britain: An Empirical Investigation and Comparison with the EU*, Aldershot: Ashgate.

Beall, Jo and Piron, Laure-Hélène (2005). 'DFID Social Exclusion Review', London: Department for International Development, May 2005.

Beall, Jo and Clert, Carine (2000). Social Exclusion and Globalisation: Implications for Social Policy and Urban Governance, Department of Social Policy, London School of Economics, Monograph prepared for the African Technical Families, Macroeconomics 2, The World Bank, London.

Berting, J. and Villain-Gandossi, C. (2001). Urban Transformations, the French Debate and Social Quality in W. Beck, L. van der maesen, F. Thomas and A. Walker (eds) Social Quality: A Vision for Europe, The Hague/London/Boston: Kluwer Law International.

Bhargava, Rajeev (2004). Inclusion and Exclusion in South Asia: The Role of Religion, United Nations Development Programme, Human Development Report Office Occassional Background Paper for HDR.

Bhalla, Ajit and Lapeyre, F. (1997). Social Exclusion: Towards an Analytical and Operational Framework, *Development and Change Vol. 28 (1997)*, 413-433, Institute of Social Studies 1997, Published by Blackwell Publishers Ltd., 108 Cowley Rd, Oxford OX4 1JF, UK.

Blair, A. (1998). Bringing Britain Together: A national strategy for neighbourhood renewal, London, UK Cabinet Office Social Exclusion Unit, CM report 4045.

Born, A. and Jensen, P.H. (2002). A second order reflection on the concept of inclusion and exclusion, in J.G. Anderson and P.H. Jensen (eds) *Changing Labour Markets, Welfare Policies and Citizenship,* Bristol: Policy Press.

Bradshaw, J., Finch, N, Kemp, P.A., Mayhew, E. and Williams, J. (2003). Gender and Poverty in Britain, Manchester: EOC.

Burchardt, T., Le Grand, J. and Piachaud, D. (1999) Social Exclusion in Britain 1991-1995, *Social Policy and Administration*, 33(3): 227-44.

Burchardt, T., le Grand, J. and Piachaud, D. (2002). Introduction, in Hills, J., Grand, J. le and Piachaud, D. (eds.) *Understanding Social Exclusion*, Oxford: Oxford University Press.

Burchardt, T., Le Grand, J. and Piachaud, D. (2002). Degrees of Exclusion: Developing a Dynamic, Multidimensional Measure, in Hills, J. Le Grand, J. and Piachaud, D. (eds), *Understanding Social Exclusion*, Oxford: Oxford University Press.

Buvinic, Mayra (2005). Social Exclusion in Latin Aamerica in Mayara Buvinic and Jacqueline Mazzaand Ruthanne Deutsch (2005) *"Social Inclusion and Economic Development in Latin Aamerica,* Inter-American Development Bank, New York.

Byrne, D. (1999). *Social Exclusion*, Buckingham: Open University Press.

Cars, G., Madanipour, A. and Allen, J. (1998). Social Exclusion in European Cities, in A. Madanipour et al. (eds), *Social Exclusion in European Cities,* London: Jessica Kingsley.

Daly, M. and Rake, K. (2003). Gender and the Welfare States, Cambridge: Polity Press.

Daly, M. and Saraceno, C. (2002). Social Exclusion and Gender Relations in B. Hobson, J. Lewis and B. Siim (eds) *Contested Concepts in Gender and Social Politics,* Cheltenham/ Northhampton, Mass: Edward Elgar.

De Haan, Arjan (1998). Social Exclusion, *IDS Bulletin*, 29 (1): 10-19

De Koning, J. and Mosley, H. (eds.) (2001). *Labour Market Policy and Unemployment: Impact and Process Evaluations in Selected European Countries,* Cheltenham: Edward Elgar Publishers.

Duffy, K. (1995). *Social Exclusion and Human Dignity in Europe*, Strasbourg: Council of Europe.

Estivill, J. (2003). Concepts and strategies for combating Social Exclusion: An Overview, Geneva: International Labour Organisation.

Evans, M. (1998). Behind the Rhetoric: the Institutional basis of social exclusion and poverty, *IDS Bulletin,* 29(1): 42-49.

Evans, Martin, Serge Paugam, and Joseph Prelis (1995). Chunnel Vision: Poverty, social exclusion and debate on social welfare in France and Britain, LSE STICERD Discussion Paper 115, Oct 95.

Esping-Anderson, G. (2002). Why We need a New Welfare State, Oxford: Oxford University Press.

EC (1994). Growth, Competitiveness and Employment, Luxemburg, Office for Official Publication of the European Commission.

EC (1992). Report on Observatory on National Policies to combat Social Exclusion, EC, 1992.

Gallie, W.B. (1956). "Essentially contested concept" in Aristotelian Society Proceedings (Oxford): 167-98.

Geyer, R. (1999). Can EU social policy save the Social Exclusion Unit and vice versa? *Politics*, 19(3): 159-64.

Goodin, R.E., Headey, B. Muffels R. and Dirven, H.J. (1999). *The real worlds of welfare capitalism*, Cambridge: Cambridge University Press.

Gore, C. (1995). 'Introduction: Markets, citizenship, and social exclusion', in G. Rodgers, C. Gore and J. B. Figueiredo (eds), *Social Exclusion: Rhetoric Reality Responses*. Geneva: International Labour Organisation.

Gore, C., Rodger, G., and Figueiredo, J.B. (eds) (1995). Social Exclusion: Rhetoric, Reality, Responses, Geneva, ILO.

Gore, C. and Figueiredo, J. B. (eds.) (1997), *Social Exclusion and Anti-poverty Policy: A Debate,* Geneva: International Institute for Labour Studies, ILO Publications.

Gough, J. and Eisenschitz, A. with McCulloch, A. (2006). Spaces of social exclusion, London: Routledge.

Hills, J. (2002). "Does the Focus on 'Social Exclusion' Change the Policy Response?" in J. Hills, et al. (eds.) *Understanding Social Exclusion*, Oxford: Oxford University Press.

International Institute for Labour Studies (IILS) (1998). Annex I, issues for discussion in: Figueiredo, J.B. & de Haan, A. (eds.) Social exclusion: an ILO perspective, International Institute for Labour Studies Research series 111, Geneva: International Labour Organisation.

Jackson, Cecil (1999). Social exclusion and gender: Does one size fit all? *The European Journal of Development Research*, 11 (1): 125-146.

Jäntti, M. and Danziger, S. (2000). 'Income poverty in advanced countries', in Atkinson, A.B. and Bourguignon, F. (eds.) *Handbook of Income Distribution* (1), Amsterdam: Elsevier.

Jordan, B. (1997). *A Theory of Poverty and Social Exclusion*, Cambridge: Polity Press.

Kabeer, N. (2000). "Social Exclusion, Poverty and Discrimination: Towards An Analytical Framework, *IDS Bulletin* 31 (4): 83-97.

Klasen, Stephan (1998). *Social Exlcusion and Children in OECD Countries: Some Conceptual Issues*, Paris: OECD.

Kronaeur, M. (1998). 'Social Exclusion' and 'underclass': New Concept for the analysis of poverty, in H.J. Andress (ed) *Empirical Poverty Research in Comparative Perspective,* Aldershot: Ashgate.

Laderchi, Caterina Ruggeri, Ruhi Saith and Frances Stewart (2003). 'Does it Matter that we do not agree on the Definition of Poverty? A Comparison of Four Approaches', *Oxford Development Studies*, 31(3), September 2003, 243-274.

Lee, P. and Murie, A. (1999). *Literature Review of Social Exclusion*, Edinburgh: The Stationery Office.

Lenoir, R. (1974). *Les Exclus: Un Francais sur dix*, Paris: Editions de Seuil.

Levitas, R. (2006). 'The concept and measurement of social exclusion', in C. Pantazis, D. Gordon and R. Levitas (eds.), *Poverty and Social Exclusion in Britain: the Millennium Survey,* Bristol: The Policy Press.

Levitas, R. (ed.) (2006). *Poverty and Social Exclusion in Britain: the Millennium Survey,* Bristol: The Policy Press.

Levitas, R. (1997). "The concept of social exclusion and the new Durkheimian hegemony", *Critical Social Policy*, 46: 5-20.

Levitas, R. (2005). The inclusive society? Social exclusion and new labour, Second edition, Basingstoke: Palgrave MacMillan.

Marshall, T. H. (1964). Class, Citizenship and Social Development, New York: Doubleday.

Mathieson, Jane, Jennie Popay, Etheline Enoch, Sarah Escorel, Mario Hernandez, Heidi Johnston and Laetitia Rispel (2008). Social Exclusion Meaning, measurement and experience and links to health inequalities: A review of literature, WHO Social Exclusion Knowledge Network Background Paper 1, Institute for Health Research Lancaster University, UK.

Moran, Ged and Simpkins, Mike (2000). Social Exclusion and Health in Janie Percy-Smith (ed.) *Policy Responses to Social Exclusion towards Inclusion?* Buckingham: Open University Press.

Nanda, Meera (2006). 'A Prophet Facing Forward', Critical Quest, New Delhi.

National Commission for Enterprises in the Unorganised Sector (2009). Report on the challenge of employment in India, New Delhi.

Nolan, B. and Whelan, C. (1996). *Resources, Deprivation and Poverty*, Oxford: Oxford University Press.

O'Brien, D., Wilkes, J., de Haan, A. and Maxwell, S. (1997). 'Poverty and Social Exclusion in North and South', *IDS Working Paper* 55.

Office of the Deputy Prime Minister (ODPM) (2004). Social Exclusion Unit, *The drivers of social exclusion: A review of the literature-summary* (Social Policy Research Unit (SPRU), University of York, 2004.

Organisation for Economic Cooperation and Development (OECD) (1997). Societal Cohesion and a Globalising Economy, Washington DC: OECD, March 1997.

Pantazis, C., Gordon, D., and Levitas, R. (2006). 'Introduction', in C. Pantazis, G. David and R. Levitas (eds.), *Poverty and Social Exclusion in Britain: the Millennium Survey*, Bristol: Policy Press.

Papola, T.S. and Partha Pratim Sahu (2012). *Growth and Structure of Employment: Long Term and Post Reform Performance and Emerging Challenges*, New Delhi, ISID, Occasional Paper Series, 2012.

Payne, S. and Pantazis, C. (1997). Poverty and Gender, in D. Gordon and C. Pantazis (eds.), *Breadline Britian in the 1990s*, Aldershot: Ashgate.

Peace, Robin (2001). Social Exclusion: A concept in need of definition? *Social Policy Journal of New Zealand*, Issue 16, July 2001: 17-36.

Percy-Smith, J. (2000). 'The Introduction: The Contours of Social Exclusion' in Janie Percy-Smith (ed.) *Policy Responses to Social Exclusion*, Buckingham: Open University Press.

Praggna, C. (2010). 'Hindu Code Bill: A Coup De Grace to systemic Gender Exclusion in India', in V. Subramanyam and K. Sekhar (eds) *Social Exclusion, Integration and Inclusive Policies*, Jaipur: Rawat.

Raday, Frances (2003). Culture, Religion and Gender, I.CON, Vol. 1(4), OUP: 663-715.

Rodgers, G. (1994). 'Overcoming Social Exclusion: Livelihood and Rights in Economic and Social Development', Discussion Paper No DP/72/1994, Geneva: International Institute for Labour Studies.

Room, G. (ed.) (1995). *Beyond the Threshold: The Measurement and Analysis of Social Exclusion*, Bristol: The Policy Press.

Room, G. (1995). Poverty and Social Exclusion: the new European agenda for policy and research, in Room, G. (ed.) *Beyond the threshold: The measurement and analysis of social exclusion,* Bristol: Policy Press.

Room, G. (1995). 'Poverty in Europe: competing paradigms of analysis', *Policy and Politics*, 23(2): 103-13.

Room, G. (1999). 'Social exclusion, solidarity and the challenge of globalisation', *International Journal of Social Welfare*, 8: 166-174.

Room, G. (2000). Trajectories of Social Exclusion: the wider context for the third and first world, in D. Gordon and P. Townsend (ed.) *Breadline Europe,* Bristol: Policy Press.

Ruspini, E. (1998). Women and Poverty Dynamic, *Journal of European Social Policy,* 8(4): 291-316.

Ruspini, E. (2001). The study of women's deprivation, *International Journal of Social Research Methodology,* 4 (2): 101-18.

Saith, R. (2001). 'Social Exclusion: the concept and application to developing countries', *QEH Working Paper Series*, No.72, May.

Saraceno, C. (2001). Social Exclusion, Cultural Roots and Diversities of a Popular Concept, Paper presented at the conference 'Social exclusion and children', 3-4 May 2001 at the Institute for Child and Family Policy. Columbia: Columbia University.

Sen, Amartya (1975). Employment, Technology and Development, Oxford: Clarendon Press.

Sen, Amartya (1985). A sociological approach to the measurement of poverty; a reply to Professor Peter Townsend, *Oxford Economic Papers*, 37: 669-676.

Sen, Amartya (1985). "Well-being, Agency and Freedom: the Dewey Lectures 1984", *Journal of Philospthy*, 82: 169-221.

Sen, Amartya (1992). *Poverty Reexamined,* Cambridge: Harvard University Press.

Sen, Amartya (1992). *Inequality Re-Examined*, Cambridge: Harvard University Press.

Sen, Amartya (1999). *Development as Freedom*, New York: Knopf.

Sen, Amartya (2000). Social Exclusion: Concept, Application, and Scrutiny. Social Development Papers No.1, Office of Economic and Social Development, Manila: Asian Development Bank.

Shah, Ghanashyam, Harsh Mander, Sukdeo Thorat, Satish Despandey and Amita Baviskar (2006). *Untouchability in Rural India,* New Delhi: Sage Publication.

Silver, Hilary (1994/5/6). Social exclusion and social solidarity: Three Paradigms, *International Labour Review*, 133: 531-578.

Silver, H. (1994). Social exclusion and social solidarity: three paradigms, *International Labour Review*, Volume 133, Number 5-6: 531-578.

Singh, K.S. (1994). *The Scheduled Tribes*, Anthropological Survey of India, People of India National Series Volume 3, New Delhi: Oxford University Press..

Singh, K.S. (1993). *The Scheduled Castes*, Anthropological Survey of India, People of India National Series Volume 2, New Delhi: Oxford University Press.

Sposati, A. (2000). Map of Social Exclusion/Inclusion for São Paulo 2000, Social Dynamics of the 1990's, São Paulo: Catholic University.

Stewart, Frances, Manuel Barron, Graham Brown and Marcia Hartwell (2006). 'Social Exclusion and Conflict: Analysis and Policy Implications', *CRISE Policy Paper*, Queen Elizabeth House, Oxford University, January 2005 (updated April, 2006).

Sunny, J. (2007). "Women, paid work and empowerment in India: A review of evidence and issues", CWDS No. 48, Aug.

Thorat, Sukhadeo (2008). 'On Economic Exclusion and Inclusive Policy', in Reservation, The Die Is Caste, *The Little Magazine*, Vol. VI, Issues 4&5. www.littlemag.com.

Thorat, Sukhadeo (2006a). 'Paying the Social Debt', *Economic and Political Weekly*, June 17.

Thorat, Sukhadeo (2006b). 'Exclusion and Poverty: Need for Socially Exclusive Politics and Development Approach', *People's Democracy*, Vol. XXX, No. 5, January 29.

Thorat, Sukhadeo and Katherine S. Newman, (2007). 'Caste and Economic Discrimination: Causes, Consequences and Remedies, *Economic and Political Weekly* (Special Issue) October 13: 4121-24.

UNDP (1997). Human Development Report, New York/Oxford: Oxford University Press.

UNDP (1995). Human Development Report, New York/Oxford: Oxford University Press.

UNDP (1992). Human Development Report, New York: Oxford University Press.

Uunk, W.J.G. and Vrooman, J.C. (2001). Sociale uitsluiting ('Social exclusion'), *Armoedemonitor 2001*, The Hague: scp/cbs (Social and Cultural Planning Office/ Statistics Netherlands).

Veit-Wilson, J. (1998). *Setting Adequacy Standards,* Bristol: Policy Press.

Walton, Fiona (2000). Education and Training in J. Percy-Smith (ed.) *Policy Responses to Social Exclusion towards inclusion?* Buckingham: Open Univesity Press.

Yepez-del-Castillo, Isabel (1994). "A Comparative Approach to Social Exclusion: Lessons from France and Belgium", *International Labour Review,* 133 (5-6): 613-33.

2

Social Ex(in)clusion and Women: An Indian Perspective

Raghunath Ghosh

The present essay has dealt at length the concepts of social inclusion and exclusion with special reference to women. In our tradition, and also in modern times, there are many evidences which show due respect and honour to the women, the sign of their social inclusion. In present times, we are well-acquainted with the concept of eco-feminism which is deserved to be mentioned here. Eco-feminism is the social movement that regards the oppression of women and nature as interconnected. It is one of the few movements and analyses that actually connect two movements. More recently, eco-feminist theorists have extended their analyses to consider the interconnections between sexism, the domination of nature (including animals), and also racism and social inequalities. Consequently, it is now better understood as a movement working against the interconnected oppressions of gender, race, class and nature. Nature and women are taken as equally honourable, adorable and inevitable for survival, which proves the social inclusion of women as well as nature. The following reference from the Atharvaveda may be taken as an example of eco-feminism in our tradition as the Earth has been considered as our Mother.

The status of Mother, among the women relations, is so near and dear to us that we do not think her as excluded from the family.

Ms. Marina L, while doing the readings on the land, said that she was struck by imagery that could have just as easily been used to describe woman. For example, when Thoreau spoke of "cutting down the forest and all large trees, simply deform the landscape, and make it tamer and cheap" (qtd. Nash 37), images of woman reconfiguring her body to conform to a "Madison Avenue" ideal through regiments of diet and exercise were called to mind. When George Perkins Marsh disparagingly used the metaphor "womb" (Nash 41) to say that "(man) is not born of her (land) (qtd. Nash), but lower forms of life are," the ideas of misogynist Greek philosophers were recalled. Then, when Swain (Nash 120) talked about *grazers still abusing and exploiting the unregulated public domain*, the connection between woman and the land was again felt, from the perspective of a female raised within the framework of Western culture. Repeatedly, I kept feeling that these authors and still others could have been describing woman just as easily as the land. That mental connection caused me to wonder whether the relationship between woman and the land went deeper. Hence society's treatment of the land is necessarily indicative of how it treats woman, which ultimately proves her value in a society.[1]

The Prthivi Sukta of the Atharaveda echoed the same theory of inclusion among men where it is prayed to Mother Earth to strengthen all in the earth to have a secular outlook. It is said: Oh, Mother Earth, give us as your children the ability to mix harmoniously without any discrimination, may we speak sweetly with one another'. The original *mantra* runs as follows: *"Ta nah prajah buhatam samagra vaco madhu Prthivi dehi mahyam"*.[2]

This sense of alienation makes a man 'self-centred' or 'narrow' which closes the door of inclusive idea. If a man thinks that he is not isolated or alienated, he starts looking 'others' as his 'own'. This sense of 'owning' generates the feeling of patriotism, nationalism, fellow-feeling, sacrifice, etc. If these feelings are developed, he will not see 'others' as excluded from 'himself' leading to the cessation of desire of exploitation, desire of usurping other people's properties, sexual exploitation, hatred etc.(*'Yadaitamanupaśyatyātmanam devamañjasā/ Īśānam bhūtabhav-yasya na tato vijugupsate'*)[3]. It is deeply felt by Swami Vivekananda while concentrating on the initial *mantra* of *Īśopaniṣad- 'Īśāvāsyamidam sarvam yat kiñca jagatyām jagat / Tena tyaktena bhunjithah mā grdha kasya-sviddhanam'.*[4] That is, whatever remains in this world is covered by the Self. Hence, one should enjoy through renunciation without being greedy towards others properties. The first line of the *mantra* is the premise and hence the second line follows from the realisation of the first one. If a man does not have the sense of 'owning', he cannot grasp the sense of inherent significance of inherent inclusion in tradition leading him to the path of exclusion resulting in human being's exploitation as well as environment's exploitation. Vivekananda, being inspired by the above-mentioned *mantra,* realized such inclusion among human beings and hence he could declare it with courage : "Forget not that the ideal of thy womanhood is Sita, Savitri, Damayantī; forget not that the God thou worshppest is the great Ascetic of ascetics, the all-renouncing Sankara, the Lord of Uma, forget not that thy marriage, thy wealth, thy life are not for sense-pleasure, are not for thy individual personal happiness; forget not that thou art born as a sacrifice to the Mother's alter; ...forget not that the lower classes, the ignorant, the poor, the illiterate, the cobbler, the sweeper, are thy flesh and blood, thy brothers." (IV.479-80)[5]

Kazi Nazrul Islam, a famous poet in Bengal had realised such inclusion among all human beings and hence he has been able to raise his voice against the man-made bad practices in the name of caste and creed (*'Jater name bajjati'*).

The sense of inclusion is also found in another poem – *'Kandari Hunsiyar'* where he has drawn our attention to consider humanity alone, not caste or creed, as the need of hour. When a man is in danger one should not consider his caste, creed, etc., but humanity alone (*Hindu na muslim oi jijñāse kon jan / Kāndāri balo dubiche mānuṣ santān mor mār).* Candidasa, a Vaisnava poet, is also of the opinion that humanity is over and above everything (*Śunoha mānuṣ bhāi, sabār upare mānuṣ satya tāhār upare nāi)*. If someone neglects the touch of human being, he indirectly hates and lies his own personal God (*'Mānuṣer paraśera ṭhekāyia dūre ghrṇā kariyācho tumi prāṇer thākure')*

Rabindranath has shown social exclusion in various manners in his dance drama Candalika and ultimately he has concluded that such exclusion is man-made and socio-logically imposed. The curd-seller refuses to sell his curd to Candalika, a girl belonging to an untouchable class. The same thing happens with other vendors like bangle-seller, etc. It has pained Candalika due to her alienation from main current of the society, which makes her feel that she belongs to downtrodden and untouchable class. She always feels pain to remember the words of her friends addressed to the curd-seller who is completely unaware of the fact of her belonging to an untouchable class. The words go like this – *'Chunyo na chunyo nā chih, se ye Candālinīr jhi, naṣta habe je doi se kathā jāno na ki ?* That is, don't touch her, because she is a daughter of Candāla. Are you unaware of the fact that your whole amount of curd would be spoiled if you are come in contact with this lady?

This discrimination has made her isolated, depressed and socially outcast or alienated called bratya. This sense of depression has been expressed by her dissociation with household work and non-cooperation with her mother as expressed in – *'kāj nei kāj nei mā kāj nei mor ghar kannāi.'* (That is, O Mother, there is no point in performing house-hold works).

At the end of the dance-drama, Rabindranath has brought the sense of inclusion among all men without having any man-made exclusive principles like caste, untouchability, etc., bringing an episode of Ãnanda, a Buddhist monk, whose thirst was quenched with the water provided by the same untouchable girl, Candalika, who was initially reluctant in offering water to a Buddhist monk (*tomare debo jal hena punyera nahi adhikarini ami je candalakanya*). At last, the monk has substantiated the fact that she belongs to human class, not to any particular caste and creed. The monk has brought her in main current of the society after conferring her honour of humanity (manaver samman). It is rightly pointed out by Ãnanda that she is after all a human being and the blood of a human being is flowing through her viens. Hence, she should not blame herself as belonging to the race of Candāla (*Tini bale gelen amai nijere ninda koro na, manaver vamsa tomar manaver rakta tomar nadite*). The property of being Candāla is a socially imposed phenomenon having no actual reality in it and hence there is reason for her exclusion.

Ultimately, Ãnanda has brought out the bond of thread of all human beings which may otherwise be called a thread of inclusion. Ãnanda has told the girl that he himself belongs to the human race which she herself belongs to. (*'ye manava ami sei manava tumi kanya'*). The Buddhists in general believes that an object is stated to be real, if it is momentary and has got causal efficacy which are followed from two premises : *'yat sat tat kṣaṇikam'* and *'arthakriyākāritvalakṣaṇam sat'* (i.e. 'whatever is real is momentary' and 'an entity is taken to be existent, if it can fulfill some purpose-oriented action'). Ãnanda has brought these theories and told Candālikā that the causal efficacy of water lies on the fact of quenching thirst of a thirsty person. If it can perform this job, it can be taken as sacred as water belonging to auspicious places (*'sei bāri tīrthabāri yā tṛpta kare tṛṣitere'*). The first point of inclusion is that Ãnanda and Candālikā belong to the same human race. The second point is that any object capable fulfilling the need of a needy person is to be taken as a glorified sacred auspicious object without considering the source or owner of the object. If 'candalatva' ('the property of being a *Candāla'*) is imposed on the dense cloud spread over the sky in the month of *Śrāvaṇa*, would it be treated as *Candāla* and its water as impure? (*Srāvaner kālo ye megh tāre yadi nām dāo candāla, ta bole ki jāt ghucive tār, aśuci habe ki tār jal'*). This honour of humanity conferred to Candālikā is a transformation from exclusion to inclusion, which is considered as a 'new birth' (*'natun janma'*). It is achieved by virtue of being included in the main stream of human race through the instrumentality of quenching thirst of the monk. (*'E natun janma natun janma natun janma āmār, āmāke dilen sahasā mānuser tṛṣnā meṭāno sammān'*). Through proper inclusion Candālikā starts thinking herself as fortunate as a flower. Just as a flower is intrinsically auspicious as it is used in the service of God, Candālikā also thinks herself pious as she has been utilised in the service of quenching thirst of a monk. So far she was excluded from the society and not allowed to serve others, which she considers as a social isolation or exclusion *('phul bale dhanya ami dhanya ami matir pare, devata, ogo tomar seva ammre tare ... nai dhuli mor antare').*[6] Rabindranath has highlighted, strengthened and developed the ethics of secularism with the spread of Buddhism that denounced social distinction between man and man, man and woman, etc. The key features of Buddhism were equality of all men irrespective of sex, language or religion, compassion (karuna) for all beings, liberation and humanity which may be taken as seeds of social inclusion.

We come across certain advertisements in the electronic and print media to highlight that all are equal – no one is superior or inferior, in so far as his/her work is concerned. When a near or dear one is in need of blood, he is given the same after collecting from other persons whose identity is not known to us. Do we really consider which class or caste the donor of blood belongs to? If not, why should we consider caste, creed, etc., in other spheres of life? Some of our modern thinkers like Swami Vivekananda, Sri Aurobindo, Rabindranath, and others have duly recognised and highlighted the equal status of men and philosophical justifications behind it. Now time has come to make others convinced regarding the views of modern thinkers about the status of men and their social position so that not a single man feels socially excluded or alienated from the main current of the society. For having a broader social inclusion, we need the change of our mindset regarding the status of women, labours and the so called down-trodden people. It has been stated by Manu that a society cannot prosper if women are not given due honour. To him gods rejoice in that society where women are worshipped *('yatra nāryastu pūjyante ramante tatra devatāh')*[7].

Now such women are looked upon as commodities and treated as instruments of a man's enjoyment. We neglect the women-labours by describing them as *'kajer lok'* ('a woman assisting in domestic work'), 'prostitutes', etc. These derogatory ascriptions to women make them socially excluded, which is undesirable. The idol of *'Ardhanarīśvara'* ('half-woman and half-man') which is a part of Hindue religious beliefs signifies the highest form of inclusion – it states that a man is basically a combination of 'man and woman'. The image suggests that a man is not complete, but half, and hence his second better is filled up by 'female'. In other traditions and also in West, the 'second-half' or 'female-half' is metaphorically described as 'better' in comparison to the first as evidenced by the word '*ardhangini*'. The term 'better' is used only to show the inevitability of this half for being a 'complete man'. So, a man's body comprises of a woman at least by half which is the paradigm case of inclusion. If this idea is nourished, the exclusion of women from men, the evil practices of witch-killing, abductions, trafficking, and the like can easily be removed. Lastly, it may be concluded that the phenomenon of social exclusion is the result of our non-education (*aśikṣā*) or mal-education (*kuśikṣā*). Our education system should have such openings where there may be a scope for teaching basic principles of moral education like, equality among men from economic, racial and social standpoints, the glorification of the deeds alone, but not of the doers. Normally, those who perform duties of sweeping, cultivating, labours, etc. are neglected in the society and thereby they are excluded. If the deeds are alone glorified in our society, there will exist no room for undermining the persons performing these jobs. In our tradition, the performance of action is called 'worshipping to God' (*karmai pûja*) and the persons performing actions are called worshippers of God giving no scope for underestimating them, which may be taken as a seed of social inclusion.

It is believed in Indian culture that the Divine Energy (*Sakti*) is manifested as the Ultimate female power in Hindu cosmology. She creates, destroys and exhibits a fierce power over all the creation. In no way the position of women was inferior in our tradition which is evidenced from the episodes of the learned women like Gargi and Maitreyi, great mathematicians like, Leelavati, and the experts of comprehensive system of medicine and surgery like Dhanvantari, etc. Considering all these, the general and most honourable term to address a lady is Devi, i.e., goddess.

It is a pity that in modern times, women have lost their glorious cultural identity and has to suffer for various reasons such as due to the over-dominance of the males or their ego-problem and many other such traits. Still, women continue to be tortured as evidenced from the reports of bride-burning, witch-killing, among many others. Many woman-related cases like rape, sexual harassment, trafficking, etc., are reported often in the newspapers. It is pathetic and disheartening indeed that a woman is burnt alive considering her as a witch. I do not know how utopian ideas like, witch, etc., have occupied the rational faculty of a modern human being. No sensible man, I think, can commit such a heinous act towards another human being in this age of science and technology. It is also very interesting that we do not get the masculine form of the word 'witch'. From this, it is presumed that if any evil spirit at all exists, it is found among the women alone. This is an invention of the superstitious male leaders alone of our society.

Today, women have been considered as commodities or the objects of enjoyment, which is evidenced from the fact of their trafficking to other places. In many instances if one comes to know that the foetus in the womb is a girl child, one does not hesitate to kill it, being unaware of the darker side of such incidents. If these things are allowed to happen or encouraged, it will surely lead to the depletion of female population. It is a matter of great concern that, in Rajasthan and Punjab, still the sex ratio is much less than other parts of the country. If this practice is allowed to continue, it will be pernicious for the mankind as it will considerably reduce the population of females due to their skewed numbers.

Now the time has come to appreciate the problems of the women which, I believe, can be realized and solved by the women themselves if they are given an opportunity. In order to prevent the women-related evils, including their exclusion from the society, women should boldly come forward, initiate a leading part and restore their glorious cultural identity. It is possible if they are given constitutional power, much of the ills plaguing them can be solved. Our country has already started reservation of women representatives in the public policy-making bodies like Panchayats, Assemblies, etc., after considering the question of their empowerment. Fortunately, now we find a considerable number of ladies as administrators, police officers, judges, pilots and soldiers. If they are encouraged with endowment of legitimate power, they can perform in a better way being free from male-chauvinism. Before considering their security in other domains, they should be provided psychological security so that they are boosted up with their full potential.

Can all-round development of our society be possible without the empowerment of women? Women have got their own ability and power, which needs an outlet of exposure. A nation should look into the matter seriously and create a situation so that they can exert their power administratively and constitutionally. Hence, they should be included in the main stream of the society.

It has already been said that through counselling and sensitization programmes, common people are made aware of certain facts like sanitation issues, ill effects of superstitions, bride-burning, dowry-system, witch-killing, etc. All the social evils including women-related ones can easily be removed through these.

References

1. Linda Marine, *Women and the Land*, Vide: www.ecofem.org/journal.
2. *Atharvaveda (Pṛthivisūkta)* 12/01/01/45.
3. *Bṛhadāraṇyakopaniṣad*-4/4/15.
4. *Îśopaniṣad, 1 / 1.*
5. *The Complete Works of Swami Vivekananda,* Vol. IV, Ninth Edition, 1966, pp. 479-80.
6. Rabindranath Thakur, *Gitavitan*, Kamini Prakashalaya, Kolkata, 202, pp. 585-601.
7. *Manusamhitā*-3/6.

3

A Jurisprudential Discussion on Social Exclusion

Gangotri Chakraborty

"Justice is the first virtue of social institutions, as truth is of systems of thought"

- John Rawls

Introduction

The need and the quest for justice in the micro and macro societies and by extension of the global world is increasingly becoming inevitable in the wake of all kinds of violence and orchestrated social disorder and break down of law that characterise our world today. Justice cuts across and assumes a high degree of importance in every sphere of human endeavour such that it is a recurrent concept, an ideal in ethics, jurisprudence, governance and every other form of human undertaking that involve human relationships, management and administration. At the intrapersonal and interpersonal levels, it is a cardinal virtue such that with it global peace is guaranteed and without it our world will remain a place of horror and discomfort. As a result of this, the concept of Justice has become real and very topical in contemporary societies. Although justice has taken the coloration of cultures, philosophies, individuals and schools of thought, still the bottom line of this concept is that it is synchronically (a historical) in terms of definition. Whatever differences there may be in the definition of justice among the scholars, broadly speaking, the concept pictures integrity, impartiality, rightness and fairness as constituting the notion of justice. However, more fundamental to the concept of natural justice are natural rights, which constitute the most original, inalienable and natural, form of justice. In the narrow sense, justice means conformity with the law. However, the limitation of this sense of justice is two-fold. One, an unjust law is no law at all. Two, conforming to written or legal law without the spirit of justice shows the inadequacy and defects of justice in the narrow sense. While in the proper sense, justice is understood as the "harmonious functioning of the constituent parts in the individual, or in the state. Access to justice can be defined as the right of individuals and groups to obtain a quick, effective and fair response to protect their rights prevent or solve disputes and control the abuse of power, through a transparent and efficient process, in which mechanisms are available. Affordable and accountable access to justice necessarily includes so-called traditional justice mechanisms, i.e., informal conflict and dispute resolution mechanisms and/or systems operating at the community level and employing local socio-cultural norms and values to reach decisions and/or work with parties to achieve mutually-acceptable results.

Inequality and Social Exclusion

Social exclusion happens when people or places suffer from a series of problem, such as, unemployment, discrimination, poor skills, low income, poor housing, ill health, family breakdowns, etc. When such problems act in conjunction, they create a vicious cycle often starting at birth. To exclude means to deny access to some place or thing. When used with an adjective term 'social', it means keeping out of the society and its organisations. The boundaries of the concept are far from determinate, but at its core, social exclusion involves being shut out from social institutions and relations in ways that matter for one's well being. The term is often used in discussion of social policies. Some key concepts in our current social policy vocabulary, such as dalit, adivasi, poverty and discrimination do not have the same resonance that they had even about half a decade ago. The concept of social exclusion has the advantage of situating individuals in a social and relational context and the experience of exclusion due to the reasons of poverty, caste, race, gender, etc., is almost universal. Moreover, the rapid social and economic changes associated with information age and globalisation have exacerbated and fostered new forms of social exclusion. Since, in the society individuals are continuously in motion, either solitary or in community, as evident from the various form of unsettlement, viz. geographic mobility, social mobility, economic mobility, political mobility and marital mobility. The impact of these mobilities is both positive and negative and they impact upon individuals as well as communities and are intensified with the advancement of knowledge, development and technological progress. The concept of social exclusion helps to provide a common language for understanding the negative effect, and as such, it has considerable potential to improve both understanding of social issues and social policies. When the term 'social' is used it means something is of or relating to society and / or its organisations. If society is understood to mean an ordered life of a community, then exclusion is the process of being excluded from hat ordered life. The ordered life of the community includes the following:

- Employment;
- Education;
- Market and related institutions;
- Public Services, benefits and institutions;
- Political and civic participation;
- Formal and informal social associations;
- Access to resources, and
- Power of decision-making.

Exclusion from one or more of this community life leads to segregation and poverty. Segregation on the basis of race, gender, disability or other immutable characteristics also result in exclusion; segregation and exclusion, therefore, are relational concepts. Segregation divides or separates groups based on their caste, tribe, race, regionalism, gender disability, poverty, etc., and exclusion refers to the process by which these segregated groups are barred from being included in the ordered life of community.

In India, there is a history of inequality and discrimination and exclusion. The most common and frequently mentioned discriminations are against the dalits (Scheduled Caste), adivasis (Scheduled Tribes), who together make up about the quarter of India's population. Their exclusion is reflected in lack of access or unequal access to resources like education, health care and other amenities and also to resources like land, water, etc. even to this day. Attempts made by dalits, adivasis to secure equal treatment and lawful entitlements are visited with resistance, violence, etc. This is further compounded by the gendered nature of the discrimination. An estimation of the National Sample Survey (NSS) in 2000 suggests that dalit constituted 20 per cent of the rural population, while 38 per cent of poor people in rural areas. The adivasis made up 11 per cent of the rural population whereas 48 per cent of the rural poor. In urban areas, dalits were 14 per cent of the population and 37 per cent of the urban poor, whereas adivasis were 3 per cent of the urban population and 35 per cent of the urban poor. The same estimate suggests that poverty was around 30 per cent for the Muslim community.[1] Across the above social groups, women face discrimination in many areas of life though their status varies significantly according to their ethnic standings. Exclusion and discrimination is magnified when identities overlap, as in case of dalit women, adivasi women, Muslim women. They are doubly excluded both as women and as adivasis. These exclusions are social, economic and political, which is also denial of the promise made in the Preamble to our Constitution, that is, of achieving Justice: Social, Economic and Political.

Due to the above reason, and also because of neglected exploitation, the Human Development Index (HDI) of the dalit, adivasi and minority Muslims are much lower than the rest of the Indian population in terms of literacy, health and access to resources.

Social exclusion describes a process by which certain groups are systematically disadvantaged because they are discriminated against on the basis of their ethnicity, religion, caste, gender, etc. Social exclusion is also about exclusion from political power. The Articles 14 to 18 of the Indian Constitution clearly set the agenda for elimination of exclusion by establishing collective rights of communities to maintain cultural identities and to pursue religious freedoms and individual rights of civil liberty to all citizens as Fundamental Rights. These objectives are also promoted through the Fundamental Duties and the Directive Principles of State Policy. This guarantees equal access in several spheres, such as, legal process, education, public employment and basic civil liberties in terms of speech, association, movement, livelihood, etc. Thus, terms of public policy relating to dalits and adivasis are three pronged – Non-discrimination, Affirmative action and Protection and Promotion of non-discrimination through a series of processes, such as, abolition of bonded labour, Indira Gandhi Abash Yojana, Rashtriya Swathya Bima Yojana, Ayushmati Yojana, Mid-day Meal Schemes, supply of uniform and books, etc.[2]

Theory of Equality, Fairness in Policy and Welfare

In Rawl's 'Theory of Justice',[3] perhaps the most important contribution was to oppose the then prevailing utilitarianism. He developed the idea of primary goods to describe a set of all purpose resources that all rational agents could agree upon as a means of furthering their aims, notwithstanding their own individual aims or conception of goods in their being a sense of justice. To achieve these all purpose ends, some all purpose means of primary goods, such as equality, freedom of thought and conscience, freedom of movement and association, free choice of occupation, equal opportunities of offices and positions of responsibilities, income and wealth and self-respect are considered to be the most important ones.[4] Dworkin[5] introduced the idea of responsibility into theory of justice. Rawls says that in terms of distribution of primary goods, distribution to the worst off in the society must be the priority. Dworkin's main point is that one should not be forced to subsidise or support. The individual choices consciously need to be made over profession or other issues. There cannot be an equality of welfare because the choices of individuals, made voluntarily and consciously, may differ in terms of their resource utilisation.[6]

Now to apply these two theories to the concerns of social exclusion and policies means the following:

- A person who loses wealth due to his habit of gambling should not have the same status of another person who is not able to earn due to social disadvantages like, caste, disability, race, gender, etc.

- The status of a person who is starving because he will only eat biriyani and no other food cannot be said with a person who is starving because he has no access to food due to his poverty or social location.

In the above context, Amartya Sen[7] argues that a handicapped individual does not have the same ability to convert resources into opportunities for their well-being and hence they require more resources. On a different stand from Dworkin, Sen argues that more resources are to be distributed to insure against potential handicaps. In other words, Sen is focusing on quality of life and well being, but for Dworkin, how well people will get on with their lives is not the concern of the theory of liberal political equality. For Sen, well-being is multi-dimensional and includes different types of freedom and agency. Thus, it can be said Sen has introduced a capability approach to the concerns of welfare and equality. But for Rawls and Dworkin, resources are meant to remove the scope of justice and equality from the subjective understanding of welfare and must be placed in relation to primary goods and resources.[8] Today, there are about 39 different capabilities in relation to welfare.[9] That list includes the following:

1. Life: Having a reasonable longevity;
2. Health: Bodily health with adequate nutrition and shelter;
3. Bodily integrity: Freedom of movement and protection from assault, battery and physical harm;
4. Sense imagination and thought: To be able to use senses, imagination and reason;
5. Emotions: Ability for attachment to things, people outside of ourselves;
6. Practical reason: Being able to from a conception of the good and to be able to be critical about the planning of one's life;
7. Affiliation: To be able to live with and among people and also environment and the world of nature;
8. Recreation: Being able to laugh, play and enjoy;
9. Decision-making and choices: Effective participation in political choices that governs one's life;

10. Ability to express one's relation to others;
11. Obedience to the law;
12. Understanding the law;
13. Recognition: Having one's value respected by others.[10]

The categories of social exclusion that have been mentioned in the foregoing pages include consumption, production, and social and political engagement. Some categories, such as life, health, integrity, reason, enables everybody to thrive on them and are worst affected by social exclusion.

Brian Barry[11] has addressed the question of what is normatively bad in social exclusion and has introduced the importance of choice in the social exclusion debate. Barry distinguished between "Fact of exclusion" and "Cause for concern" with social exclusion because as mentioned earlier, there are voluntary exclusions by individuals who should not be forced to include themselves. In other words, in a society there will be individuals who voluntarily exclude themselves. Such individuals should not be forced to socially include themselves. But if such individuals wanted to socially include themselves, they should not lack the authority to do so. If such an opportunity is denied, it would amount to social exclusion. Moreover, social exclusion, even if voluntary, should be minimized by presenting ample opportunities for inclusion.

The issue of fairness in the above context arises when the behaviour of a person having self- imposed exclusion leads to unfair cost on the person who is excluded on the ground of reasons mentioned in the foregoing pages. Therefore, there is also an element of priority which may *prima facie* appear to be a violation of norms of equality. Justice in transition requires rationalizing these various demands and models of exclusion before adopting remedial measures.

Conclusion

Justice in transition, therefore, is a complex issue and relational in nature. It largely depends on the relations and patterns of segregations and isolations and the respective remedial choices made in respect to them in order to create a society where there is equal respect regardless of whether there is any actual material equality of condition. To create such a society, it is required that there should be sufficient capabilities and no one is forced to be ashamed of their condition and standing in life. Remedies to social exclusion, is to provide sufficient levels of capabilities, which in turn is justice in transition.

References

1. Kabeer Naila (2006). "Social Exclusion and the MDSs: The Challenge of 'Durable Inequalities' in Asian Context", paper presented at the Asia 2015 Conference.
2. Sheth, D. "Caste, Ethnicity and Exclusion in South Asia: The Role of Affirmative Action Policies in Building Inclusive Societies", Human Development Report Office, Occasional Paper, UNDP, New York.
3. Rawls, John (1971). A Theory of Justice, Harvard University Press.
4. *Ibid.*
5. Dworkin, Ronald (2000). Sovereign Virtue: The Theory of Practice and Equality, Cambridge University Press.
6. *Ibid.*
7. Sen, Amartya (1980). "Equaity of What?", The Tanner Lecture on Human Values I, University of Utah Press (1980); Amartya Sen, "Social Exclusion: Concept, Application and Scrutiny", Social Development Papers No. 1, Asian Development Bank, 2000.
8. Shepley W. Orr (2005). "Social Exclusion and the Theory of Equality: The Priority of Welfare and Fairness in Policy", University College, London.
9. I. Robeyns (2002). "Review of Sabina Alkaire; Value in Freedom, Sense Capability Approach and Poverty Reduction", 2003 Economics and Philosophy, 19:371-377.
10. *Ibid.*
11. Barry, Brain (2002). "Social Exclusion, Socil Isolation, and the Distribution of Income", in HILLS, LeGrand and Piaschaud (Eds.).

4

Exiled Indoors: Divine Discourses and Social Exclusion/Inclusion of Women

Shelly Parul Bhadwal

Introduction

At times divine, and at times insignificant; at times a pillar, and at times nothing but dust. It is between such extreme positions of power and powerlessness that the portrayal and the identity of a woman oscillates within the Indian society. Such a polarity within the social structure finds its bearing in religion, or more precisely, in the Brahmanical-Sanskritic texts as far as Hinduism is concerned. In other words, it is the written word that has ever since determined and influenced the dynamics of social existence. For instance, a treatise such as the *Manusmriti* is considered as one of the significant structuring forces behind social stratification, as it presently exists.

Enlisted under the rubric of the *Dharmashastras*, the *Manusmriti* enumerates a number of prescriptive verses regarding social conduct, to be adhered to, by an individual. It categorises the society into four classes and enumerates a catalogue of dos and don'ts for each class. At the level of the individual, the treatise divides the human life span into four stages and once again prescribes the appropriate way of conduct for each. Similarly, the treatise also mentions the duties and rights of men and women towards one-another, and so on. This systematisation of the society has however, empowered certain individuals within the community while marginalising the rest. It is for this reason that in the recent times this treatise has faced immense criticism, especially for its proposition of the caste-based stratification of the society. Similarly, it can also be held responsible to some extent, for excluding women from the social and the political domains of the social framework, or in one word, the public sphere.

It would however be inappropriate to single out one treatise for having pushed women towards the periphery. For it is not only the Manusmriti, but a range of texts and divine discourses, which constitute the corpus of the scriptures that may be held responsible for exiling women indoors. Primarily patriarchal and elitist treatises, they are framed in a way that indicate inclusion and exclusion of women within the social structure. Interestingly, both these processes take place as a simultaneous event. Seen as oppositional ideas, it might for once seem difficult to look at the two as being interdependent. It is however, the recognition of this mutual reliance that helps understand the subtlety of the working of the patriarchal discourse.

She is 'Devi', she is 'Durga', and she is 'Lakshmi' and 'Mohini' too. In one word, she is divine. It is in this way that the religious discourses portray women. She is the goddess who should be revered and worshiped in every house. The house thus is the temple where the goddess resides. Reinforcing this revered stature of the women the *Manusmriti* states,

> *"Yetra nayarsh tu pujayante ramantey tatra devta:*
> *Yetra-yatas tu na pujayante savarsh tatra-a-fala: kriya:"*
> *3&56 (Manusmriti, 3.56)*

(Where women are honoured, there the gods are pleased; but where they are not honoured, no sacred rite yields rewards. Buhler, 3.56)

Offering such a high pedestal to women certainly provides a safe and strategic upper-hand to the patriarchs, helping them strengthen their armour of arguments which is potent enough to tackle even the slightest ripple of revolt. While the women bask in their divine glory, it is the men who exercise the actual divine powers. This is certainly a smart move. By defining women as divine, the patriarchs give them an entry into the social realm and yet have planned their subtle exit already. For, the 'divine' is a problematic territory. In the flesh and blood realm of the human, the divine appears as frozen. It implies that conferring divinity to someone carries with it the ideas of immobility. Lying at the centre of social life in a culture dominated by religion, it is yet removed from it. Therefore, while the labelling of women as divine gives them an honourable position within the social framework, their power is restricted to the premises of their temple, i.e., the confines of their house. The women are positioned in a way that they can neither complain nor act. They are goddesses, meant to be decorated and worshipped, but not allowed to step out.

Though goddesses of great strength, capable of driving away all evil forces, women are prescribed a life protected by male guardians all the time. As is clearly mentioned in the Manusmriti,

> *"Pita rahkchati kawmarey varta yuoaney*
> *Rahkchanti swastabirey putra na stree swantranayam aharti" 9&3 (Manusmriti, 9.3)*

> (Her father protects (her) in childhood, her husband protects (her) in youth, and her sons protect (her) in old age; a woman is never for independence. Buhler, 9.3)

In this way, they are sentenced to a life which is constantly under the panoptic patriarchal surveillance. Thc romanticism of divinity gets punctured in the light of such powerlessness on the part of the goddess, who needs her guardian angels at every stage in her life. This lends ambivalence to a divinity that deprives its recipient, of freedom.

Analysing the idea of female divinity, Bose (2010) observes that within the Indian culture, "The need for emphasising the domestication of goddesses seems paramount." He examines the various goddesses and women icons within the Hindu tradition and lays bare a clear patriarchal strategy which marginalises women through divinity and also defines the roles of 'mortal' women through such unquestionable models, for instance, the 'pativratya' Parvati, the submissive and surrendering Sita, the nurturing Prithvi, the protector Durga, the graceful Saraswati, etc. An examination of the icons also leads to the question of the social identity of women, as individuals in their own right. Bose (14) interestingly observes that,

> In traditional Indian society, even powerful goddesses are seldom imagined – just as mortal women are seldom imagined – as single, self-determined persons unattached to a male figure as his mother or wife or daughter or sister, which suggests that her very identity rests on her relationship with males, with rare exceptions.

It is crucial to note how, in terms of the social presence of women, the divine discourses make marriage paramount. According to Smith (2003).

> In the traditional brahminic culture, man enjoys four life stages, from student, to householder, to forest dweller, to wandering ascetic, while woman has only two, girlhood and marriage.

This holds true not only for women in the human world but also in the realm of the superhuman. Marriage becomes one of the easiest criterions of classifying the range of goddesses within the Indian tradition. The goddesses are either married such as Parvati and Lakshmi, or are unmarried like Durga and Kali. Distinguishing between married and unmarried goddesses, Smith adds,

> Married goddesses are mild and controlled; unmarried goddesses are wild, uncontrolled, dangerous — Kali is the supreme example here. All this is exact transposition of the belief that unmarried women are dangerous, superheated by their rampant, unsatisfied sexuality, while married women are so to speak, damped down (Smith, 2003).

In the light of this reflection, it does not take much effort to understand the reason behind the emphasis laid by the patriarchs on marriage. The 'mild and controlled' suits best to the working of the male-order, as opposed to the 'wild and uncontrolled'. According to Mrinal Pande,

> Goddesses are presented through word and image as overdressed, bejewelled and fawning mothers, givers of wealth and gentle imposers of discipline. Those unpredictable outbursts of temper, that fury of wild hair, those rolling eyes, the lolling tongue and other manifestations of an inexplicably complex presence, are all being erased from Goddess-lore (Pande, 1996).

Thus, by creating knowledge of the docile married goddess, the wild is kept in check. It is the promotion of this idea of matrimony that may serve as an explanation for the eulogized married female icons. Once again the notion of the female divinity as a self-reliant construct is deflated and the patriarchal control over female identity, even in the realm of the divine, let alone the world of mortals, is exposed. This control over the female has been justified, arguing that the inherent nature of the female itself makes control a necessity and thus their social exclusion. For instance, the Manusmriti states,

> *"pawsrayliyache chalchitach cha naysreyayach cha swavawatah*
> *Rakshita yatnatho api-eha bhratiswa atha bikuvarthe" 9&15 (Manusmriti, 9.15)*

(Through their passion for men, through their mutable temper, through their natural heartlessness, they become disloyal towards their husbands, however carefully they may be guarded in this (world) Buhler, 9.15)

> *"ayum sambawh gyatatwa-ansha prajapatinisargjahm*
> *Param yatnam atisasteytam purushu rakshan prati" 9&16 (Manusmriti, 9.16)*

> (Knowing their disposition, which the Lord of creatures laid in them at the creation, to be such, (every) man should most strenuously exert himself to guard them. Buhler, 9.16)

Along with the idea of matrimony, is associated another important idea, that of motherhood. Therefore, the second best way to show reverence to women within the Indian tradition is to term them as 'mother'. According to Mrinal Pande,

> Men have eternally tried to convince the Goddesses that they too are their worshippers and so the divine beings must come to them as loyal and gentle mothers. Since few Goddesses have children, in their secret wishes men want to take their children's place and so reinvent the perfect mother, wild and fierce, yet loyal and all-pardoning (Pande, 1996).

This once again restricted the women within the confines of the household and sets their social function to that of bearing children. The glorification of the roles of a woman as a mother and a homemaker therefore also act as strategies of inclusion and exclusion. It does not require much effort to recognise motherhood, to be the primary function of a woman, as also prescribed by the Manusmriti and various scriptural texts. These treatises repeatedly reiterate this notion as an assertive prescription for all women to follow. Moreover, it is not simply about bearing children but about bearing sons. Here it is interesting to note that while women play a significant role in the working of the patriarchal social sphere, by giving it its heirs; motherhood limits them to the confines of the house. Similarly, the idea of a woman being the 'grihalakshmi' and the 'homemaker' also demarcates the domestic domain as her area of existence and thus hinders her entry into the social sphere.

The hide and seek of inclusion and exclusion is also visible in the fields of education and economics. There is hardly any dispute on the fact that capital, both intellectual as well as monetary, are sources of power within the social sphere. An individual in possession of any one of them, or both, automatically climbs up the ladder of social hierarchy. Women once again are conferred a position which appears questionable. While religion looks up to female deities such as Saraswati and Lakshmi as sources of knowledge and material comforts respectively, women in the mortal world are deprived of both to a large extent.

The education of women is mostly considered irrelevant and their economic independence is hardly thought about by a majority. Even the Brahmanical-sanskritic texts do not seem to lay much emphasis on the learning of women. As Vijaya

Ramaswamy observes, that "...most of the important high tradition texts such as Manusmriti and Yajnavalkyasmriti say that marriage takes place of education...for women" (Ramaswamy, 2003). In this way, the paradox of inclusion and exclusion persists in the sense that while these traditional texts confer divinity to a female and make her the residing deity of learning, in the mortal world, the education of women rarely encounters support in terms of any scriptural sanction. Also, by equating marriage to education in the case of women, the women are once again confined to the household and exiled indoors.

This callous attitude with regards to the promotion of scholarship among women seems to have existed ever since. While retracing the mythical past, it is interesting to note that though the past may boast of a handful of learned women, there is hardly any significant text attributed to them. The well-known Brahminical-Sanskritic texts today have been authored by men and it is these texts that are cited and used as benchmarks for structuring the society. The *Dharmasutras* and the *Dharmashastras* that are considered to be the sources of the Hindu law have been attributed to male authors. For instance, the six major contributors of the *Dharmasutras* include, *Gautama, Baudhayyana, Apastamba, Vasistha, Vishnu* and *Harit*. Similarly, the six major contributors of the *Dharmashastras* are well known sages like *Manu, Yajnavalkya, Parashara, Narada, Brhaspati* and *Katyayana*. The two Indian epic namely the *Ramayana* and the *Mahabharata* are once again attributed to men. It is also worth noting that the mythological legend regarding the creation of the universe mentions the creation of ten *maharishis*, namely *Mariki, Atri, Angiras, Pulastya, Pulaha, Kratu, Praketas, Vasishtha, Bhrigu,* and *Narada* (Buhler, 1.35) in particular, but there is no mention of any specific female sage being created. It was these great sages who created and developed the discourses of social conduct that have persistently exercised influence till date.

On the other hand, the learned women or Brahmavadinis, who find a passing mention during the Vedic period, have hardly any substantial contribution to make to the corpus of the Vedic texts. According to Vijaya Ramaswamy,

> Out of the thousand hymns which come down to us from the Vedas, only ten were authored by the Brahmavadinis, i.e. a ratio of 1:100 (Ramaswamy, 2003).

One is hardly left with much to say after such a revelation. The statistic speaks volumes regarding the participation of women within the social working of the society — a scenario that has still not improved by and large. It is clear that the texts as well as the society are explicitly as well as implicitly governed by a perspective which is primarily male, despite the divinity conferred on women. It is this absence of women as writers, within a literary canon which instructs, condemns and eulogises them every now and then, that may be seen as stark instance of the social inclusion and exclusion taking place simultaneously.

In terms of the female voice within the canonical religious texts, the deified representation or iconization of women once again serves as an interesting site of contention. On the one hand, women are canonized as 'devi' while on the other hand they become victims of their own divinity. Despite their stature, the iconized women within the Indian textual tradition exhibit a sense of powerlessness as far as their voice within the social sphere is concerned. Moreover, the perspective visible in these texts is primarily male. The female voice, though mostly silenced, reiterates patriarchal norms even when allowed to speak. Then, be it Sita or Savitri, Draupadi, Ahalya or any other iconic woman of the mythical past, their conduct is divine only till they adhere to the norms of patriarchy.

The divine aura created around these women is fed with the patriarchy-approved discourses of female virtues, such as loyalty towards their husband, selfless service towards them, adherence to their commands without questioning, enduring hardships of their behaviour, sacrificing all it takes to ensure their well-being, and of course, bearing sons. While Sita followed Rama during his exile and later left the royal palace to live in the forest, when her husband commanded, *Ahalya* bore her husband's curse for ages, waiting for her redeemer *Rama*, (the mere touch of whose toe would turn her back from a stone to the human form). *Mandodari* too, gave in to the whims of her husband *Ravana*, and agreed to welcome *Sita* into the family. These virtues are further strengthened by treatise such as the

Manusmriti, which direct women to be with their husband in every condition.

> "ashil kam-britho wa gunyar wa parivarjit
> Upacharya streeya sadiyouwa sa-taha dewbat pati"5 and 154 (Manusmriti, 5.154)

> (Though destitute of virtue, or seeking pleasure (elsewhere), or devoid of good qualities, (yet) a husband must be constantly worshipped as a god by a faithful wife. Buhler, 5.154)

In relation to the scriptural prescriptions regarding the duties of women, Smith states that,

All the Hindu law books agree that the foremost duty of a wife is to obey her husband and to honour him as her god. The good wife pativrata, remains always devoted to her husband. Whether or not her husband is worthy of her is irrelevant. As long as she honours him, she is honourable — though this is not usually explicit — goddess to her god (Smith, 2003).

Therefore, women as a presence within the social sphere primarily exist due to their association with men and their honour rests in their being exiled indoors, attending to the needs of their husband and family. For, there is hardly any instance where the iconic women are remembered for being wise politicians, economists, policy-makers, etc.

This dependence of women on men in order to claim social visibility is more explicit in the case of widows. For in this case, the death of a woman's husband means 'social death' for the woman. As Rajul Sogani (2002) observes, "In the case of a widow, 'pativratya' entailed a complete withdrawal from participation in the social life of the community and the imposition of a severe discipline which made her existence a virtual social death." The situation becomes all the more worse if the woman has no sons. Sogani (2002) further adds that,

> A young childless widow had no status in the family and was treated as an unpaid drudge and a useless drag on resources as she had no direct or manifest economic role. She was considered ritually impure, inauspicious and dangerous—someone to be shunned and treated with suspicion.

Therefore, without her husband and her sons, a woman has no utility within the household. In this way, in the absence of men, she no longer remains a presence. She becomes a mere shadow that has no claims over even being considered a human, let alone being divine.

Within the discourses of divinity, womanhood and matrimony, the notion of purity also commands authority. Purity of the mind, body, thought and action, have been considered as one of the highest virtues to be possessed by any individual. But, women in particular are expected to cultivate them and make them an essential part of their existence. This is important for them not only at an individual level, but also at the level of the family, since they are vital as a presence in the domestic sphere. And it is only by maintaining domestic sanctity that women can claim reverence and well-being within the social sphere.

Divinity demands purity at every step. For instance, at the level of the body, "For higher castes, a menstruating woman is held to be impure. She does not cook, nor does she enter a temple during her period" (Smith, 2003). This seems to be a paradoxical instance, for, on the one hand a woman is conferred divinity and on the other she is condemned for defiling it on the basis of a phenomenon which is purely biological. Here, the idea of purity and impurity gets further complicated with the association of another couple of concepts, namely that of auspiciousness and inauspiciousness. As Smith observes, "The opposition between pure and impure exists in tandem with another pair of concepts: auspicious and inauspicious" (Smith, 2003). In this light, while a menstruating woman is impure, she is also "the potential creator of new life" and thus "she is auspicious....The menstruating wife glories in her potentially fertile condition. The red tilak mark, and even more the line of red painted on the parting of her hair, directly relate to the auspicious redness of menstruation. The red powder placed on images worshipped by women is an indirect glorification" (Smith, 2003). On the other hand, "The pre-menopausal widow, having no male partner, cannot give birth and is on that account inauspicious" (Smith, 2003).

The discourses of purity and auspiciousness also entwine the discourse of virginity. A girl is considered as a manifestation of the 'devi' before she attains puberty. The worship of the '*kanya*' is a common practice within the tradition (Ironically and unfortunately, female infanticide is as prevalent.) But while on the one hand, religion deifies the girl child as an image of the divine, on the other hand, by giving the son prominence within the social framework, it inadvertently pushes people to eliminate female individuals, sometimes even before they are born. And for those who survive, guarding their virginity becomes a major concern. For, it is the safeguarding of their virginity which is considered the sole parameter of a woman's merit. In this respect, Rajul Sogini's observation aptly highlights the strategic control of female sexuality both through coercion as well as consent. She states that,

> [W]omen were jealously guarded and their freedom severely restricted. The ideology of pativratya or satitva (chastity and devotion to the husband) was designed to make them control their own sexuality and avoid transgressing patriarchal norms.

After being fed with such an ideology since childhood, women start believing that, they can claim social respectability only if, they are virgin before their marriage and remains loyal to their husband thereafter—thus becoming custodians of their own enslavement.

In the light of the above discussion, one factor which can be recognised as a major shaping force behind a strategic inclusion and exclusion of women within the social sphere is the patriarchal desire to control female sexuality. From the importance associated with virginity, to the stress laid on marriage, from conferring divinity and aura to motherhood and fidelity, to the eulogizing of icons of female domesticity, all have been different means to attain the same end, that of keeping women in control, by keeping their sexuality in check. In other words, "The essence of a woman is reduced to her hymen" (Ali, xi).

Women have been excluded from the public realm and exiled indoors in the name of protecting their 'honour' which is once again solely understood in terms of their sexuality. Then, whether as a girl, a married woman or a widow; a woman's existence is confined within the four corners of the household for honour's sake. It is the protection of this 'honour' that has claimed several lives in the past and continues to do so even in the present. For instance, it is in the name of honour that women were forced to perform *sati* and were later deified for other women to take inspiration from. Even today women are killed in the name of honour, at the slightest hint of transgression.

Despite having entered the modern era, the situation of women has not improved to an appreciable level. While the patriarchal control has played its part, women themselves too have been responsible for their own state. With the constant indoctrination over the ages, women have eventually become custodians of their own enslavement. According to Ayaan Hirsi Ali (31-32) women,

> [H]ave internalised their subordination, they no longer experience it as an oppression by an external force but as a strong internal shield. Women who have mastered the survival strategies derive a certain pride from living this way. They are like prisoners suffering from Stockholm syndrome, in which hostages fall in love with the hostage-takers and establish a deep, intimate contact with them. But it is an unhealthy intimacy, comparable to slaves who are subordinate not only in body, but also psychologically, and who preferred the certainty of their existence in slavery to a freedom that they perceive as treacherous.

This attitude certainly needs rectification. In order to emancipate women from the claustrophobic bondage of patriarchy, which is safely obscured within the divine discourses, it is important that the distinction between the natural and the naturalised roles of women is made clear. The frozen iconic notions need to be broken and women need to be realised as individuals in their own right. Though some change in the condition of women is visible in the present times, the society at large still has a long way to go in order to ensure equality to women in every sphere and liberate them from being exiled indoors.

References

Bose, Mandakranta (2010). Women in the Hindu Tradition: Rules, Roles and Exceptions, New York: Routledge.

Buhler, G. Manusmriti: The Laws of Manu. Web. http://www.hinduism.about.com/library/weekly/extra/bl-lawsofmanu9.htm

Pande, Mrinal (1996). Devi: Tales of the Goddess in our Times, New Delhi: Penguin.

Ramaswamy, Vijaya (2003). 'Re-searching Icons, Re-presenting Indian Women' in Vijaya Ramaswamy (ed.), *Re-searching Indian Women*, Delhi: Manohar.

Saxena, Surendranath (2011), trans. Manusmriti, Delhi: Manoj.

Smith, David (2003). Hinduism and Modernity, Blackwell.

Sogani, Rajul (2002). The Hindu Widow in Indian Literature, New York: O.U.P.

5

Conflict Induced Widowhood and the Right to State Assistance: A Case Study of Manipur

Upasana Mahanta and *Samrat Sinha*

Introduction

It is generally acceptable to state that the Northeastern region of India has been historically affected by the phenomenon of armed conflict. While the veracity of the statement made above cannot be denied, it is critical to point out that "armed conflict" is an extremely problematic lens to view developments in the region for two particular reasons. Firstly, conventional understandings of armed conflict define the phenomenon as consisting of "a contested incompatibility which concerns government and/or territory where the use of armed force between two parties, of which at least one is the government of a state, results in at least 25 battle-related deaths."[1] The definition further goes on to explain that the two types of incompatibility consist of the following:

- Incompatibility concerning government: In this case, the incompatibility concerns the type of political system, the replacement of the central government or the changing of its composition.

- Incompatibility concerning territory: In this case, the incompatibility concerns the status of a territory, for example, the change of the state in control of a certain territory (interstate conflict), secession or autonomy (intrastate conflict).

As will be demonstrated consequently, conflict in the region does not necessarily conform to the assumptions held by the definition, primarily because of changes in the nature of the means being used, the direction of the violence and the perpetrators. While many of the conflicts originally began with the essential philosophy of state-contestation whereby the armed resistance movements (through their ideology and mass mobilisation) sought to carve out autonomous territories and replace the state through secession, the nature of the response of the state by itself led to certain transformations in the dynamics of the various conflicts in the region. The militarised approach towards combating the insurgency has indeed been stated as being a successful strategy in reducing levels of overall violence (as shown in the data below) whereby reduction in fatalities among security forces and civilians (and increasing arrests and fatalities among members of armed groups) are used as an indicator of success of counter-insurgency initiatives.[2] However, this transformation in the intensity of the conflicts addressed in the data especially, seen only in terms of formal indicators, overlooks several other processes which are closely connected to the nature of violence that is being witnessed in the region. As will be argued in the paper, there is a marked inconsistency between the "conflict indicators" and what can be termed as "conflict burdens." Moreover, by focusing our attention on the overall volume of violence leads us to ignore in many ways the seriousness of the problem of estimating "conflict burdens" especially given the assumption that "conflicts" in the Northeast are being transformed or are ending. A reflection of this particular stance can be seen in the increasing attention being paid to the increasing number of ceasefire arrangements that are being established between the central/state government and armed groups as also the number of members of armed groups surrendering (or being rehabilitated). While these developments are important, it must be pointed out that the organizational structures of many non-state actors remain resilient. Moreover, many of the groups are now treading the continuum between the "greed" and "grievance" models of behavior whereby they engage in both ideological justifications for their actions but also have a significant economic motivation.[3] As Ballentine and Hero state:

Much of the academic debate on the economic causes of contemporary armed conflict has become polarized around the *greed* versus *grievance* dichotomy, juxtaposing "loot-seeking" with "justice-seeking" rebellions, and, more generally, the significance of economic versus socio-political drivers of civil war. There is growing recognition, however, of the analytical limits that this dichotomy imposes on what are in reality highly complex systems of social interaction. While there is overall agreement that economic factors matter to conflict dynamics, there is little consensus as to *how much* they matter relative to other political and socio-cultural factors. The answers to these questions are not merely academic. Improved understanding of the causes, character, and dynamics of intra-state conflict can lead to more effective policies for conflict prevention and resolution; conversely, inadequate analysis may result in inappropriate policy responses and ill-conceived solutions."[4]

As stated above, interpreting the current state of violence through overall reductions in fatalities (and other quantitative indicators) and engaging in negotiations with armed actors does not necessarily lead to transformation of the conflict in its entirety. Rather, what we have until now perceived are changes in the *political* drivers of the conflict and not necessarily transformations in the *societal* consequences of conflict. What must be remembered is that the *societal* consequences of conflict can outlast in many ways the political grievances or ideological motivations that marked the origins of a particular conflict. It is the derivation, measurement and disaggregation of these societal impacts that require explication and in-depth study in order to design well-conceived solutions to the complex nature of conflict dynamics in the region. In summing up, three major approaches or standpoints are taken in the paper, which will be addressed in the course of the writing:

- First, it is important to understand the characteristics of the changing nature of conflict in the region and their interrelationship with conflict-burdens.
- Second, analysis of the conflict must not be limited to the political or ideological environment, but must be broadened to include the direct and indirect consequences of insecurity. Moreover, disaggregating these consequences must be rooted in evidence-based empirical approaches that establish the extent of unrecognized processes that are part of the overall conflict-burden.
- Third, evidence-based approaches have to be integrated into long-term advocacy measures that seek to bring about long-term change in the alleviation or reduction of conflict-burdens.

In the next two sections, we seek to achieve the following. First, we provide certain insights into the characteristics of the overall nature of violence in the Northeast and certain unrepresented thematic areas. This section integrates available data in the public domain and also findings from micro-level dataset constructed by our field research project on conflict dynamics in the state of Manipur. Following this, we describe certain specific direct and indirect consequences of conflict that have remained understudied in the literature of the region. Second, we discuss the nature of conflict-induced widowhood and provide certain qualitative narratives and extract themes that are indicative of the nature of vulnerability faced by conflict widows. A central argument in this section is that conflict creates categories of persons and emergent vulnerabilities that did not exist earlier which are part of the conflict-burden. Widows of persons who have been killed as a result of the conflict are a neglected category of persons who require special attention. At the same time, they are sub-sample of other vulnerable populations whose lives have been directly (or indirectly) affected by conflict such as: the elderly, children, orphans, wives of those who are incarcerated, and persons who have been disabled (due to injury). While we are of the view that these other populations also require systematic attention, we focus our attention on widowhood for two particular reasons. Firstly, as a category of persons, conflict widows have not received special attention even in the literature on gender impacts of conflict. Thus, very little is known about the manner in which widows evolve coping mechanisms and are able to improve their life-chances. Conversely, the manner in which widows face obstacles to accessing government services (including justice mechanisms), the new vulnerabilities they face in terms of domestic conditions, and the nature of psychological trauma after losing their husbands remains completely unknown. At the same time, we do not seek to portray widows as being passive and only as victims of life-changing circumstances. Rather there is an active negotiation with the environment in which they exist and contribute actively to changing or coping with their circumstances. In many cases, individual widows become instrumental in organising and mobilising civil society support in terms of access to justice mechanisms but also in terms of livelihood support, health education and social welfare.

Characteristics of Conflict Processes in the Northeastern Region with a Focus on Manipur

In characterising the conflict processes in the Northeast, it is extremely difficult to provide an overarching framework to interpret the nature of the phenomenon. The multi-dimensionality of the process implies that every conflict-affected state or district has unique contextual causal factors. As stated by Phanjoubam (2009):

The broad brush, any painter will testify, is a tool often used to shroud and mystify a subject so as to disguise and give credence to ignorance of the inner dynamics of the subject. And so, in the portrayal of the insurgency in not just Manipur but the entire northeast region, the popular resort has been to rely on images of primitive clannish tribal loyalties, mutual and irreconcilable atavistic hostilities among tribal groups, primordial xenophobia reminiscent of the days of savagery, etc. This approach leaves little room for a resolution apart from keeping the warring parties separated from each-other (just as the instinctually determined hostility between cats and dogs is resolved by keeping them apart).[5]

In reaffirming the need to guard against the danger of essentialist narratives, Das (2009) states:

> Social scientists working on the region have a tendency of blowing conflicts out of proportions in a way that inter-ethnic conflicts are conventionally taken as the mark of the society and politics of the northeast. Conflicts are sanitised of their complexities and are defined in simple black and white terms. The absence of conflicts is read as cooperation and vice versa. We, on the other hand, plot conflict and cooperation along a continuum and there are vast grey areas that spans between them. If there is one hallmark that is said to characterise these societies, it is conflicts between communities in the region. The history of conflicts in the region written by the scholars becomes so overbearing that it hides the history of cooperation and turns our attention away from the intricacies of conflicts that may have told a different story had they been studied in depth. Seldom are their works informed by any microstudies in conflicts and violence in the region.[6]

The two views presented above are extremely critical when we present the overall data on fatalities in the Northeast, for both indicate a need to conduct rigorous sub-state studies in order to provide an accurate description of the situation. We, thus, present below two types of data that provides the context for the study. The first pertains to the overall number of fatalities in the states of Assam, Manipur, Meghalaya, Mizoram, Nagaland and Tripura since 1992. These are compiled from the South Asia Terrorism Portal (SATP) which uses both news sources and official figures. We then present a disaggregated analysis of findings from a micro-level dataset which examined 22538 insurgency related events in 2008-2009 and also a study conducted by Regional Institute of Medical Sciences (RIMS) Hospital, Imphal.

In terms of descriptive statistics it can be seen in the SATP data that 19507 persons have died as a result of insurgency related incidents in the six-states mentioned above. Excluded from this data are the number of victims of ethnic riots and also the number of injury victims (who are a significant, yet unknown

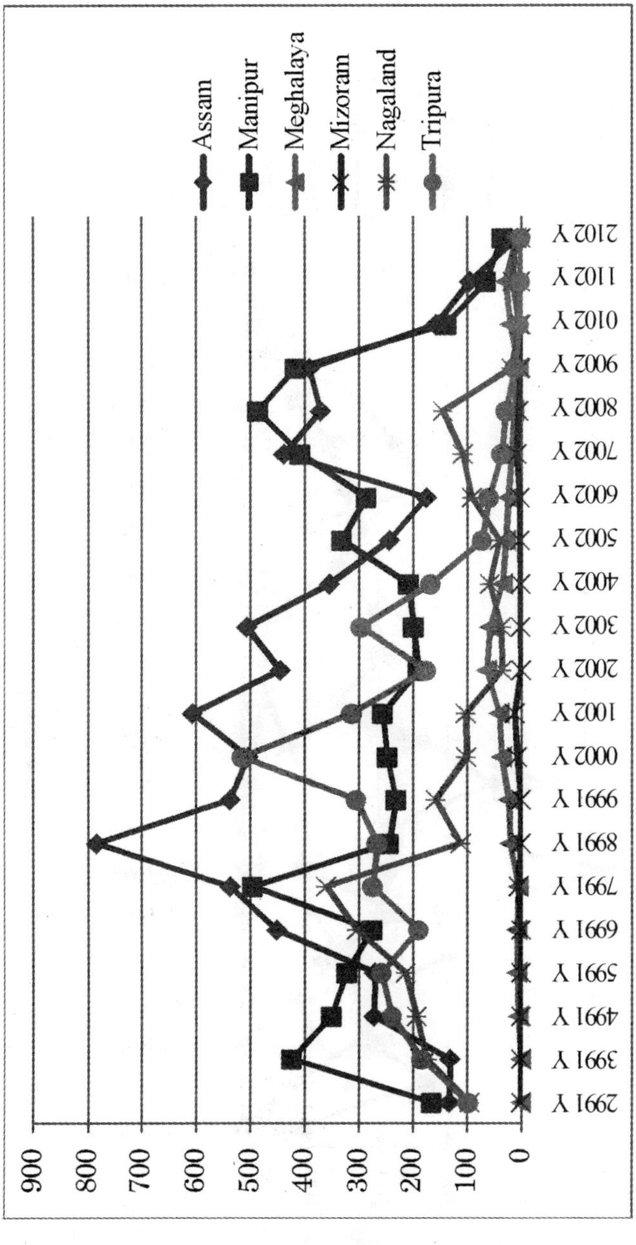

Fig. 4.1: Overall Trends in Violence 1992-2012[7]

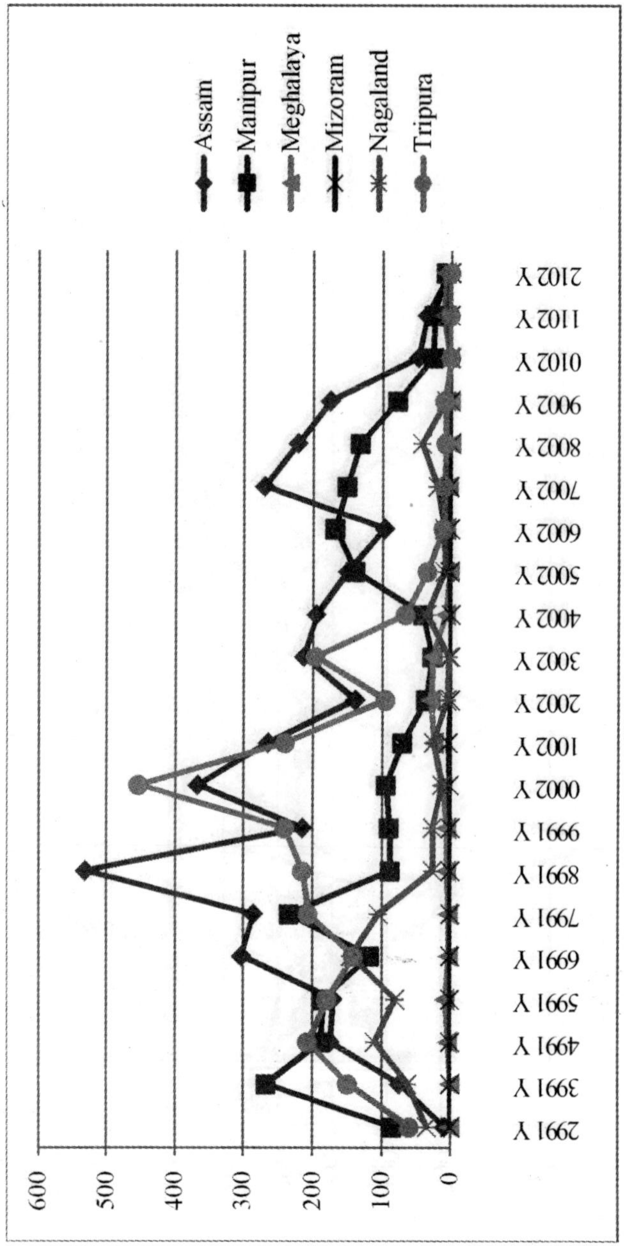

Fig. 4.2: Overall Civilian Fatalities[8]

number of persons). In terms of civilian fatalities, the following can be seen below.

In terms of civilian casualties, it is important to point out that, of the 19,507 estimated overall fatalities, 9,605 are civilians and constitute a striking 49.23 per cent of all fatalities. The high numbers of civilian fatalities that in the data raise a critical question: if conflict processes are about the control over state and territory and essentially involve incompatibilities between the state and armed groups, then why are there such a high proportion of civilian victims? One possible explanation lies in the changing nature of insurgency itself whereby the strategies of the security forces has meant that a lot of violence by non-state actors is directed towards civilians. As stated by Lacina (2009) in describing patterns of insurgency in Northeastern India: "A more important factor behind ongoing insurgency is the weakness and corruption of formal political institutions in the region. Many of the small insurgent groups in the Northeast lack the capacity to launch attacks on central government targets. Instead, they flourish by simultaneously partnering with and preying on weak local governments through extortion, partisan clashes, and criminality."[9] Even more important is what we cannot infer from the data: what are the demographic patterns underlying these distributions and moreover what about injury victims?

In attempting to shed light on these questions, the "Manipur Micro-level Dataset on Insurgency Events (2008-2009)" showed certain significant patterns. The study recorded 1,010 fatalities and 416 injury victims over a two-year period and some of the inferences pertaining to demographic distributions are given below and will be discussed subsequently.

It would also be important at this juncture to present some of the important findings by a study done by RIMS hospital which we had mentioned previously.[10] The study was a retrospective study of homicidal fatal firearm injury cases brought for autopsy in the Department of Forensic Medicine, RIMS from Imphal-East and Imphal-West districts for the period 1986-2003. It was found that out of the 3,947 medico-legal cases brought to light from these two districts for the time period, 1,248 (or 31.62 per cent) were caused by firearms.[11] The following findings were also stated by the authors:

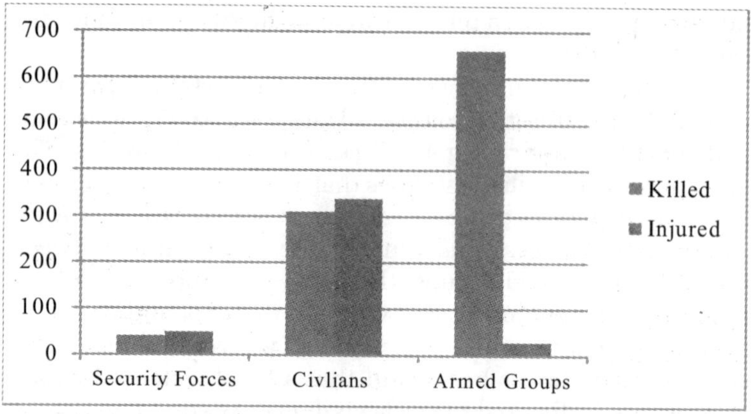

Fig. 4.3: Comparison of Victims Manipur 2008-2009[12]

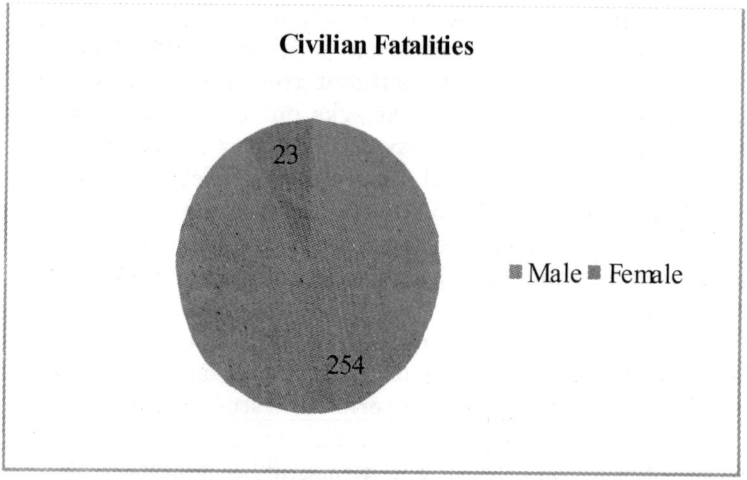

Fig. 4.4: Gender Distribution of Civilian Fatalities[13]

Out of those 1,248 victims, 35.98 per cent were killed by militants, 32.13 per cent by security forces and 31.89 per cent by unknowns. 53.77 per cent of the victims were civilians of which 28.29 per cent were killed by the unknowns, 21.23 per cent by militants and 4.25 per cent by security forces. 98 per cent of the victims were male and 50.56 per cent were of the age group 21 to 30 years, which was followed by the age group 31-40 (20.51 per cent) and then 11 to 20 years (16.27 per cent). 6.25

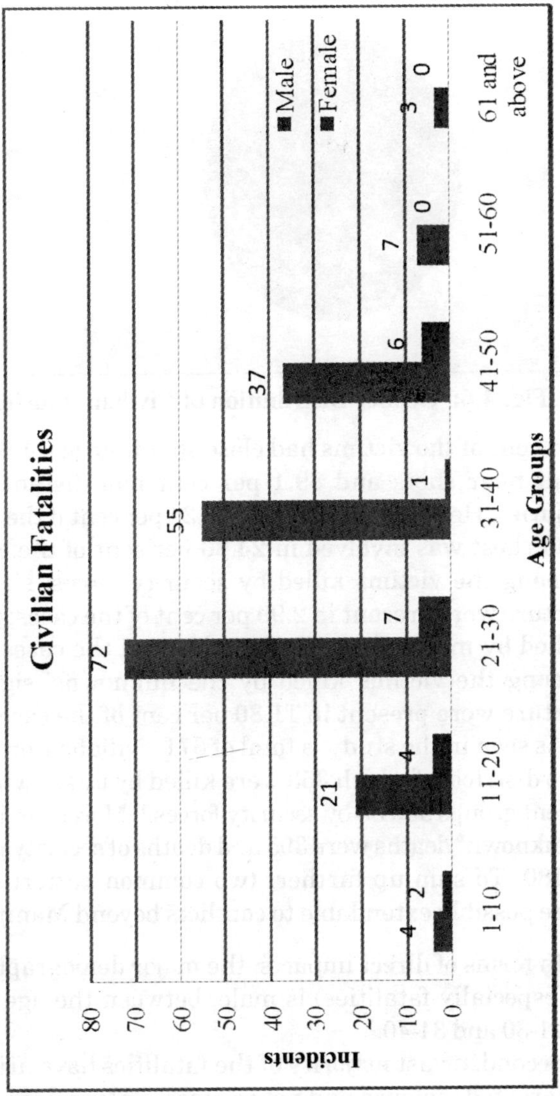

Fig. 4.5: Age-Wise Distribution of Civilian Fatalities[14]

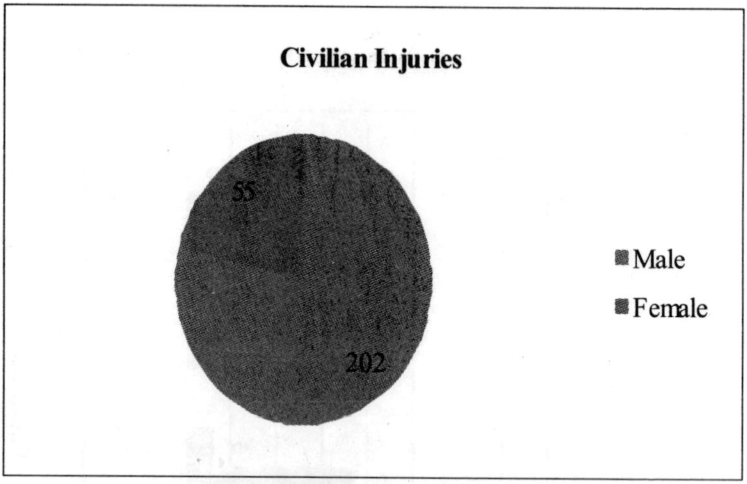

Fig. 4.6: Gender Distribution of Civilian Injuries[15]

per cent of the victims had close shot injuries, 4.65 per cent near shots and 89.1 per cent had distant shot injuries. Head was involved in 60.34 per cent if the cases and chest was involved in 24.36 per cent of the cases. Among the victims killed by security forces, signs of torture were present in 2.99 per cent of the cases; those killed by militants in 10.25 per cent of the cases, and among the victims killed by the unknowns' signs of torture were present in 11.80 per cent of the cases.[16]

As seen in the study, a total of 671 civilians were killed in the two districts of which 353 were killed by unknowns, 265 by insurgent groups and 53 by security forces.[17] Moreover, insurgent and "unknown" deaths were 395 and deaths of security personnel were 180. To sum up further, two common patterns emerge that are possibly extendable to conflicts beyond Manipur:

- In terms of direct impacts, the major demographic group (especially fatalities) is male, between the age range of 21-30 and 31-40.
- Second, a vast majority of the fatalities have arisen from targeted violence and not in mass-scale violence.

The fact that we were able to infer the above patterns is extremely problematic for the simple reason that the focus of

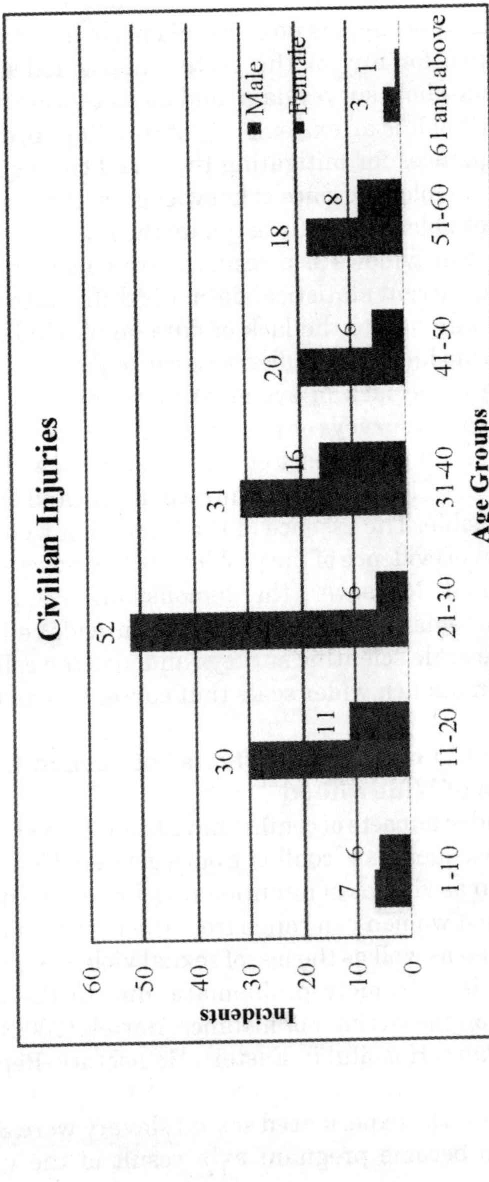

Fig. 4.7 : Age-Wise Distribution of Civilian Injuries[18]

our work has been more event-based. As a result, what we have presented above are only "direct" impacts of the violence and are unable, till now, to grapple with the more serious "indirect" consequences of the casualty patterns described above. In other words, the fact that there is no comprehensive list of victims of armed violence for any of the states mentioned above (or systematic household survey data) and no state-wide records of affected households is an extremely problematic gap, which has major consequences for mitigating the social consequences of conflict. This complete absence of knowledge on the issue means that it is impossible to actually estimate the number of persons who have become widows as a result of armed action. Rather, even with the current statistical data it is difficult to make an indirect estimate due to the lack of data on marital status of those males who have been killed as a consequence of conflict. In many ways, the lack of systematic attention to casualty recording (through surveys or passive surveillance techniques) has meant that an entire part of the population, which bears the brunt of conflict, has gone unrecognised and has been rendered invisible. The essence of the issue in our view is the demonstration of evidence of the problem, before policy solutions can be designed. Moreover, the demonstration of evidence, requires a systematic state-wide (or region wide) effort that involves large scale scientific surveys and also the collation of testimonies on a much wider scale that currently exists.

The "Indirect" and "Direct Effects" of Armed Conflict: The Problem of Widowhood

The gender impacts of conflict have been studied in depth. The direct consequences of conflict from a gendered lens revolve around women as victims of intentional violence. The nature of violence against women can range from the use of armed force to target women as well as the use of sexual violence. The latter phenomenon is extremely problematic due to the adverse consequences on the victim. For instance, Bartels (2006) in their study of the Panzi Hospital in Eastern Democratic Republic of Congo state:

Survivors who experienced sexual slavery were 37 times more likely to become pregnant as a result of the violence.

Previous work from Panzi Hospital demonstrated that sexual violence survivors who become pregnant as a result of the attack were more likely to report psychological symptoms than were women who did not report a resultant pregnancy. Since abortion is illegal in DRC and since adoption is rarely considered an option in Congolese society, most pregnant sexual violence survivors find themselves responsible for raising a child. Because many sexual slavery survivors are single and because identification as a "rape victim" usually impedes a woman's chances of marrying, many pregnant survivors are single parents. Not only does this impede the survivor's ability to continue school or to pursue a career, but without the economic support and protection traditionally provided by men in DRC, it also increases her vulnerability.[19]

In the case of gender impacts of violence, the underlying difference between "direct" and "indirect" impacts is a definitional one. While "direct" impacts essentially revolve around patterns and effects of victimization and type of violence, "indirect" impacts tend to go beyond the immediate, to the short and long-term consequences of the act of violence. In addition, many of the "indirect" effects tend to be aggravated with the larger breakdown of health-systems, livelihood structures, schooling and other societal systems. Conflict-induced widowhood has both individual level and societal level consequences which require systematic attention. While patterns of violence can be studied and defined, widowhood is a subject that has not received adequate attention in the broader literature. One of the primary reasons behind this is that studies attempting to derive patterns of armed (and sexual) violence are generally based on individual-level information (or testimonies). On the other hand, a study of widowhood would not only require individual level information but also require "household" level information as well. In other words, widowhood is not only constituted by the individual's experience of widowhood but is also constituted by shifting gender roles (especially in case of women-headed households) within the larger household/family unit. This is not to say that there have been no findings on the conditions of widows. While very little is known about the intra-household changes, studies are indicative of enhancement of vulnerabilities of widows at the individual. For instance, a study on Rwanda[20] (Turhsen, 2001) found that Rwandan widows in the post-genocide era are more vulnerable to extortion and expropriation of their husband's land while it was found that widows in the same country in the post-genocide context are vulnerable to discrimination which significantly affects their living standards.[21] The increasing vulnerability of widows to predatory behaviours was also seen in a study in Northern Uganda where they found widows in an internally displaced community were compelled to engage in High Risk Sexual Behavior (HSRB):

> Even after coming out of displacement that came about due to ensuing conflicts and wars, most people in the study population were still mourning the loss of their property which had always been a basis of their livelihood. Apparently, this had forced some of them to adopt HRSBs to acquire basic necessities of life. With the maltreatment of men during the conflicts who are traditional breadwinners, many widows and vulnerable girls were reported to have ended up with no viable alternatives of supporting their families. Engaging in transactional sex was reported to have become a choice for many. Many of them took to engaging in HRSB to get money to buy food or to get physical food from those privileged to control or own it. Even after the 'guns had fallen silent', many widows and vulnerable girls were known to have continued with the HRSB adopted during the time of active conflicts. Findings from an FGD of 12 men aged 24-35 years and a 45 year old female who was a case study showed that impoverishment associated with the conflict had increased HRSB.[22]

In terms of possible outcomes, Scindler and Bruck (2007) put forward certain postulates that are relevant for intra-household level dynamics. Four significant conceptual points emerge from their work:[23]

- Intra-household relations and gender roles are affected by conflict. The allocation of tasks within the household may change across gender whereby women may perform productive activities that are confined to men, during times of peace.

- Gender roles have the greatest impact when women become the head of a household.
- The impact of conflict-induced changes in gender roles, in addition to the allocation of resources, income and decision-making power on widows, depends on household constellations they live in. For example, widows who become head of household may become the principle caretaker of other household members, and therefore, assume responsibilities in decision-making and productive tasks.
- At an individual level, because of their sex, widows are more vulnerable to attacks and sexual violence in both the conflict and post-conflict period.

In the context of Northeast India (especially pertaining to Manipur), the above conceptual points require further elaboration. The question of state assistance becomes extremely important primarily because of the following: first, it provides a possible pathway by which women-headed households can improve welfare outcomes for themselves and those members, whom they support; second, going beyond financial gains, welfare assistance can allow the enhancement of coping mechanisms for widows with their current vulnerabilities; third, even in cases where the widow is not the head of household, welfare assistance can possibly provide a degree of agency to the beneficiary that allows them to overcome their existing situation. Some of the problems faced by widows in Manipur were highlighted by the Conflict Widows Forum. On 19th September 2011, the Conflict Widows Forum called a conference at the Manipur Press. As the report from the *The Sangai Express* states:

> "Conflict Widows Forum member Ambrabati Takhelchangbam said that bandhs and blockades have compounded the woes of the people who have already been enduring the brunt of the conflict situation. The ongoing blockade which is now almost 50 days old has been causing immense misery to widows. On account of the prolonged blockade, prices of all essential

commodities have skyrocketed beyond the reach of impoverished people. HIV widows have been suffering the worst with ART drugs running short. Besides ART drugs, many other drugs prescribed by doctors are no longer available at the market, Ambrabati said. Under such situation, widows struggling for their square meal a day are at their wits end. On the other hand, these widows have not been given benefits entitled to BPL families on the ground that they are not heads of families." The Government has issued an order declaring that HIV widows would be given MGNREGS job cards. This is most welcomed. But the question, what would the Government do for other widows", Ambrabati said. Decrying the stoic silence maintained by the State Government rather than working to end the blockade, she lambasted the Government for turning a blind eye to the plight of the common masses in general and widows in particular. If the situation persists, the helpless widows would be forced to go begging even if the rich families do not feel any pain of the blockade, she added.[24]

In many cases, widows themselves become victims of direct violence. For instance, an example of this was reported on 10th April, 2008 by *The Sangai Express*. According to the report:

A young widow was found killed in an suspicious manner and her body abandoned at a paddy field located on the northern side of the Loushipat Main Canal, about 7 km north-east of Kakching Police Station in Thoubal district last night. According to police sources, the deceased woman has been identified as Laishram Ningol Laimujam Ongbi Shantibala alias Inaothoibi (24) w/o late L Rojen of Tentha Tuwanband. She was staying at her maternal mother's place at Tekcham Mayai Leikai along with her two sons and mother. Two of her younger brothers are reportedly working and staying at Imphal. Her husband, LaimujamRojen had been reportedly shot dead by unidentified gunmen near the Buffalo farm at Keirak some two years back on alleged charge of working as an informer.[25]

In another case reported by the *Hueiyen News Service* on 30th March, 2009:

> A widow sustained bullet injury when suspected gunmen which were perhaps underground fired at allegedly for refusing to deposit the gun to her home last night at around 8.30 pm at Khurai Konsam Leikai under Porompat police station. Decrying the act of the gunmen, locals, mostly womenfolk, of the locality carried out a sit-in protest today at Khurai Konsam Leikai.The injured widow was identified as Wahengbam Bilashini (55) wife of late Brajamani. She sustained bullet injury at the right armpit near the chest. According to the injured Bilasini, last night at around 8.30 pm two unknown youths entered to her house and requested to help them in carrying a small gun with them upto Salanthong. When she refused to do so, the two youths again requested her to deposit the arm to her house. This time also she turned the request. When she closed the door and remained inside the house and was trying to respond to a phone call, the miscreants fired a bullet inside the house from a window.[26]

The fact that widows are facing such serious problems requires consideration. As can be seen below, while the central government responded through a broad-based measure, there are several exclusionary aspects that obstruct the implementation of the policy in a judicious and equitable manner.

Central Government-led Assistance Programme: Assistance to Civilian Victims

The most prominent program developed by central government is the Ministry of Home Affairs (MHA) 'Central Scheme for Assistance to Civilian Victims/Family of Victims of Terrorist, Communal and Naxal Violence.' The scheme was formulated in April, 2008 and a final revised version was drafted in 2010. From the perspective of inclusion, we see that the scheme states that:[27]

- "Financial assistance would be given to the family member(s) in the event of death or permanent incapacitation of the victim" and that "assistance would be given to the surviving spouse in case of death/ permanent incapacitation of the husband or the wife, as the case may be."

- Moreover, an "amount of Rs. three lakh would be given for each death or permanent incapacitation to the affected family under the scheme" and that beneficiaries would be given a health card by the District Health Society, functioning under the National Rural Health Mission (NRHM). This card would entitle beneficiaries to free medical treatment in respect of injuries and all other major illnesses caused due to violence.
- Medical care would also be provided to the beneficiaries of the scheme as a special case under the on-going schemes of the Ministry of Health and Family Welfare such as the National Trauma Care Project.

At the same time, it is important to indicate that, while seemingly extensive in its applicability, the key to understanding the policy lies in its procedural requirements. However, looking at the policy from an exclusionary perspective indicates there are four major structural barriers that need to be redressed.

- *First*, the criteria of disability is highly problematic whereby the victim should have suffered a disability of "50 per cent and above." Moreover, the disability should be of a permanent nature where "there are no chances of variation in the degree of disability and the injury" and that the disability renders the "victim unfit for normal life for the rest of his life." These are types of injuries that do not necessarily fall within the 50 per cent range and hence claimants may not be eligible.
- *Second*, while the District Committee is responsible for verification, a number of documents have to be furnished by the claimant. These include the Police Report (First Information Report), Death-Postmortem Certificate in the event of death, and Medical Certificate in the case of permanent incapacitation. If the victim is a minor then the birth certificate is required, while an "eligibility certificate" issued by the District Superintendent of Police

is required in the case of naxal violence. In most conflict areas, with the collapse of governmental systems, many of the claimants would not necessarily be able to acquire the required documents thus affecting the claim.

- *Third*, the scheme is not applicable for the families of those who have been termed as a "perpetrator of violence." This implies that if a person has been killed by security forces, they would not be eligible for any assistance, a point which will be discussed later. Most databases and testimonies on conflict in India, in fact show that there have been high proportions of both civilian victims, and also casualties among alleged members of non-state armed groups, arising out of the actions of security forces.
- *Fourth* and most important, despite widowhood being such a prominent aspect of conflict, there are no provisions that deal specifically with long-term assistance to widows, in terms of livelihood support, medical care and psychological counseling. In other words, victim assistance pertaining to support for widows is essentially a long-term endeavor; the policy on the other hand views the issue through one-time short-term measures.

Organising beyond the State: The Necessity of Civil Society Approaches to Widow- Assistance

Given the nature of exclusion and inclusion into the central government scheme discussed above, it is extremely important to discuss assistance to survivors, that are *community-led or civil society-based.* Indeed, given the absence of long-established state-based schemes, community or individual-led assistance becomes a crucial mechanism that requires some degree of examination. Organising beyond the state is also a matter of concern, for in many ways, these initiatives though having a long-term perspective on rehabilitation of widows, work under severe resource and other constraints, including that of non-recognition. At the same time, these initiatives, by having their origins in the community, need to studied as they might provide means of support that are more context-driven, versus the top-down policy-driven approaches (with their high degree of exclusionary criteria). Two types of community-driven assistance can be seen in the case of Manipur. In the first type, these grass-roots initiatives tend to provide both livelihood and psycho-social assistance. In the second type, more formal legal support to families of those who have been alleged to have died in extra-judicial manner at the hands of security forces. This can be seen for instance in the *Ongbi Latani Devi* case which was decided by the Guwahati High Court in July, 2010 whereby litigation-support was provided by the Human Rights Law Network (HRLN) to the petitioner.[28] While the second type of assistance can become a subject of study by itself, we focus on the first for two reasons: (a) they represent an area of community organization that "emerged" outside the formal parameters of the state institutions; (b) they provide assistance to include moral and financial support to their members (and thus engage in long-term advocacy to cope with societal impacts in addition to facilitating access to justice). At the outset, it must be mentioned that the impact of these initiatives (and other similar movements in the other Northeastern states) have been understudied and hence been given very little recognition. Six of these community-led mechanisms have been described below in terms of their scope, aims and significant activities. Of these six, detailed information of only three initiatives is available, while being unavailable for the other three. The latter three initiatives occur very much at the micro-level, and their strategies and constraints, require detailed primary field work.

(i) Manipur Gun Survivors Network (MGSN)

MGSN was formally launched in 2007 and is currently steered by Ms. Binalakshmi Neparam. As stated in an official document of the MGSN, the genesis of the movement began in 2004, whereby Ms. Neparam witnessed the killing of 27-year old Buddhi Moirangthem (of Wagbai Lamkahi village, Thoubal) by unknown gunmen. In the aftermath of the incident, community members raised Rs. 4500 for the widow of Buddhi, Ms. Rebika Akham to purchase a sewing machine. After a steady evolution, it has emerged as an important model of victim assistance. The significance of the movement is that it provides assistance to widows of those who have been killed by both state and non-state actors. In terms of their work, the MGSN helps gun survivors to open bank accounts and provides small loans ranging from Rs. 3000-9000. In many cases, women are supported to engage in entrepreneurial work related to silk reeling, weaving and other occupation such as fishery or mushroom farming.[29] Apart from several consultations and advocacy initiatives (including collection of testimonies) on the issue of gun survivors, the MGSN in its future endeavors seeks to also draw on the support of doctors and psychologists, to professionally counsel women gun survivors and deal with their mental trauma.[30]

(ii) EEVFAM(Extrajudicial Execution Victims Family Association, Manipur)

EEVFAM is an extremely important initiative that requires mention, as it partly emerged in the context of the exclusionary aspects of state assistance discussed above. Formed in 2009, the association is formed by those women, whose husbands were killed by security forces. Moreover, due to the nature of the death of their husbands, they are excluded from any of the central schemes (including those extendable to orphans of conflict) whereby the impact not only falls on the widows, but also the children of the deceased. In addition, the widows are also excluded from schemes offered by the state Social Welfare Department. One of the core philosophies of the organisation is narrated by Renu Takhellambam (Secretary, EEVFAM) who is the wife of Mung (who was killed in a suspected extrajudicial killing by Imphal-West police commandos on 6th April 2007. According to Ms. Renu:

> EEVFAM is first and foremost about self-empowerment and mental support. Every time someone in this region is killed, we go there. We sit with the survivors in their houses, we share their sorrow. The depression, the trauma is sometimes so severe that women cannot even talk, let alone stand up for themselves, their children and their murdered husband. I know only too well that as a widow, for the first months or even years you feel completely isolated and you think that you will be standing alone for the rest of your life. We show them that this is not so. We help women come out of that

> depression. But we also try to give financial support. The little that we have, we share so that they can send their children to school, for example. Else, we help them to get a job or an income. And we offer legal support, by referring them to pro-bono lawyers we know, by organising informational meetings with human rights organisations, by sorting out what kinds of compensation and support they are entitled to from the government. More and more, widows in the city are getting access to this information. They know their rights as human beings, as women and as widows. But in the country, that is by no means the case. Here again, we share everything that we have: information, knowledge, financial resources, sorrow and compassion. When we give workshops today, sometimes the local press sends someone. That shows that we are getting there. But it also means we have to watch out. Because, the more you act out in the open, the more you demand your rights and the rights of your murdered husbands, the more you are known as a critical organization of troublesome widows, and the more you risk the government, the army or the police making your life difficult.[31]

One of the critical aspects of EEVFAM is that it functions in an informal manner, primarily due to the fact that the association has not been given permission to register under the Societies Registration Act by the Government.[32]

(iii) Gun Widows' Survivor Association (part of Integrated Rural Development Social Organisation-IRDSO).

The IRDSO project was conceptualized under the "Supporting Gun Widow Survivors for Sustainable Livelihood" Project, an outcome of which was the formation of the Gun Widows' Survivor Association. As stated by IRDSO (2011):

> IRDSO initiated this project with the goal of strengthening the single women (gun-widow-survivors) as an important stakeholder in Peace Building rather than remaining as a victim, and bringing economic

liberation through creation of SHGs. Its aim is to bring about a change in the way the single women view themselves and their future, the society's and their respective families' prejudice and attitude towards them, and to enable them to cope with their irremediable loss. In a bid to bring about positive attitude and changes so as to help the single women to move forward in rebuilding their lives, IRDSO planned a series of gender rights and human rights education programmes. Additionally, capacities were built for formation of self-help groups (SHGs) to support livelihood initiatives.[44]

As IRDSO (2011) further goes on to describe its strategies:

As a result of IRDSO's effort, the single women from Yairipok, Wangjing and Irong villages were organised. To build their morale, strengthen their confidence and self-image frequent sharing meetings were conducted wherein women could share their hardships and discuss both domestic and societal attitude towards them. Initially, women just came together and cried and cried. Slowly, they opened up. Later on, to capacitate and broaden their perspectives, workshops on gender rights, human rights, conflict analysis and the Protection of Women from Domestic Violence Act, 2005 were conducted. IRDSO facilitated the women in forming 3 SHGs and after training them on accounts management and other SHG practices, each group was supported with a revolving fund of Rs. 50,000/- from which the SHG members were given small loans ranging from Rs. 2,000 to Rs. 5,000 to start income generating activities such as kitchen-gardening, poultry, piggery, detergent and soap-making, weaving, etc. The women have started earning and are now able to support their children and family. Their in-laws have started treating them with care and respect. As part of the effort to make them stakeholders in peace-building process, these single women groups initiated a network called "Gun Widow Survivors Association" and have appointed their Convener and Co-convener. The Gun Widow Survivors Association have also networked with a State level

Association called Extra Judicial Execution's Victim Families' Association, Manipur (EEVFAM), which is fighting for rights, justice and peace-building in the State of Manipur. This enables them to participate in the district and state level discussions on conflict resolution.[45]

Three major characteristics sum up the approach of the IRDSO intervention. Moreover, in striking contrast to the state-based programs these three characteristics possibly indicate a possible process which requires further mainstreaming (beyond the context of Manipur as well):

- First, it an intervention for which "breaking the cycle of armed conflict is very important for reducing violence."
- Second, this is made possible only by making the victims stakeholders in peace-building initiatives.
- Third, the method by which the above is to be achieved is through involving them in framing programmes and policies that ensure human security as a fundamental right.

(i) Gun Victims' Survivors Association (GVSA)

The Gun Victims' Survivors Association seems to be an additional initiative of the IRDSO and could possibly be seen in conjunction with the Gun Widows Survivors Association. Demands by the GVSA include the: provision of livelihood for widows, the ending of violence and a halt on the manufacturing of guns. What is striking about the GVSA-provided testimonies (GVSA 2011) is that their members consists of widows of state security personnel including those killed outside Manipur, persons killed by security forces, and even persons killed by non-state actors (thus providing a wider definition of conflict-widowhood).

(ii) Conflict Widows Forum

In terms of the organizational aspect of the Conflict Widows Forum, it has been difficult to locate information. However, a prominent example of their advocacy was their drawing attention to the plight of widows during the economic blockade of Manipur in 2011.

(iii) Association of Bomb Blast Survivors

Similar to the above, in terms of the lack of information on activities, the association's membership and coverage is more narrowly defined in scope. The association was formed after the Ragailong bomb blast of October 21, 2008. The Association of Bomb Blast Survivors advocates for provision of required expenditure for treatment of the Ragailong blast victims who have not received proper care. They also asked the State Government to provide compensation to the families of 18 persons killed in the blast as well as to 38 individuals who sustained injuries. They further asked for provision of jobs to the injured victims to support their livelihoods.

Conclusion and Discussion

As seen in the descriptions above, there are significant (yet underexplored) mechanisms that have involved enhancing the agency of widows, as opposed to treating them as recipients or non-recipients of welfare schemes. Indeed, the fact that the political context has in many ways shaped even a non-political issue of the right to welfare for widows of conflict, is a characteristic of the restrictive and exclusionary nature of conflict dynamics. At the same time, the initiatives mentioned above are significant because they confront exclusion in a direct manner, and seek to provide solutions that are not only victim-oriented but also in many ways victim-led. Moreover, by examining the issue of rehabilitation in a more holistic manner, these types of initiatives require more in-depth examination. Moreover, cross-cutting work that includes examination of similar initiatives across the Northeast, Jammu and Kashmir, Chattisgarh and other formerly conflict affected regions (such as Punjab) is required. Conflict-induced widowhood in other words, is a subject that goes well beyond the duality of the conventional approaches to conflict analysis, which treats the conflict and post-conflict period as a distinct set of processes. Rather, by looking at the topic from a victim-centered lens implies that analysis will have to go beyond the duality as in many ways the "indirect" effects of conflict can go well beyond the end of a conflict. Thus, while the Northeastern region may witness declining trends of armed violence, it does not mean the disappearance of the issue of victimization. Rather, there is a strong risk that the reduction in violence, might lead to the neglect of the vulnerabilities of those who have been affected by the conflict-contexts, especially widows, the elderly, orphans and the displaced.

References

1. Wallensteen, P., Sollenberg, M. (2001). Armed Conflict 1989-2000, *Journal of Peace Research*, Vol. 38(5): 629-644.
2. See Ministry of Home Affairs Annual Report 2010-2011. Available at <http://www.mha.nic.in/pdfs/AR(E)1011.pdf> Accessed 23/03/2012.
3. See "Militants extort about 160 crores a year", Imphal Free Press, 22 June 2008.
4. Ballentine, K., Nitzscheke, H. (2003). Beyond Greed and Grievance: Policy Lessons from Studies in the Political Economy of Armed Conflict," 2003,International Peace Academy: Program on Economic Agenda in Civil Wars, p. 2 Available at *<reliefweb.int / ... / 6765C3D3477FE91C8525742400689BD7. IPA_ArmedCoflict_Oct03.pdf.> (20 June 2011).*
5. Phanjoubam, P. (2009). 'Fragmented Civil Society: Problems and Prospects' in P. Singh (ed.) Tribalism and the Tragedy of the Commons: Land, Identity and Development: The Manipur Experience, New Delhi: Akanksha Press p.75.
6. Das, S.K. (2009). "Land Identity and Conflicts: A Plea for Rebuilding Civil Society in Manipur" in P. Singh. (ed.) Tribalism and the Tragedy of the Commons: Land, Identity and Development: The Manipur Experience, New Delhi: Akanksha Press p. 30.
7. Compiled from <http://satp.org/>Accessed 28/04/2012
8. *Ibid.*
9. Lacina, B. (2009). The Problem of Political Stability in Northeast India: Local Ethnic Autocracy and the Rule of Law", *Asian Survey,* XLIX No. 6, 998-1020..
10. Pradipkumar, Kh. et al. (2004). Homicidal Fatal Firearm Injuries, *Journal of the Indian Academy of Forensic Medicine* Vol. 27(4): 222-225.
11. *Ibid.* 223
12. Unpublished Report: The Burden of Insecurity: A Case Study of Conflict Dynamics in the State of Manipur (Tata Institute of Social Sciences: 2010).
13. *Ibid.*
14. *Ibid.*
15. *Ibid.*

16. Pradipkumar, Kh. et al. (2004). Homicidal Fatal Firearm Injuries, *Journal of the Indian Academy of Forensic Medicine* Vol. 27(4): 222-225.
17. *Ibid.* 223
18. Unpublished Report: The Burden of Insecurity: A Case Study of Conflict Dynamics in the State of Manipur (Tata Institute of Social Sciences: 2010).
19. Bartels, S et al. (2010). Patterns of sexual violence in Eastern Democratic Republic of Congo: reports from survivors presenting to Panzi Hospital in 2006, Conflict and Health, Vol. 4 (9):1-10.
20. Turshen, M. (2001). The political economy of rape: An analysis of systematic rape and sexual abuse of women during armed conflict in Africa, in Moser, C. and Clarke F ed. Victors, Perpetrators or Actors: Gender, Armed Conflict and Political Violence, London: Zed Books.
21. Nowrojee, B. (1996). Shattered Lives: Sexual Violence during the Rwandan Genocide and its Aftermath. New York: Human Rights Watch.
22. Muhwezi, Wilson W. et al, (2011). Vulnerability to High Risk Sexual Behaviour (HRSB) Following Exposure to War Trauma as Seen in Post-Conflict Communities in Eastern Uganda: A Qualitative Study, *Conflict and Health*, Vol. 5(22):1-15.
23. Bruck, T. and Schindler, K. (2007). The Impact of Conflict on Households: A Conceptual Framework with Reference to Widows, pp: 10-11. Available at <http://community.eldis.org/dsa/042 Schindler. pdf>Accessed 22/03/2012.
24. "Blockade exacts steep price from widows" Available at <http://www.thesangaiexpress.com/sangai-express-news.php?newsid=9043> Accessed 24/03/2012
25. "Young widow found dead, abandoned at Kakching" Available at <http://e-pao.net/epRelatedNews.asp?heading=2&src=110408> Accessed 27/02/2012.
26. "Widow hurt" <http://e-pao.net/GP.asp?src=Snipp18. 310309.mar 09>Accessed 27/02/2012.
27. 'Central Scheme for Assistance to civilian Victims of Terrorist, Communal and Naxal violence, Available at <http://mha.nic.in/pdfs/T-Guide141008.pdf >Accessed 5th March 2012
28. See "Compensation Awarded through HRLN Manipur to Victim of Unjustified Killing by Assam Rifles" <http://hrln.org/hrln/hrln-in-news/press-release.html?start=10>

29. Manipur Gun Survivors Network, 2009, p.5, Available from < http:/ /cafi-online.org/report/MWGSN_details.pdf>Accessed 20/03/2012.
30. Manipur Gun Survivors Network, 2009, p. 9, Available from < http://cafi-online.org/report/MWGSN_details.pdf>Accessed 20/03/2012.
31. Lierde, F. (2011). We, Widows of the Gun, Cordaid, The Hague, p.88.
32. India Status of Human Rights in Manipur: Joint Stakeholders Report (2011). Available from<http://lib.ohchr.org/HRBodies/UPR/Documents/session13/IN/JS13_UPR_IND_S13_ 2012_Joint Submission13_E.pdf> Accessed 23/03/2012.
33. See <http://www.fstindia.org/content/integrated-rural-development-service-organization>Accessed 27/04/2012.
34. *Ibid.*

6

Social Exclusion and the Tribes of Bankura in West Bengal: A Note on Violation of Human Rights

Sandip Kumar Ghatak

Introduction

Social Exclusion remains a malaise in all societies. Social exclusion is a process by which individuals or groups are wholly or partially excluded from full participation in the society within which they live. The term "social exclusion" was originally coined by Rene Lenoir, in France in 1974 to refer to various categories of people such as "mentally and physically handicapped, suicidal people, aged invalids, abused children, substance abusers, delinquents, single parents, multi-problem householders, marginal, asocial persons, and other social misfits" (Silver, 1995). But this term encompasses many dimensions: social, economic, legal and political. In India, unique forms of exclusion are observed where certain groups like the dalits, experience systematic exclusion in regard to accruing the benefits of development, and institutional inequality and discrimination have been prevailing in the society. It hampers democracy, development, and social integration. Dalits are excluded in every walk of life. The Indian social system, which was based on the principle of purity and pollution, was a system of inequality. This system denied equality before law, equal opportunity of the law and equal protection of the law. Thus, it was a source of social exclusion, and thereby a source of violation of human rights as well.

Social Exclusion

Exclusion as a social phenomenon is expressed in different forms all over the world. Social exclusion and discrimination are practiced on the basis of ethnicity, gender and religion. In Indian society, mainly, the caste and patriarchal systems are the source of social exclusion. Social hierarchy of traditional social system in India presents inequality between the highest and lowest castes. But in reality, the downtrodden communities are excluded from interaction and denied access to resources through inequitous social arrangements.

The concept of social exclusion has been defined differently among social scientists, both by western and Indian. According to Silver (2004), social exclusion is multi-dimensional process of progressive social rapture, detaching groups and individuals from social relations and institutions and preventing them from full participation in the formal, normatively prescribed activities of the society in which they live. As Amartya Sen (1997) observes that social exclusion emphasizes the role of relational feature in deprivation. Bauvinic (2005) summarises the meaning of social exclusion as the inability of individual to participate in the basic political, economic and social functioning of society and goes on to add that it involves "the denial of equal access of opportunities imposed by certain groups in society upon others." On the whole, social exclusion may be termed as a process by which, certain groups are wholly or partly denied full participation in the development activities-social, economic, cultural and political life of societies. Thus, social exclusion refers to process in which individuals and entire communities of people are systematically blocked from rights, opportunities and resources (e.g., housing, employment, health care, civic engagement, democratic participation and due process) that are normally available to members of society and which are key to social integration.

In India, exclusion is embedded in social interrelations that exclude, discriminate, isolate and deprive some groups on the basis of group's identities like caste and ethnicity. The Indian Hindu social system is a unique system of inequality sustained by religious and ritual concepts of purity and pollution. In Indian social system, inequality is accepted as a fundamental value which is against the very spirit of human rights.

Dalits, the untouchables were placed at the bottom of the Indian society and are excluded in most of the developmental process which reflected with respect to a number of development related indicators. In 2000, about two-thirds of the SCs rural householders were landless, compared to one-third among the non-SCs/STs, less than one-third of SC household had acquired access to capital assets, compared to be present among the non-SCs/STs, about 60 per cent of the SC household still had to depend on wage labour compared to one-fourth of the non-SCs/STs, which is indicative of a much higher level of dependence on wage employment. Employment rate and literacy rate have also tended to be low. Disparities of similar magnitude exist in the health status of SCs. The incidence of anemia among women and mortality rate among children are high as compared to the non SCs/STs population. They continue to suffer from untouchability and atrocities. A numerous cases of human rights violations and atrocities are registered by the SCs with the police annually. Dalits of India (2009) in its report revealed that, 7,099 or 18.7 per cent of the crime against dalits were pending with police at the end of 2002. The number of cases pending with the courts was at the same time 126,009 or 77.69 per cent of all cases brought to court. It appears that only 21.72 per cent of the total cases were disposed of during the year 2002.

In recent era, they have been facing different types of disabilities in their life cycles. These disabilities are as follows:

1. Denial or restriction of access to public facilities such as wells, schools, roads, post offices and courts.
2. Denial of the right to learn the Vedas.
3. Denial or restriction of access to temples.
4. Exclusion from any favourable and profitable employment and subsequent relegation to menial employment.

5. Residential segregation that required them to remain outside the village, etc.

So, above mentioned disabilities have legitimised the violation of human rights of human dignity. The traditional Hindu social system was based on purity and pollution. The system subverted equality before law, equal opportunity and equal protection of the law. Thus, it was a source of exclusion and thereby a source of violation of human rights. Every human being by virtue of being human is entitled to certain human rights for development. But, in reality dalits are denied minimum basic human rights such as right to equality, right to work, right to live, right to health, etc. Thus, due to social exclusion, dalit populations have been denied in different forms of social, economic, cultural, political rights in their life cycles. If we peep into the reality we will find the pathetic condition of the dalit population in every corner of the society.

With the advancement of civilisation the concept of Human Rights has come into focus. This important concept today is based on individual's inherent dream for a dignified, worthy, secured and respectful life irrespective of race, sex, religion, occupation and social status. In fact, these fundamental liberties mark the very foundation of a modern civil society and are placed above all kinds of socio-political narrowness and discrimination.

Growing concern for human rights clearly indicates their gravity and importance both in national and international community. In the face of the extremist challenges and the crisis of the modern civilisation, the concept of Human Rights receives high importance not only among the academicians, but also policy makers. At present, man's life is in question and struggling for existence. Thus, time has come for the establishment of human rights for the sake of human existence.

Human Rights often described as, to quote President Jefferson, "inherent and inalienable rights of man" refer to those minimal rights that every individual should enjoy by virtue of being a human being - a human being irrespective of any other consideration. They attach to all persons equally, simply by virtue of their humanity, irrespective of race, nationality or membership of any particular social group. They specify the minimum condition for human dignity and a tolerable life.

By human rights, we mean the recognition of rights and prerogatives irrespective of race, caste, colour, creed, social status for all round development of personality. As a human being, we need food, shelter, security, and liberty. For the sake of our existence, we want to enjoy civic, political, economic and cultural privileges and opportunities in full measure. These are basic needs for civilised existence. In fact, human rights provide a man to live as civil man.

The concept of human rights has been evolved to a large extent by the historical struggles, mainly in Western countries, for the acquirement and enhancement of individual civil and political rights. Originally, it developed as an instrument for limiting the use of autocratic power within the state, one of the ancient manifestations of which can be traced back to the "Magna Carta" (1215). After that the concept has developed through the evolutionary process in which the remarkable incidents were the Glorious Revolution (1689), the October Revolution (1917), The Virginian Declaration of Rights of 1776, etc. In fact, human history witnesses an ascending order of evolution of human rights. Thus, while the first generation of human rights laid emphasis on civil and political rights; the second generation emphasized on social and economic rights. There is now emerging a third generation of human rights born of human solidarity: rights concerning development, environment, peace, humanitarian assistance and the like.

Recognition of and respect for human rights is now regarded as the foundation of freedom, peace and justice in the world. Of course, denial of human rights is a personal tragedy. But it has a wider implication for creating conditions of social unrest and political turmoil even with the potential of leading to conflict between societies and nations. That is why the United Nations did not make much delay in adopting the Universal Declaration of Human Rights.

At least from the constitutional point of view, our country has taken a lot of steps. The Preamble of Constitution has assured equality of status and of opportunity for all. Chapter III of the Constitution deals with some important fundamental rights for the citizens of India so that each and every man can develop their personality and individuality to the fullest. Chapter IV of the Constitution is also very important in this regard. For the preservation and protection of the rights of the minority community, our Constitution has constituted National Commission for Minorities, National Commission for Scheduled Castes and Scheduled Tribes, National Commission for Women, etc. In 1993, the protection of Human Rights Act was passed and in the same year, The National Human Rights Commission was formed. In West Bengal, through a gazette notification, West Bengal Human Rights Commission was formed on 31st January, 1995.

The enjoyment of rights by the people is one of the most important components of modern civilisation. In a civil society, it is expected that each and every individual will enjoy their rights as a human being with a view to develop their personality. We have already come out from the slave and feudal society where the ruler has frequently smothered the human rights. But, with the growth of civilisation and democratic institutions and values, the span and area of the rights of the individual also extended immensely.

But, the present reality gives us a different picture. The rights of the man are being violated both by the state and the non-state actors. In the face of modern civilisation, really it is a great crisis faced by our society. Particularly, the condition of the grass root marginal people of our society is very worse and pathetic.

Thus, the study of the violation of Human Rights among the tribes of Bankura gives us the nature and extent of the crisis of modern civilisation.

Against this background, the present study is to examine the crisis of modern civilisation from the context of the violation of Human Rights among the tribal community of the district of Bankura. Keeping this in mind, this study also analyses how the Santhals of Bankura, a dominant tribe of not only in the district of Bankura, but also all over the country, are enjoying their rights and dignity in the existing civil society. It is also the purpose of the study to see how the Santhals of Bankura acknowledge Human Rights as a part of their life. In fact, whenever we study some aspects of Human Rights Declaration and the present state of position of the Santhals, then we can understand how the Santhals of Bankura are enjoying the rights as mentioned in the Human Rights Declaration.

Since pre-independence days, the Santhals have been the dominant tribe not only in West Bengal but also in Bankura. In 1872, the total number of Santhals in Bankura was 6,954 only. Again in 1901, the number of Santhal population rose to 47,221.

According to the Census Report of 1971, the total number of Scheduled Tribes in West Bengal was 25,32,969, out of the total population of 4,43,12,011, which formed 5.72 per cent of the State's total population. In Bankura, the western part of West Bengal, the Santhals constitute a major part of the total population, numbering 1,12,725 according to the Census Report of 1971. In 1981, the total number of the Santhals increased to 1,57,108; and in 1991 it further increased to 1,88,006.

Thus, the abovementioned statistics is enough to state that, numerically the Santhals constitute the dominant tribe in Bankura.

Methodology

Both primary and secondary sources of data have been utilised in this study. Primary source data have been collected through interview of the respondents and from reports of committees and commissions appointed by the Government, archival materials, Government publications, etc. Secondary sources include newspapers, published books and scholarly articles published in journals and periodicals.

The survey has been conducted among two hundred Santhals of different age and sex groups who belong to six villages situated in three different Blocks of Bankura. These villages are Baghmundi and Nunia Para under Khatra Block; Tulunga and Masra under Onda block; Joredihi and Sattore under Chatna Block. These villages are predominantly Santhal-oriented villages from the very beginning of their settlement and still now continue to be so.

For extensive field work for this survey, a sample survey method has been adopted. For this purpose, a total number of two hundred Santhal villagers were selected for interview. The selected individuals belonged to different age and sexes. For example, out of these three hundred Santhals fifty (30 males and 20 females) belonged to 18-30 years age group, one hundred (77 males and 23 females) to 30 to 50 years age group and one hundred and fifty (96 males and 54 females) to the age group of 50 to 70 years.

The selection of the Santhals has been made in such a way that a fairly representative idea of Santhal community of Bankura regarding their enjoyment of Human Rights in general may be gathered from their responses to the interview schedule.

Violation of Human Rights: The very first article of the Universal Declaration of Human Rights starts with, "All human beings are born free and equal in dignity and rights. They are endowed with reason and conscience and should act towards one another in a spirit of brotherhood." What about the effect of this article among the Santhals of Bankura? To provide food, cloth, shelter and security for all equally is the prime job of modern Welfare State. When, more than 80 per cent of the Santhals of Bankura are still passing their days with inadequate food and are being exploited and tortured by the non-tribal community, then can we say that the Santhals are born free and equal in dignity and rights? "We are living in a democratic and civil society, but still to this day, the Santhals of Bankura are being exploited by the money lenders and contractors. It seems that they are not living in a democratic society but in the medieval period." This community who is struggling for their existence, has no time to think about their rights and dignity. Extreme poverty, limitless ignorance and regular negligence are the common feature of this community, though they are living in a civil society. Mr. A.K. Basu, a Schedule Castes and Scheduled Tribes Welfare officer has said that, if we study not only the tribal life of this district but also the tribal life of our entire society, then we will find that we are standing far behind the human civilisation.

According to the article, three vital rights of the Human Rights Declaration are enshrined in the statement, "Everyone has the right to life, liberty and security of person."

Now the question arises that what is life? Is it just to remain alive, or something different from that? During the period of survey, it has also been found that the earnings of the most of the Santhals (nearly about 86 per cent) do not exceed Rs. 40 per day per individual, and for that earning, they have to toil, more or less, ten hours in a day. They mostly work as wage laborers either in the agricultural land of a landowner or under a contractor. But wherever they work, the employer is exploiting them without giving them real wages. Again, under this abject poverty they have no other alternative but to borrow money from the moneylenders at a high rate of interest. The moneylenders are trapping this gullible people and they are never able to come out from the vicious circle of the moneylenders due the exorbitantly high rate of interest. This is the right to life that the Santhals of Bankura are enjoying in this democratic and civil society. The very core of the civilisation is that, in a free world, man will live a free life and without any bondage. Thus, the study of the life of the marginal section of the society very clearly reveals the nature of the crisis of modern civilisation. And liberty? Their liberty was first axed in the 19th century by the introduction of "Indian Forest Policy" by the British Government. Since then, several forest acts have been interfering into civil liberty, i.e., the symbolic relationship between them and forest. In this connection, it should be mentioned here that the Santhals still depends on forest for their food, fuel, fodder-corps, housing materials, medicines and all other things essential things for their existence. In short, the entire life of the tribes revolves round the forests. But unfortunately, after independence, in the name of nation building, they are gradually losing their right over the forests. For the greater interest of the national development (?), they are being rendered shelter less. "For the spread of industrialisation and urbanisation in Bankura, the Santhals are uprooted from their own places. This situation is a severe blow against them. The authorities should earnestly think for their rehabilitation which is the basic human right of the tribes as a human being."

Article 4 of the Human Rights Declaration says that, "No person shall be held in slavery or servitude; slavery and the slave trade shall be prohibited in all their forms."

The real agony is that, the Santhals of Bankura are still under the firm grip of exploitation of the non-tribal community of this region. The local merchants, traders and contractors are continuously exploiting the vast labour power of the Santhals. The primary occupation of the Santhals is to work as daily wage labourer in a stone-crushing factory or in the agricultural land of others. But they are not getting real wages from their work place. Even the rate of wage also differs from one place to another place. "The nature of exploitation among the Santhals of Khatra block of Bankura by the Mahajan and money lenders is really inhuman. They treat the Santhals as their slaves. The administration should immediately take strong measures against this sort of practices." Thus, in this so-called free world, a significant section of the community is still being exploited and treated like slaves by another section of the people. We are standing far away from the touch of humanity and gradually loosing our moral values.

The subject matter of Article 17 of Human Rights Declaration is the recognition of right to property. Article 17 says, "(a) Everyone has the right to own property alone as well as in association with others, (b) No one shall be arbitrarily deprived of his property."

The concept of property is a myth to the Santhals. Though most of the Santhls have their own house and also possesses some domestic animals but it is really very meager and inadequate. It has been found that, in most of the cases the land upon which they build their own house is a vested land. Thus, from the technical point of view, ownership over the agricultural land among the Santhals is very pathetic. During the survey period among the Santhals, it has been found that more than 80 per cent of Santhals have no agricultural land of their own. These large number of the Santhals are forced to work either as daily wage labourer or work in other land as agricultural labourers. What they get from that, as their wage is so insignificant and paltry that it is very hard for them to maintain their livelihood. Though, more or less, some of the Santhals own agricultural land but that so insufficient that they are still compelled to work either as wage labourers or agricultural labourers to fulfill the basic needs pertaining to their day to day life.

Article 24 says, "Everyone has the right to rest and leisure including reasonable limitation of working hours and periodic holiday with pay."

Rest, leisure and limitation of working hours are synonym to hunger for the Santhals of Bankura. A Santhal has to work hard from dawn to dusk to acquire his bread. Due to the exploitation by the employer, the Santhals have no particular working hours. It has found that the working hours in a particular job are different in different work places. In fact, majority of the Santhals of Bankura are not in any way related with any government job or company job. As a result, the word "pay" has no relevance for these tribes. Even if they are provided with a holiday, then they are compelled to do so without food and hunger.

Article 26 states that, (a) "Everyone has the right to education. Education shall be free, at least in the elementary and fundamental stages. Elementary education should be compulsory. Technical and professional education shall be made generally available and higher education shall be equally accessible to all on the basis of merit."

(b) "Everyone shall be directed to the full development of the human personality and to strengthening the respect for human rights and fundamental freedom. It shall promote understanding, tolerance and friendship among all nations, racial or religious groups, and shall further the activities of the United Nations for the maintenance of peace.

(c) "Parents have a prior right to choose the kind of education shall be given to their students."

As per Census Report of 2000, the rate of literacy among the tribes of Bankura is 0.67 per cent. Even during the time of survey, it has been found that more than 98 per cent Santhals are not literate. Indifference to education becomes quite a common and natural feature in the life of the Santhals. They have come to believe the hard fact that education is a thing which is beyond their reach. The drop-out rate among the Santhals is also very high. In 2003, the drop-out rate among the children of Santhals was 86 per cent. In fact, after reading upto the third or fourth standard, majority of the Santhals have to enroll themselves in some mills or factories with a view to assist their family financially. They consider a career of a daily wage labourer, either in agriculture or in a factory, much more profitable than to continue their studies on a meager pittance of Rs. 40 per day. Their abject poverty has alienated them from the education. Again, the Santhals are totally unaware about the value and importance of education. No one cares to give the Santhals the light of knowledge. The children are allowed to maintain a carefree life and none of the children are convinced to take education.

There is no infrastructural facility for the Santhals for education with a view to spread literacy among this community. The nearest primary school is (at least 10 km.) far away from their village. Even, they do not have the slightest idea about the governmental assistance regarding the education for the tribal community. No one has evinced any genuine interest for spread of education among the Santhals of Bankura.

The concept of Human Rights is a foreign term for this community. They do not know what is right and they have no interest about this. In fact, their world is confined to their community. They only know poverty, torture, ignorance, hunger, etc. and all kinds of hardship of life. Every day, they are struggling for their existence and so they have no time to think about their rights.

Mere declaration is not enough. Time has come to understand them properly, help them honestly and sincerely. They never beg to anyone. Still we can save them by our healing touch. To fight against this crisis of civilisation, the following steps can be taken:

Approaches

(a) Continuous and integrated awareness programme on rights among this tribal community is the utmost necessity.

(b) Need-based economic programme to arrest the problem of poverty of the tribes is to be taken along with the mass participation of the tribes.

(c) Administration should be more honest and sincere and active to protect the rights of this marginal people.

(d) NGOs should come forward more actively with a view to stand in favour of this community in all circumstances.

(e) Laws protecting the rights of the tribes should be rigidly implemented.

References

Ananda Bazar Patrika, 20th November 2001, p. 7.

Ananda Bazar Patrika, 3rd March 2000, Kolkata, p. 7.

Bauvinic, Mayra (2004). 'Social Inclusion in Latin America', in Bauvinic Mayra and Mazza Janquline (ed) 'Social Exclusion and Economic Development', Baltimore: John Hopkins University Press.

Census Report of India, 1971, Government of India.

Ghannshyam Shah (2001). 'Social Movements in India', New Delhi: Sage Publications.

Gupta, S.K. (1985). 'The Scheduled Castes in Modern Indian Politics: Their Emergence As a Modern Power', New Delhi: Manohar Publishers.

Interview of Mr. A.K. Basu is taken on 4.9.2004 at Bankura.

Majumdar D. West Bengal District Gazetteers, Bankura, Calcutta, 1975, p. 171.

Omvedt, Gail (1994). 'Dalits and the Democratic Revolution: Dr. Ambedkar and the Dalit Movement in Colonial India, New Delhi: Sage Publication.

Pradhan, Atul Chandra (1986). 'The Emergence of the Depressed Classes, Bhubaneswar: Bookland International.

Rao, Y. China (2010). 'Social Exclusion in India', Concepts and Contexts', in Exclusion and Discrimination: Concepts, perspectives and Challenges, Kaniskha Publishers.

Rarh Katha, 26th June 2001, Bankura.

Rarh Katha, 3rd April 2000, Bankura.

Sambad Protidin, 10th August 2001, Kolkata, p. 7.

Sen, Amartya (1997). 'On Economic Inequality', Oxford: Clarendon Press.

Sidhu-Kanu Swaranika, 30th June 2001, Published by the Office of the Information and Culture, Suri, Birbhum.

Silver, H. (1995). Reconceptualising Social Disadvantage: 'Three Paradigms of Social Exclusion in Rodgers, G. Gore, C. and Figueireds, J. (eds), 'Social Exclusion: Rhetoric, Reality and Responses, Geneva: International Institute of Labour Studies.

Silver, H. (2007). 'Social Exclusion: Comparative Analysis of Europe and Middle East Youth', Middle East Youth Initiative Working Paper.

Thorat, Sukhadeo (2009). 'Dalits in India: Search for Common Destiny, New Delhi: Sage Publications.

7

The Confluence of Praxis: Ex/Inclusion, Development and Gender

Priyanka Nandy

[The] average third world woman leads an essentiaily truncated life based on her feminine gender (read: sexually constrained), and being "third world" (read: ignorant, poor, uneducated, tradition-bound, domestic, family-oriented, victimised, etc.).

Chandra Talpade Mohanty, "Under Western Eyes: Feminist Scholarship and Colonial Discourse."

Introduction

The best part of an action film – or a superhero film, or a thriller, or a war retrospective – is when the hero and his band of Good Guys burst onto the screen, brandishing flaming swords (or their contemporary equivalents) at evil villains, rescuing the downtrodden, and making the world safe for freedom, democracy, and happy endings. Sadly, said happy ending lasts only till the next instalment of the franchise, in which commerce dictates the world must be saved all over again, from another set of evil villains. Then again. And again.

There is no dearth of villains in this narrative. In the better-written ones, in fact, they turn out to be former best friends or brothers of the heroes.

Before we get to the explosive climaxes, though – and indeed to carve a path to it – we must sit through the back story: The narrative of who the people were, who they are, and why there was, or must absolutely be, a war between them. And, while connoisseurs of the genre might scoff at these dull details, they're vital if one is to know which set of sword-wielders (or similar) stand bathed in glory, and which must be consigned to the darkness. Because in *modus operandi* and context-detached snapshots of climactic action, they are almost impossible to tell apart.

To understand clearly why the social exclusion of women in India has become the central point of public policy, social justice and development concerns, therefore, we must first look back in quick recapitulation. How did gender – or, to take ambiguity away, 'women' – become a key development concern? And why, after several decades of investments in various forms – aid, policy changes, activism, academic studies – is there a general consensus that there has been little widespread, sustainable, positive change?

International Development: The Mechanisms of Exclusion

In 1970 – five years after her first major work, "Conditions of Agricultural Growth[1]", was published and construed by some as a denunciation of the Malthusian theory of population[2], and at the beginning of the decade that saw the formal introduction of WID, women in development – Danish economist Ester Boserup published her newseminal work, *Woman's Role in Economic Development*[3]. Boserup's work was remarkable in 1970, and it is remarkable now, but for entirely different reasons. And in this difference, lies the crux of our original questions – why has 'the gender problem' proved so persistent in international development?

By 1970, 'development' was a concept at a crossroad. Or perhaps, more appropriately, a disintegrating idea in an ideological stews pot. After the Second World War, European colonial powers gradually withdrew their spheres of influence – or so it appeared – back within the borders of their native lands. Public statements by leaders of the victorious Allies, in particular the United States of America, indicated a spirit of generosity and amiable advancement of aid to the third world[4], aimed at building a modern, peaceful, politically stable, and economically flourishing world. Making a direct reference to eschewing structures of European colonialism in his inaugural address in 1949, President Truman insisted that "[t]he old imperialism – exploitation for foreign profit – has no place in our plans. What we envisage is a program of development based on the concept of democratic fair dealing". A primary tool in the reification of this inclusive vision in the third world was the modernisation theory of social evolution, based on W. W. Rostow's 'stages of growth' model[5] (in war-ravaged Western Europe, it was the Marshall Plan). Rostow, like many of his contemporaries, saw, 'development' as a linear progressive model, in which 'traditional' societies – existing in a 'pre-Newtonian science and technology'[6] age – make certain adjustments to their economic structures to achieve economic and political modernity. These adjustments are calculated to push the society through four successive stages of 'growth'[7], changing it from an agrarian economy to one based on high mass consumption of goods and services. In the 1960s, Rostow postulated that the United States was already emerging from the last stage into an yet-undefined sixth; Europe and Japan were slowly grasping the joys of stage five; and the third world was still largely languishing in stage one (and needed all the help it could get).

In the two following decades, however, scepticism about the true intent and efficacy of post-War world-building efforts grew rapidly. The modernisation theory, being one of the most prominent ideological tools of this enterprise, came under particular scrutiny, and by the late 1960s, critique of it had been condensed into the 'dependency theory', deconstructing its alleged underbelly. Proponents of the dependency theory asserted that the 'end' of colonialism was not, as Truman expounded, an end of 'exploitation for foreign profit', but indeed a reinforcement of it, without the moral encumbrances of political responsibility that colonialism required – or at least created a theoretical expectation of. If bringing the light of civilisation into the world's dark corners was imperial colonialism's excuse for political and military action on foreign shores, then post-war US (and eventually, Western Europe's) was bestowing democracy and engendering development/ alleviating poverty in the third world. Under the altered rhetoric, however, dependency theorists pointed out, the structure of global power relations and political/economic dominance remained unchanged. The third world continued to provide labour, resources and a market, without having access to capital, advanced technology, or decision-making powers in the global process, even when it involved them directly.

It is in this context of doubt, dissent and development that Boserup's work was published, and must be read. Despite a rising awareness of political, economic and social exclusions and exploitations social groups were being subjected to worldwide (the term 'third world' would soon be frowned upon), and despite the concurrence of second-wave feminism[8], women were not yet a considered unit of analysis in development practice. According to Lourdes Beneria and Gita Sen, who analysed her contribution a mere decade later, Boserup's primary legacy in this context was that she "emphasised gender as a basic factor in the division of labour, prevalent across countries and regions[9]". Unlike most of her peers in economic policy-making, she also noted and emphasised the *differences* in gendered division of labour across countries and regions – particularly the "male" and "female" farming systems of Asia and Africa, respectively (Boserup's specialisation was agrarian methods). Above all, however, it was her awareness of the frequently negative social impact both pre-war colonialism and post-war 'development' had on third-world societies, that made her gender-consciousness effective and actionable. For instance, she observed that European colonisers found the female farming systems of many of their colonies peculiar – and even morally objectionable – because of their patriarchal cultural belief that farming was 'properly' a man's work. Consequently, land reforms imposed upon these colonies as part of their 'civilising' process stripped women of their culturally-granted land rights, and made farming a male domain. This meant that while hundreds of men *and* women lost their land to the colonisers, the few who did prosperusually with cash crops, and by using imported agricultural technology – were all men. While it is certainly important that several women lost their financial independence thus, it is perhaps even more important to note that with such land reforms, agricultural success became almost inextricably linked to men, cash crops, and technology-aided large farms. Women, locally – consumed food crops, and domestic farming, despite their society's continued dependence on them for survival, lost economic priority, social status and cultural centrality.

Of course, Boserup's work is not a comprehensive guide to inclusive social policy. Amongst the more prominent flaws of her work, her lack of a cohesive theoretical framework and her complete acceptance of the modernisation theory of international development are particularly glaring. She also perceived 'economic development' as the sum of extra-domestic forms of productions – a significant omission in the calculation of female productivity, given the gendered structure of labour in most cultures. However, as even her detractors admit, Boserup emphasised the economic contribution of women at a time when this was not formally recognised, and indeed, when their primary identity in policy-making – as we shall see in the next section – was of an exploited, oppressed people in need of rescuing.

Women in Development: A Flawed Inheritance

Given the confluence of scholarship and advocacy in the decade – outlined in the previous section – the explicit inclusion of women, as a unit, in development priorities in the 1970s is barely remarkable. What has drawn immense critique – divided nearly equally between the inevitably-male policy planners and almost inevitably-female women's rights activists – is the nature of this inclusion. The primary problem with the overt inclusion of women with the WID (women in development) desks at the UNDP was this: It rendered women invisible. Of such contradictions, WID critics pointed out, are minority-inclusion policies made. Their argument, really, was simple. If, in the 1970s, governments and international organisations say "We shall from now onwards include women in the processes of international development" (they would, of course, say this in impressively complex ways), then they are also effectively saying, "Women have had no contribution so far to the development process, and therefore, to national economies". And thus, although women would be recognised and included within the development paradigm and would continue to do the work they always did, their status as producers would be officially negated, and they would be consigned to the periphery of the development narrative as a non-productive, beneficiary group.

This apparent inclusion, by essentialising the self and excluding such contributions from it as does not fit within the development paradigm, has been a persistent conundrum in the narrative of international development.

This basic exclusionary structure apart – although this alone discredits the 'inclusive' approach the UNDP sought to espouse – WID has been widely criticised on yet another slightly complex ground. The flaw in WID's design, its critiques claimed, was that it focused exclusively on women, to the extent of decontextualising them. This might seem unfair criticism to level at a programme that is, after all, called 'women in development', but the critics' point was precisely that to understand the position (and, unfortunately, the plight) of women in any given society, one must necessarily understand the gender dynamics of the society as a whole. Especially, since gender is the point of confluence for several concurrent institutions within the same society – religion, ethnicity, nationality, and so on. To be visibily and measurably effective, a programme aimed at empowering a marginalised group – in this instance, women – must first understand the nature of their productions, consumptions, exchanges and negotiations within the community. These, according to its critics, WID failed to do. It was eventually replaced by the GAD – or *gender* and development – approach, which sought to address WID's gender-analysis deficits.

However, although GAD does make some effort to understand the role of social institutions in assigning specific values and duties to specific genders, it has been criticised as well for limiting itself to the discourse of difference between men and women, instead of exploring the negotiations and accommodations that enable their daily coexistence. GAD also suffered, though this has not been widely discussed, from being deployed during the peak of the structural adjustment phase of development. This phase, while promising greater equity and personal freedom to restructured national economies, had in actuality, quite the opposite effect. Income gaps widened, labour laws were relaxed, state and welfare services were withdrawn, and the cumulative pressure was felt most keenly by those in the lowest rungs of social privilege, women across regions and communities amongst them.

Monoliths and Neo-Colonialism

[Contemporary Western hegemonic position is rooted in] control over the orientation, regulation and decision of the process of world development on the basis of the advanced sector's monopoly of scientific knowledge and ideal creativity
Anouar Abdal-Malek, Social Dialectics[10]

In 1984, nearly a decade and a half after Boserup's work, Chandra Talpade Mohanty published "Under Western Eyes[11]", subtitled "Feminist Scholarship and Colonial Discourse". If Ester Boserup had touched briefly upon the negative social impact of European dominance in Africa and Asia – with particular reference to the loss of organic forms of autonomy for women – then Mohanty explores its legacy in considerable detail, focusing especially on the influence these socio-political inequalities has had on the vision of development the first world had for the third. The concerns somewhat loosely articulated by Boserup and her contemporary minority and women's rights activists (including WID advocates), are still the centres of concern in Mohanty's text. Taking contemporary development rhetoric to be an index of this vision, and the vision as an index of the third world, as constructed in the mind of the first, Mohanty unveils, in this essay, the anatomy of a phenomenon she terms 'discursive colonialism'.

In his inaugural address, mentioned above, the then-US President Harry Truman outlined the United State's four proposed contributions towards a better world. The first was a commitment to the goals of the United Nations. The second was a commitment to world economic recovery, especially to Western Europe, so that they may once again take "their rightful place at the forefront of civilisation". The third contribution was a detailed description of the military and financial aid that would be extended to all nations who opposed the Soviet Union and communism. The fourth, however, was this:

> [W]e must embark on a bold new programme for making the benefits of our scientific advances and industrial progress available for the improvement and growth of underdeveloped areas. More than half the people of the world are living in conditions approaching misery. For the first time in history, humanity possesses the knowledge and skill to relieve the suffering of these people... I believe that we should make available to peace-loving peoples the benefits of our store of technical knowledge in order to help them realise their aspirations for a better life.

Technology, therefore, was to be the main charitable export of the West, since, as Truman emphasises in the same speech, "The material resources which we can afford to use for assistance of other peoples are limited. But our imponderable resources in technical knowledge are constantly growing and are inexhaustible". This should, on the surface, have appeared a welcome move, and yet for many scholars of colonialism, it was not. After all, it was widely held then – and in pockets, still is now – that European colonialism began and succeeded because of the Industrial Revolution, which gave the colonial powers a scientific edge in both economic production and warfare that was quite literally 'imponderable' earlier. Indeed, it was not just scholars who sought to establish a link between knowledge – scientific, in particular – and political power. Imperialist colonialism had its root in West Europe's certain knowledge that the barbaric world beyond its borders existed in intellectual and spiritual darkness, rescuing them from which was a moral Christian duty (instead of, for instance, an enterprise of violent territorial greed). The colonial government in India, a product of said duty, made quite an effort to limit their native subjects' access to higher or specialised 'occidental' knowledge. While the richer local families were, at later stages of colonial rule, able to send their sons (and in very rare instances, daughters) to England – and eventually to the larger cities of the Raj – for degrees in law, engineering, medicine and so on, they would seldom find employment within the public or private institutions. Higher public offices, of course, were legally reserved for British subjects, and private sector appointments above the glass ceiling, such as it was then, were predominantly Europeans. It is this history of control over knowledge for power that Mohanty invokes when she speaks of 'discursive colonialism'. In certain influential instances of feminist scholarship, she says, this colonialism manifests itself in the monolithic production of the 'Third World Woman' – at this point, at least theoretically an important development priority – where real heterogeneity is eschewed in favour of constructing her as a homogeneous, non-Western body of lack, which the West, with its superior knowledge of social progress, is morally compelled to fulfil.

The tension here can be summarised as the structural domination of Woman – an ideological construction of the developed world, hegemonic/universalised via cultural capitalism – over women, who are gendered products of specific geopolitical and cultural histories, suppressing their heterogeneity. Being similar, structurally, to the conflict between third world realities and the idea of the third world in the first, this tension also indexes the dissonance between actual gendered needs in the developing world (that is, of 'women'), and the *modus operandi* of women-centric international development programmes, crafted on an understanding of 'Woman'. This, as Mohanty points out, is considerably more complex than depictions of dominance during pre-war, imperialist colonialism, and therefore more difficult to dismantle. Most of authors she finds guilty of discursive colonialism are, in fact, critical of European colonialism and global domination of the West. They should, therefore, be the polar opposites of colonialists. Where, then, is the problem? According to Mohanty, the problem lies in their assumption of globally homogeneous female needs and desires, rooted in their own cultural parameters of what is necessary and desirable. In some instances – particularly in activism – these assumptions are blatant. Poor women of colour from the global south (or from minority groups in the developed world) are considered disempowered by default because they do not belong to 'right' confluences of class, ethnicity, and nationality. Now, this is certainly a lived reality for many such women, but what such activism fails to grasp is that there is considerable variety in contextual meanings of such abstract concepts as 'freedom' and 'poverty', which must be taken into account. They also tend to ignore the ability of such women to negotiate with local institutions for small slices of opportunities and freedoms. Mohanty – and other scholars of the subaltern – do not advocate remaining within this unstable, insecure *status quo*, but they do advise learning from the nature of such negotiations, and learning about what different groups of women in any given part of the global south want. Good intentions and an awareness of history, although commendable and more than what most possess, are not sufficient to decolonise minds of hierarchies involuntarily internalised by social osmosis, by people in both the First World and the Third.

This persistent chasm between reality and constructions of it – in matters of identity, local institutions *et al* – is one of the answers to the question we began this article with: Why does gender inequality continue, indeed, appear to worsen, despite investing resources in ending it? One should, of course, further explore the nature of this chasm, and institutional interests in not bridging it. In the next section of the paper, we shall attempt to do this contextually for a few instances of development-in-practice.

The Confluence of Praxis

In instances of 'writing back' to the centre of development planning, scholars and activists working in the Third World have attempted to demonstrate how an imposition of western 'modernity', as it was in the early decades of the development enterprise, has resulted in the regression of societies that were, in fact, more inclusive and less rigid than a post-Victorian West. Mohanty's essay yields the the example of *Women of Africa: Roots of Oppression,* by Maria Rosa Cutrufelli. Studying post-colonial changes in social exchange amongst the Bembas of

Zambia, Cutrufelli notes that marriage in this matrilocal and matrilineal society required the prospective groom to integrate with the bride's community, living and working with her people. Their sexual relationship would vary, depending on her changing physical maturity, but intercourse would not be sanctioned till she reached puberty and had her initiation ceremony. The colonial economy, however, introduced the idea that cash could be substituted for various traditional forms of value and thus, says Cutrufelli, many young men were beginning to pay a rough equivalent of their labour in cash to the bride's family, and earning the right to take her away in exchange. This, in Cutrufelli's analysis, alienated these young women from the support system of their natal communities, and made them vulnerable to potential exploitation or abuse (Mohanty, 1984). Mohanty, of course, critiques the simplistic nature of this analysis[12], but similar arguments have been made against male-centric land reforms favouring the middle-class, legally limiting the definition of a family to a parent-child nuclear structure[13], reducing and concretising arguably fluider caste/tribe/other social identities via the census and other enumerating processes, and so on. The plight of transgendered and non-heterosexual people in certain communities have been particularly ironic and tragic, as local acknowledgement and accommodation of their difference were made illegal by colonial 'civilisation' (pre-war) and continued in 'modernity' (post-war), till the hegemonic influence of the West successfully obliterated memories of more fluid gender relations, deeply stigmatising everything except closely-monitored heterosexual behaviour. So deeply, in fact, that late twentieth and twenty-first century activism for gendered equality and freedom – sourced, again, from the West – have not been able to make a dent, or even reach, these formerly inclusive communities[14].

In the case of women in India, this 'writing back' has been rather more insistent than in the case of sexual minorities, yet oddly, so has been the persistence of their representation as the Third World Woman, as Mohanty would have it – a monolithic, homogenised construct created largely in negation of the West's majoritarian view of its own women. To compound Mohanty's view, however, it is largely Indian policy-makers, policy-analysts and development workers who espouse this stereotype. Therefore, the Indian woman in policy statements – and, from personal experience, at many gender-centric seminars, conferences or workshops – remain shrouded in terms of marginalisation, disempowerment, exploitation, dependency, and worst of all, restricted capability. Quite apart from structural limitations placed on women in a socially conservative, predominantly rural, patriarchal society, the Indian state refuses to recognise the immense economic contribution of its women, because it occurs 'informally'. The Census of India, till 2011, recorded women in charge of households as 'unemployed', and consequently as 'dependants', and shows no signs of changing this exclusionary concept of productivity, by which domestic labour, child-rearing, tending to the elderly, domestic/garden agriculture (an important source of sustenance in a country plagued by hunger), contribution of both labour and capital – especially in the form of jewellery or inherited property – to the family enterprise, are all rendered invisible, and therefore undocumented. As a farmer's wife from Bardhaman, West Bengal told me during a field visit, "I have been up since three to cook rice for my husband and brothers-in-law, take out the lunch allotment for the [agricultural] labourers from the pantry, wake up the children and make them sit down with their books, supervise the cleaning of the house before my mother-in-law gets up... it is now afternoon, and this is the first chance I have had to sit all day. I have not even had time for my bath yet. But the men of the house? They will never believe we do any work. What work do *we* do? We sit at home all day and do nothing!"

This idea that 'women who sit at home do nothing' has been termed the 'ideology of the housewife' by many scholars, activists and development professionals working in South Asia, because the ideology has had a wide – and interestingly varied – impact on the exclusion, and inclusion of women in the narrative of development. The most basic difference of interpretation of the 'housewife ideology' has been between tradition and 'modernity'. Traditional gender roles, of course, glorify the housewife, and within the Hindu discourse – if she fulfils the traditional criteria of obedience, hard work, and necessary matronly sternness with a gentle, nurturing demeanour – elevate her to the position of Lakshmi, the patron deity of prosperous households. The narrative of modernity, on the other hand, epitomises housewives as wasted opportunities, patriarchal capitulation, intellectual lack or laziness, and voluntary female dependency on the male. Both these categories, although they may not be aware of it, are very class and space-specific. The first is very middle-class, urban/suburban in nature. This becomes evident when the discourse of modernisation fails to include the ubiquitous cook or cleaning woman[15], or for that matter sex workers or fishwives or female vegetable sellers, within its purview of 'working women'. Neither does it include affluent women without formal jobs, but with an active and visible participation in social and cultural life, in its category of housewives.

Another basis of interpretation – not necessarily detached from the traditional but distinguished from it – is the question of honour, gendered spatiality, and the woman's body. Making women or their specific behaviour responsible for the prosperity of the household (as in the traditional Hindu glorification of the housewife) or the honour of the family has long been a common mode of patriarchal dominance. We have already seen that the former does not prevent women from participating in economic production – quite the opposite. Indeed, the average 'housewife' in non-urban India has a far longer duty roster than the one indicated by my informant. These include supervision of labour, keeping account of daily harvests during the season, manufacturing snacks and condiments for domestic, social or market exchanges, assisting in the process of transforming harvested crops into food grains, and so on. The latter, which prescribes keeping women inside the house, and away from the gaze of unrelated men, should technically not pose a problem either, since most of the work listed above occur within the household. And it does not, with a few omissions. However, not all families observing veiling practices own land. Neither do they all live in agricultural areas where – taboos of touching household products between castes and communities permitting – farm-owning families can outsource their work to them. Till relatively recently, the only socially productive activity available to such women were the non-remunerative, largely unacknowledged domestic sort[16]. Some employers, however, have seen the benefits of employing such a socially disempowered, fragmented workforce, with no capability of comparing the market-worth of their labour or unionising for better conditions. In doing so, they can also represent themselves without impunity to their socially-conscientious First World consumers as equal-opportunity employers who respect local gender ideologies.

These conflicts between the traditional and 'modern' views of gendered labour, spatiality and honour is yet another manifestation of the cognitive dissonance we have already seen throughout the discourse of development and gender – between organic rurality and westernised urbanity, knowledge and constructs, praxis and ideas – that is inevitable in a space like India, with concurrent multiple doxa. Compared to the housewife of a prosperous rural farming family, a middle-class urban housewife may indeed have very little to do physically, because the social and economic structures within which they exist are completely different. An *adivasi* woman who has to leave her home and family four times each year to work as an agricultural labourer in another state might envy the ability of a Narsapur lace-maker to work without leaving her room. Although they may be only a few tens of kilometres apart from each other, one inhabits what Rostow would term a traditional society, another a 'high mass consumption' one, and the first and fourth are possibly poised in between at the take-off phase of economic growth. And none, except the alleged urban middle-class consumer, quite fits his model, because clearly, although he had in part engineered it, Rostow failed to clearly envision a world where, to enable high mass consumption in the parts that could afford it, the rest of it would have to engage in long hours of poorly-paid labour, and likely consider themselves lucky for having found work at last.

And this, in effect, is why development policy designed for India and its women have failed consistently: The nation-state exists only politically, and as an abstract sociological idea. Necessarily, therefore, there are no 'Indian' women, except again as a politically identifiable group. India a not merely a collage of diverse, disjointed geo-social fragments, it is a collage of diverse, disjointed geo-social fragments living in different bits of time. This makes the planning for it at a national level, or planning locally with a national 'Indian' identity in mind, a project destined for failure. To plan for, implement and achieve effective projects of social change in India, especially those with a gendered focus, policy-planners would ideally be advised to pick either small areas, or a social group within a given area. The social, economic and cultural borders of that area, along gender, caste, class, religion, ethnicity, language-group *et al*, must then be carefully mapped, and the nature of their porousness evaluated. Without this basic, local understanding of the various levels of interactions and negotiations between all social groups present, their relative social capitals, and the interaction of (potentially conflicting) institutions in any given area – and on a larger scale, the locus of that area on the political and economic map of India – it is impossible to step out of the cyclical structure of analysis we have inherited, where 'realities' are constructed, acted upon, critiqued, reconfigured, and then the entire circle repeated.

Of course, the question that remains is this: having established early in this article that the charitable intentions of the international development project was probably suspect, and that its true intentions are quite possibly a cunningly-veiled neo-colonial plan of, to put it simply, world domination, can we expect its support in serious efforts to empower fringes of the global south? Or must a true project of social inclusion begin with considered exclusions?

And the bigger question that *that* question begets is, despite decrying its 'true' intentions of oppression and exploitation, is the global south capable of sponsoring international development programmes without help from those whose best interests, allegedly, are in suppressing it?

Of such conundrums, as we had occasion to note earlier, is development made.

References

1. Boserup, Ester (1965). The Conditions of Agricultural Growth: The Economics of Agragarian Change Under Population Pressure", London: George Allen and Unwin.

2. Briefly, the Malthusian supposition about population of a certain society was that its growth depended upon its food supply, and therefore upon its agricultural practices. The population in places of plenty would grow, till it outstripped the land's ability to provide for it. Poverty and hardship would then ensue. Boserup's research suggested that the opposite was the case. The size of a society's population did not depend on its agricultural production, but the agricultural methods certainly depended on the population of the society. When population density is low, it is efficient for the community to cultivate land periodically, allowing it to lie fallow. Very low-density groups might even favour a migratory lifestyle, choosing agricultural methods like slash and burn, considerably lightening the entire group's workload. A higher population density would require greater supply of food, for which land has to be cleared, fields prepared, and a much larger workforce engaged in production on a semi-permanent basis. This would increase agricultural production (as well as invested resources), but drastically reduce efficiency.
3. Boserup, Ester (1970). Women's Role in Economic Development, London: George Allen and Unwin.
4. The use of the term 'third world', a taboo in formal discourse, is a considered one. While many object to the term as derogratory and homogenising, censoring its usage has neither reversed – or evened out – the global hierarchy of economic and political power, nor has it addressed the undifferentiated, monolithic approach taken by those at the top of the hierarchy towards the bottom.
5. Walt Whitman Rostow (1960). The Stages of Economic Growth: A Non-Communist Manifesto, Cambridge: Cambridge University Press.
6. *Ibid.*, p. 4.
7. Roscow's Stages of Growth model, also know as the Roskovian take-off model, proffers the idea that economic development happens in five stages (of varying lengths, each). In the first stage, the society is 'traditional' and lives in an approximation of pre-Enlightenment Europe. They are primarily agrarian, though not scientifically so, and limited in production capability. The next stage is transitory, in which the society prepares – perhaps without clear prescience – for the "take off". In this

stage, comparable to Europe of the late 17th and early 18th century, society begins to realise the economic benefits of scientific discoveries. Then comes the take-off, described by Rostow as "the great watershed in the life of modern societies". 'Old blocks of resistance' to the harnessing of science and technology for economic growth are overcome, and the production methods which has sparked in fits and bursts during the second stage now come to dominate the society. Rostow points to Britain in the beginning of the nineteenth century as an example of a take-off, and to India and China at the time of writing of the book. Stage four, the 'drive to maturity', is a long period of sustained, if occasionally fluctuating growth, when the developing economy moves beyond the original sectors that powered its take-off, and diversifies further. In the fifth, 'post maturity' stage, the formerly agrarian, largely rural society has become an urban economy consisting primarily of 'white-collar' professionals, "anxious to acquire the consumption fruits of a mature economy". The development focus shifts too. Acquisition of technological advancement ceases to be the society's primary object, and greater resources are allocated to its welfare and security.

8. The terms 'first wave feminism' and 'second wave feminism' were, in fact, coined in the 1970s, when women's rights activists — fighting for both social and legal equity — traced the roots of their ideology back to the women's movement of the 19th and early 20th century, which focused primarily on *de jure* reforms.
9. Beneria, Lourdes and Gita Sen (Winter 1981). "Accumulation, Reproduction and Women's Role in Economic Development: Boserup Revisited" *Signs,* Vol. 7 No. 2, Chicago: University of Chicago.
10. Anouar Abdel-Malek (1981). Social Dialectics: Nation and Revolution, Albany: State University of New York Press.
11. Mohanty, Chandra Talpade (Spring-Autumn 1984). "Under Western Eyes: Feminist Scholarship and Colonial Discourse", *Boundary 2,* Vol. 12 No. 3, North Carolina, Duke University Press.
12. She points out, for instance, that the description of the traditional marriage contract does not actually document the lived experiences of Bemba women with it. Cutrufelli also falls into the trap of homogenising a group on the basis that they do

not belong to her social milieu – a classic othering paradigm. This makes her overlook the critical difference in response uninitiated and initiated girls might have towards the marriage ritual, since by its dictum, uninitiated girls could be kidnapped, abused or carried away with impunity, as they could not take part in biological reproduction and had little consequential value to the community (according to Cutrufelli's text). The other methodological flaw was in valorising traditional marriage contracts to the extent that tracing the trajectories of inter-gender negotiations in a changing socio-economic environment were almost completely ignored, which could have been the most valuable contribution of such a study to gender equity activists and policy planners.

13. Variance of legal definitions of family and kinships with those practised culturally continues to a crucial area of contention between developmental 'modernity' and 'organic' social structures of a community, even in the first world. In an anecdotal instance, a teenage daughter of a single mother was removed from her great uncle and aunt's care after her mother passed away. Although the couple had been involved in the girl's life from a very young age and considered themselves her only living family, the law found their kinship to her too weak to sustain an automatic transfer of care. The girl lived in a state-sponsored facility and then in foster homes before being reunited to her legally-disregarded family when she was almost eighteen. This is not an isolated incident.

14. As with the Bembas, a point can be made here about the actual lived experience of non-heterosexual or transgendered people within traditional inclusive societies. One might ask how free a society can claim to be, if those in the minority – and here we speak only of the sexual/gender minorities – have specific roles, or a limited spectrum of it, assigned to them, as was often the case in these societies pre-colonisation. The example of the two-spirited amongst some Native American groups, and that of the *hijras* in India come to mind. This is certainly a valid question. However, in such lines of enquiry it is also useful to question our instinctive comparative baselines – in this case, the idea of a 'free society' – and examine it closely for influences and their sources. A monolithic, and for most of the Third World, an imported idea of a free and equal society might not be a

hindrance to contemporary battles for social justice, for such battles must be fought within a similarly imported socio-legal structure. But it does get in the way of understand how, via what political and market forces, a traditionally inclusive society can be transformed, within a couple of centuries into a rigid, exclusionary one eager to change those socio-economic structures that allowed sexual/gender minorities to be of some value socially via ascribed roles, and instead become delegitimised, tabooed bodies. And such questions are vital, if social justice is to be historically informed and comprehensive, instead of being employed as scattered band-aids on the body politic.

15. Domestic labour in India, which, till even the middle of the last century, consisted of both men and women, has increasingly become a female domain. The causes behind this merit discussion.

16. The commonest example of this category of employees are Muslim women lace-workers, although recently people studying them have wondered their mode of economic participation is purely exploitative, with no benefit to them. It is true that sometimes all women provide in this set-up is labour. Terms are decided and the money is kept by their families. However, even if they don't always have access to the money their labour earned, they are becoming aware of their capability for remunerative work, and if domestic labour is destined to go unrecognised, then this is a good way for girls and women to start recognising themselves as contributors to the economy and society.

8

Negotiating Gender: An Account on the Struggles of Dalit Women Activists in Kerala

Deepika Rose Alex

Introducing the Context: Dalit Women as the 'Market Women'

An important feature of the social reform movements of the early 20th century in Kerala is that it was driven by casteist and community based interests[1] (Jacob and Bandhu, 2009). These reform movements were lead by upper caste educated men (Devika and Sukumar, 2006) for attaining better job opportunities for their communities in government services and internal reforms and modernisation of their community. Voices of Dalit reformers like Ayyankali and Poykayil Yohannan were alienated in the social and political spheres. The much hailed Ezhava reformer Sri Narayana Guru was also not accepted in terms of his principles of questioning caste hierarchy. Thus the social transformation of Kerala society in the early 20th century did not question the fundamental basis of social organisation of the society, i.e., caste. Also patriarchal family order was accepted by these reformers unanimously. Matrilinial family organisation came under strict scrutiny[2] (Kodoth and Eapen, 2005). An important outcome of this model of social reform was that it created a notion of 'Kulastree' (Devika, 2010) in Kerala society which connotes the notion of ideal womanhood. Important criteria to attain this ideal womanhood were upper caste birth and confinement to domestic affairs. In order to emphasise the idealness of the notion of 'Kulastree', the terminology of 'Chanthapennu' or market-woman was also created. According to Devika and Sukumar (2006), 'Chanthapennungal (plural form of chanthapennu) 'or market-women refer to 'women who get their way through loud and vociferous argument, with caste connotations as well. Women, who support themselves through labour and reject dominant norms of feminine modesty'. Needless to say, Dalit women who were not confined to domestic sphere, who, because of their economic necessity participated along with their men in social labour came under this category of 'Chanthapennu' or market-woman. Market-women mainly signify two related meanings. Firstly, women independent of any sort of patriarchal control. Secondly, women who participates in social labour along with men. An important enquiry that this paper undertakes is to critically analyse these stereotypical perceptions, from the perspective of Dalit women. The dominant image of Dalit women in Kerala society, which is still prevalent, is one of women who does not confine to the norms of feminine modesty, who are not controlled ideally by their husbands. Thus significance of Dalit women as a social category is that they have been denied the right to selfhood right from the period of Kerala social reforms and renaissance.

The Experiences of Dalit Women Activists within the Organisation: A Critical Exploration

None of the Dalit women activists and the organisation they are part of, i.e., Kerala Dalit Federation (KDF), have the legacy of any of the Dalit movement in Kerala. The person who formed KDF, P. Sudhakaran was a very active Congress worker and leader and when he had some conflicts with congress leadership, he formed KDF. Since the last 14 years, right from its formation, he is the state level leader of KDF. KDF is a very good example of a popular pattern of formation of caste-based political organisations in Kerala; Dalits who are part of political parties leaving it to form their own groups to protect their interests. KDF is also an example of the experiences of women workers in leader centric Dalit organisations formed by men to fulfil their political aspirations which were unsuccessful in the previous political parties and organisations they were part of.

KDF is an organisation formed by men and women joined later. It was formed in 1997 and a year later, the women's wing, Kerala Dalit Mahila Federation (KDMF) was formed. KDMF was formed along with other wings of KDF like youth wing and employee's wing. KDMF is just a symbolic of the participation of women in KDF, which is largely modeled as per the structure of political parties and it aims mainstream political negotiations. In short, KDMF does not mean that KDF has a feminist agenda. This point can be further illustrated. None of the wives of the main leaders of KDF are actively involved in the struggle fronts of KDF. The reason that is given is that family affairs will not run smoothly if both husband and wife are active in politics. Thus, women are not considered the natural and accepted members of politics and their sphere of activity is considered the sphere of domestic by the male leaders of KDF. Another important aspect is the perception of KDF leaders regarding the nature of role of women in KDF. According to them, women are more kind hearted and are less corrupt than men. Thus, the role of women is conceived as more moral and less political. Their sense of justice and their political consciousness which are results of the harsh realities they face at the intersection of caste and gender are not considered.

In the case of KDF, the leadership structure is very elaborate. The state is divided into districts; each district is subdivided into Mandalams which are further divided into Mekhalas, according to the size of the population. Each level has a president, general secretary and secretaries. The same hierarchy is in KDMF and other wings also. Men and women participate in the organisation's (KDF's) work in the field equally. And women are not excluded in addressing any issue. But a separate wing for women has meant that women's representation in leadership will be limited to the women's wing. There was an absolute absence of women in KDF state level leadership before, even though women participated equally in KDF activism. P.K Vanaja is the first women to raise voice against absence of women's representation in the state level leadership of KDF. When P.K. Vanaja became the State level general secretary of

KDMF in 1998-99, she noticed that women were completely absent from the leadership levels of KDF. She protested against it and even pressurized that if women are not represented in the leadership level of KDF, she will leave the organisation. Hence, in the next state level meeting, the then president of KDMF became the vice president (the post of vice president existed before) of KDF and Vanaja was selected as the president of KDMF. Since then, KDF gives a token leadership for women in the state level.

P.K. Vanaja also believes that voices of Dalit women are not heard in the public meetings of KDF. Also in KDF, leadership and decision-making are considered more like an arena of men. P.K Vanaja says, *"Many times I have felt that KDF men were insecure about KDMF women emerging as leaders through protests. They are afraid that whether they will lose their positions of power"*. According to P.K. Vanaja, in showing patriarchal tendencies, KDF is not different from any other organisation. She says, *"They will use women for struggles, to march etc. But in meeting stages and infront of media, men will be there. They will never share the power with women"*. When one observes the meetings of KDF, one can clearly see this tendency. During the 'Dalit Christian reservation state level meeting[3]' on August 2011 organised by KDF, in which various Dalit Christian organisations participated, the stage was filled with men leaders. Few women present sat at the back row as audience and some with children. When the children cried, the men asked these women to go out along with the children. Although KDMF leaders like Ramani and P.K. Vanaja were present, they were not given a chance to speak. P.K. Vanaja was quite offended with this. Also, in the notices those were printed for the state level meeting of KDMF conducted in august 2011, the front page contained the photo of P. Sudhakaran, and not of any women leaders of KDMF which makes one wonder whether it was a meeting of KDMF or KDF. Thus what we can observe is that, KDF follows the much older tradition of giving roles for women in the field and excluding them from leadership roles. KDF has responded to more women entering the collective by giving them more roles in the field and keeping their leadership limited to KDMF. But, even when it comes to meetings of

KDMF, Sudhakaran gets importance. Women's absence in public meeting stages as speakers, in media conferences, etc., gives one the impression that although they are inevitable in the field, there is a presupposition that women are not as well articulate as men.

For KDF members, P. Sudhakaran, the president of the organisation is their father, and men and women of the organisation are brothers and sisters to each other. The gender hierarchy in family is copied to the collectives also. And the father-son-daughter hierarchy in the organisation, in a way legitimizes the role divisions in KDMF, especially when it comes to leadership. The way father is the head of the family, P. Sudhakaran is the head of KDF family, with all its wings. And beings brothers and sisters makes the women undertake duties and men to decide, control and protect. P.K. Vanaja says, "*Sir (P. Sudhakaran) is like our father, and any KDMF woman is safe with KDF man. We are one blood. We are confident to stay with these men even the whole night*". It is a fact that women feel more confident working in such environment and it may promote more mobilisation of women. But at the same time, by extending the gender hierarchy and gender roles that are followed in the families to the organisation, traditional roles within the families are routinised within the organisation and gender hierarchy within the organisation is legitimised. And it creates a remarkable twist in the self-definition of women as Dalit women activists, back into their traditional roles as wives and mothers, and vulnerable people who need protection and guarding.

KDF addresses women's issues also like any other issue, responding to the particular incident at the time of its occurrence, and does not create any gender-based perspective of caste oppression within and outside the organisation. An illustration of this fact is the way in which the guest house protest by women of KDMF was handled by KDF. KDMF women protested against the harassment of a Dalit women sweeper in the guest house. They protested in the guest house manager's room. They were carrying brooms also, signifying their protest. Later, this protest turned out to be a fight when other guest house workers interfered to protect the manager. Police arrived and arrested the women. They were remanded for thirty days. Next day newspapers reported the incident as the attack of Dalit women on guest house manager and other workers. No one reported regarding the sexual harassment the Dalit woman sweeper was undergoing in the guest house. The background of KDMF women who protested, why they protested, what will happen to the livelihood of the families if these women are remanded etc. also went unnoticed. And media succeeded in creating a public opinion against these Dalit women. KDF was not able to tackle this with a discourse in support of these women.

Life of the Dalit women Activists within Families

An important finding emerged from the research is the experiences of Dalit women in their familial sphere. The women I interviewed as part of the research were the most important income earners of their family. They were solely responsible for domestic work, and they engaged in income earning activities outside home as well. There were wage labourers and cashew factory workers among them. Some of them earned a living through animal husbandry. Contrary to the popular image of being free of patriarchal control within families, and sharing an equal relationship with husbands because of their equal role in livelihood earning, family and marriage proved to be oppressive in the case of these women. For all of them, their first experience as Dalit women was in their family itself, in the form of poverty and violence. Poverty was very much a result of their state of absolute absence of productive resources and it proved to be suppressive for women as this poverty was combined with violence from their fathers and husbands. Violence emerged from the alcoholic behaviour of men.

Needless to say, from a very young age, as early as 12-15, many of them became wage labourers in exploitative work conditions. And some of the research participants, as old as 75 years, are also engaged in wage labour. The research proved wrong the well accepted perception regarding Dalit women's labour that the labour of Dalit women is the symbolic of the freedom they enjoy. For these women, their indulgence in wage labour is totally forced upon them, without an option, which is an illustration of the exploitation of these women because of their caste, mediated by gender. Many times they are forced to go out and work even though their health does not permit it, since many of them have husbands who are drunkards and will not look after family properly. And women opined they will prefer to sit at home and look at household matters, and children's future if they are given a chance. Shobhana an activist says, *"The so called freedom of Dalit women is a myth. That freedom needs rethinking. If you ask a Dalit woman, whether she want to go out and work or sit at home, she will say she wants to sit at home. They are really happy to sit at home".*

What is mistaken as freedom by the outside world is exploitative labour which is enforced on them, on which they have no choice. They have no choice on the kind of work, their working conditions, their wages etc. Because of unhealthiness and children's education, they may want to sit at home. But they have no other option than becoming wage labourers. They have many reasons to go out and work, but no option at all to withdraw from labour. Before their childhood ends, they get oriented to the labour class. It is an enforced condition on them. Women unlike men take the additional task of keeping together the disintegrating family, undertaking domestic labour and wage labour and also negotiate with men's violence. This is the most important factor in the survival of Dalit families and communities.

The research proves that control and violence of private patriarchy on the lives of these activists is immense. This point can be illustrated through many examples. Although these women and their family have the tradition of political participation especially along with left, and they have a very strong political consciousness against oppression which is directly informed by their experiences, the immediate reason behind their joining KDF is not simply their urge to fight caste-based discrimination. They joined the organisation seeking help for some problems faced by their family. Among the women interviewed, two prominent family crises because of which women joined were the unlawful arrest of their sons by police based on the complaints of upper caste people and secondly fear of being displaced from their land. When male members of their family were not taking responsibility for solving these issues these women sought help from the Dalit leaders and joined their organisations. An important point to note is that women were able to join only with the permission of their husbands. Women were permitted by their husbands since they were joining not to become leaders or act as change makers but for the sake of their family. Although there is caste based violence involved in the crisis their family faced, women prefer to say that they joined the organisation for the sake of their family.

Another important aspect is that the level of engagement of women is directly linked to the marital status of these women. Two important leaders of KDMF S.P. Ramani and P.K. Vanaja are unmarried. Vanaja decided not to marry since she wanted to be active in the political sphere. Ramani is unmarried and wants to marry, but she is not getting alliances because of her activism. She was the leader of the women who were arrested in relation to the guest house protest and her marriage which was almost fixed did not materialise because of this incident. Women who are married prefer to be ordinary members attending the meetings of the organisation. Protest marches and arrests are unthinkable for them. This is clear from the experiences of married women who were arrested along with Ramani with regard to the guest house protest. The protest turning violent and the arrests that followed were quite unexpected for these women. After the arrest of the women protesters, KDF leader P. Sudhakaran had to convince the angry husbands of the women by reasoning that the women went to jail for the sake of the organisation. One woman is still facing violence from her husband and he is threatening to divorce her as he suspects that she had illicit relationship with the police men while she was in jail. And these women protesters who had to face rejection from their husbands, family members and neighbours said that they went to jail 'for the sake of their sons'. The organisation helped their sons who were framed in a police case and they went to jail for repaying that gratitude towards the organization. Here, women activists are taking refuge in their traditional roles as mothers to face rejection. Thus, their self definition is still under the control of their men and their roles as activists and the main income earners has not made any positive impact on their status within families.

Resistance of Confrontation and Negotiation

KDMF activists are known for their militant activism in Kerala's Dalit politics. The activism these women were engaged in, are clear examples of their fearless attitude and protest against casteist and patriarchal practices. They have fearlessly entered police stations to protest against unlawful arrest of Dalit men, and also caste discrimination they face from police officials. They have manhandled men who have misbehaved with women and have practiced corruption. They have entered toddy shops and have destroyed them completely. The most recent example of the spirit of struggle of KDMF activists is a protest organised by KDMF women in Kollam guest house against the sexual harassment of a Dalit women sweeper. For this protest, the activists were arrested and jailed for a month. In short, their activism expresses a sense of urgency, and boundless commitment towards the cause they represent. They have their sense of justice which they express by giving punishment to the transgressors, before negotiating and taking the path of law. But these acts are not a connotation of the popular belief about Dalit women, being the market women and enjoying the absence of patriarchal control. But it is derived from their experiences as Dalit women. Both the direct experiences they have as Dalit women; experiences of poverty and exploitation and indirect experiences which are derived by imagining the slavery and exploitation their foremothers and forefathers have underwent. This is expressed in the following words of P.K. Vanaja, "*Dalit women suffered the worst effects of slavery. Men were treated like cattle and used to plough the land along with cattle. When they marry, they have to give their wife to their Nair and Namboodiri landlords first. It was not considered rape then. Those experiences are the secret behind the extraordinary militant spirit of Dalit women, even now. They are the most spirited women among all castes. Histories like this are our energy. Before going to participate in any struggle, I remember the struggles of my mothers and sisters, who fought for their chastity. I think that is what makes me a violent activist.*" Such experiences give meaning and legitimacy to their existence as activists. What is manifested in the activism of these Dalit women is a real and rooted political consciousness. Their activism is directly informed by their experiences of discrimination they had as Dalit women.

On the contrary, as we have already seen, the life and experiences of these women in their intimate spaces, their family and organisation they are part of, shows that they are negotiating with the oppressive structure of Dalit patriarchy. Negotiation is an important concept used in the study. It is based on the finding of Franco, Macwan and Ramanathan (2000) that the peculiar nature of South Asian cultures which are largely traditional, demand resistance of negotiation rather than resistance of confrontation. Negotiation happens when a group of oppressed withdraw from active mode of confrontation for the sake of survival. This mode of survival strategy also signifies that agency of the subaltern and self perceptions of the subaltern are not totally subsumed by domination. Similar is the conceptualisation by Bernice Johnson Reagon (as quoted by Mohanty, 1998) which explains this tendency in a wider context of political coalition. When survival rather than shared oppression becomes the priority, coalition occurs, even between groups who have named their difference with each other.

In this study, negotiation becomes an important concept since the entangled caste and gender oppression put Dalit women in a situation of choosing an alliance which offers comparatively more choices of self-expression. Because of the close and intimate relationship with Dalit men and since the association gives them more chances of exercising their agency, women tend to negotiate with the oppression happening in that association. The act of negotiation becomes more manifest since even after recognising their differences with Dalit men and the oppression that happens in their relationship with Dalit men, women withdraw from any sorts of active mode of confrontation. But in their field of activism, as we have seen, they have very militantly confronted all sorts of oppression, including sexual oppression of Dalit women by upper caste men.

Dalit Women in Struggle Fronts: The Act of Negotiation

Within the organisation also, women withdraw from active confrontation, and negotiate with the powers of oppression, as this is also an arena they recognise as basic for their survival. Women workers of KDF repeatedly admit the fact that male workers are their brothers, who will not harm them but will protect them. But at the same time, women of KDF are very clear about the fact that, the same men exclude them when it comes to leadership position. Thus, accepting men as brothers is in a way, a deliberate negotiation within the collectives from the part of women. They compare their organisation to their own family, where the leader is the father and other men brothers. This normalises the domination of men in leadership positions. This also gives women confidence to work in the organisation and this way they convince outsiders, their husbands and themselves that the organisation is a safe space. These acts of women are only negotiations, as these women completely realise the patriarchal tendencies within the organisation. Thus, placing men at the top of the family, and copying the same hierarchy in the field of activism for these women is a way of negotiating the patriarchal oppression and the conflict of private and public divide along with the possible scandals and suspicions that emerges from it.

Negotiating Oppression: The Case of Family

The influence of the private-public divide which confines women to the private sphere is increasing in the lives of these women. But because of the various material hardships, they are very much active in public labour and organisation activities. In fact, women are behind the survival of their family. They perform domestic labour, look after the life and future of children, and also joined KDF seeking support for their family. But this research reveals that women negotiate with patriarchal ego and the pressure to confine to the ideal womanhood, by invisiblising their roles within and outside the family. For example, KDMF women explicitly expresses that ideally men should be the head of the family and should take important decisions. S. P. Ramani says, *"I always think men should take the control of family. In my home also my father takes important decision"*. But when one looks deep into the lives of these women one can realise that this is not an absolute principle that these women believe in, but rather this is an ideal typical situation they create and thereby negotiate with the patriarchal power relations in their life to make their family and field of activism safe spaces. Even though Ramani says men should take control of the family, in her family she and her mother look after the family economically and also by taking important decisions. Her father is old and visually handicapped. Ramani does animal husbandry and real estate business to look after her family. Her ancestral land is illegally occupied by some rich people and she is the one who is running the case. She came to KDF for a support regarding the case and also did a hunger strike for obtaining the legal documents of the land. She and some other women of KDMF guarded the land against the illegal occupants. She travels all over Kerala and also many times reaches home late. In the family, Ramani has the control over decision-making. But still, she says it is her father who is more important.

Again, the negotiation that Dalit women have to make in the families is evident from the words of Jalaja and Mini. Jalaja and Mini say, *"We don't think Dalit women are more hardworking and active than Dalit men. Even if we say something like that they will not recognise it and it will destroy family peace. We never say such thing. Women always stand behind them. They take all decisions. If we say we are smarter, it is against god."* Thus, it is evident that explicitly admitting, the authority of men is a way they maintain family peace. Praising their men and showing happiness and pride in accepting their dominance is a way in which the women negotiate with the overarching reality of patriarchy. Without directly confronting it, they device ways and means to reduce its intensity.

Why do Dalit Women Negotiate with Oppression in Spaces of Struggle?

Although the women activists of KDF are unsatisfied with it in many ways, these women have never thought of leaving KDF. The main reason is the support and confidence this organization gives them. And taking part in meetings and listening to the speeches have made them stronger. "*Whenever Ramani calls us we go for committees. They send vehicles. Till now, we have attended 7-8 committees. We listen to the speeches. Big people come and give speeches. In meetings, we have heard about Ayyankali and the issues of Dalits. Before, we did not use to talk much against people who try to harm us. But now we give them answers. We are stronger. We know that if anything happens to us Ramani will help us*". Further, for the first time, this organisation has given them space to represent their agency. It gave meaning to the many experiences they had as Dalits and as woman. Dalit women who are part of KDMF have worked or have seen Dalits working with political parties, especially communist party of Kerala. And coming to an organisation which values them and their potential, giving them spaces to listen, teach, discuss and write, these women also are not seeing any chances of asking for more.

We can also see that since KDF is an organisation that stands for the benefits of Dalit family and community, a separate space and initiative for women centred reforms loses its scope. Women do not feel the need of a separate mobilisation against the patriarchal relations within their families or within the organisations. What becomes important is the interest of the community and peace and security in the family and the role women can play in it as mothers and sisters. The space, efforts, and time to address the specific issues of women becomes absent when family and community becomes the focal point. Another important aspect is the solidarity that activists of KDMF have with Dalit men co-activists. They believe that Dalit men were the only allies of Dalit women in their fight against oppression and that Dalit men and women should work together to end the oppression of their community. Thus, the feeling of oneness emerged from the strict casteist nature of society has an important role in Dalit women negotiation with Dalit patriarchy within collectives.

As such, although there are insufficiencies in the women's representation in these organisations, Dalit women consider them the most important part of their survival. It represents and accepts their agency, which is devalued by the society and most of the political parties they have worked with before. And there is a confidence in these women arising from the security, that they are working with Dalit men and it can bring a change in their family and community. It gives a meaning to their existence and identity as Dalit women. And for most of them, they are the only arenas of their self expression.

Reasons for Negotiating Oppression within Families

The oppression and negotiation that happens in relationships between Dalit men and women within family need to be understood in the light of dominant gender ideology which has been internalised by both Dalit men and women and also the material and ideological oppression of caste system, that has given women little scope to confront the oppressions in the intimate spheres of their life. The conflict over Dalit women's engagement in public sphere and violence against Dalit women and children often becomes the standard to measure male supremacy. In that way, Dalit men objectify themselves and the women.

Two important themes emerge from the relationship between Dalit men and women within and outside their family. One is the evident antagonism that Dalit women experiences in their relationship with Dalit men and second is the feeling of love, support, and strength that they derive from Dalit men. There is a sense of solidarity they feel with Dalit men, their only ally in the struggles against slavery and untouchability. And it puts them in a very difficult situation, that is, liberation from the antagonism and oppression in their relationship with men may make them negate the basic aspect of their survival, family and community and the love, support and strength it offers. This relationship has been characterized by Collins (2000) as the love and trouble tradition[4]. And to her, this love and trouble tradition needs to be understood in the light of the gender ideology propagated by dominant group and its influence on the work and family experience of the oppressed group, in this case, Dalits. It's the inevitable outcome of intersectional oppression of caste, gender and class. And this overarching gender ideology is rarely challenged by women, but negotiated. This negotiation, even amidst physical and mental violence, is normalised because the dominant gender ideology legitimizes and routinises it, it happens in spaces which are considered intimate, and are considered very basic to the survival of Dalit women and children, it's everyday nature makes it look less like a violation, and moreover, these women are silenced by themselves and by their image as the most strongest women among all categories of men and women.

Conclusion

Although Dalit women activists have perceptions regarding their differences with Dalit men, and have experiences of oppression and exclusion, it is not leading to an active discourse and acts of resistance. No separate space for an active discourse against gender ideology, no freedom from household chores, roles as mothers and wives, lack of roles in leadership and decision-making, all make their oppression a normal aspect to deal with. Without any long term agenda for the emancipation of their status in family and community, which may help them to acquire self-worth and importance, they concentrate on reactionary politics those are mostly agendas of men. Their closeness with Dalit men and the routinisation of this closeness through Dalit movements has affected their self-definition and limits it to their traditional roles in domestic sphere; mothers, wives and sisters.

At the best, all what can be said is that, 'regardless of whether movement ideologies overtly represent attacks on or a reinforcement of patriarchal norms, the call for women to break out of their traditional household roles and assume responsibility for social action in itself represents at least the beginnings of an attack on patriarchy' (Kishwar, 1988) and 'taking major steps towards their own (women's) liberation' (Omvedt, 1977).

Endnotes

1. For a discussion, see Mathew, George (1989). Communal Road to Secular Kerala New Delhi: Concept Publishing Company. Ezhavas were the first to establish their reform movement in 1903, which was named as Sri Narayana Dharma Paripalana Yogam. All Kerala Catholic Congress, an attempt to organise

Syrian Christians was formed in 1905. Namboodiri (Malayali Brahmins) Yogakshema Sabha was founded in 1908. Nair reforms dates back to Chattambi Swamikal who raised his strong voice against the Brahmin dominance of Kerala society and asserted the Nair glory. Mannathu Padmanabha Pillai took initiative in forming Nair Service Society in 1914, which aimed ending Brahmin supremacy, Nair kinship system of Marumakkathayam (Nair matriliny), and also ending expensive social rituals like Thalikettu Kalyanam (Mathew George, 1989). Thus, although these attempts of community reforms started as a common protest against Brahminic domination, it never attained an anti-caste nature.

2. See Kodoth, P. and Eapen, M. (2005), Looking beyond Gender Parities: Gender Inequities of Some Dimensions of Well-Being in Kerala, Economic and Political Weekly, Vol. 40 (30), pp. 3278-86. 'The social and legal reforms were instrumental in sanctioning a new form of marriage, grounded in modem patriarchal relations. The abolition of matriliny and strengthening of patriarchy among all social groups were important aspects of this process'.
3. I attended the meeting to observe the proceedings.
4. For a discussion, see Collins, Patricia, Hill (1991), Black Feminist Thought: Knowledge, Consciousness and the Politics of Empowerment, New York: Routledge.

References

Collins, Patricia Hill (1991). Black Feminist Thought: Knowledge, Consciousness and the Politics of Empowerment, New York: Routledge.

Devika, J. (2010). Kulastreekalum Chandapennungalum Undayathengane, Adhava Adhunika Malayali Streekalude Charithrathinu Oru Amukham, Thiruvanathapuram, Center for Development Studies, Prasanth Nagar.

Devika, J., Sukumar, M. (2006). Making Space for Feminist Social Critique in Contemporary Kerala, *Economic and Political Weekly*, Vol. 41 (42), October 21-27: 4469-4475.

Fernando Franco, Macwan Jyotsna and Ramanathan, Suguna (2000). The Silken Swing: The Cultural Universe of Dalit Women, Calcutta: Stree.

Jacob, T.G., Bandhu, P. (2009). Reflections on Caste Question, the Dalit Situation in South India, Bangalore, NESA Publication.

Kishwar, M. (1988). Nature of Women's Mobilisation in Rural India: An Exploratory Essay, *Economic and Political Weekly*, Vol. 23, No. 52/53 (Dec. 24-31): 2754-2763.

Kodoth, P., Eapen, M. (2005). Looking beyond Gender Parities: Gender Inequities of Some Dimensions of Well-Being in Kerala, *Economic and Political Weekly,* Vol. 40 (30): 3278-86.

Mathew, George (1989). Communal Road to Secular Kerala, New Delhi: Concept Publishing Company.

Mohanty, Chandra Talpade (1998). 'Feminist Encounters: Locating the Politics of Experiences', in Philips Ann (ed.), *Feminism and Politics*, New York: Oxford University Press.

Omvedt, G. (1977). Women and Rural Revolt in India, *Social Scientist*, Vol. 6, No. 1 (Aug): 3-18.

9

Narrations of 'Exclusion': The Autobiographical Accounts by Women of Alternative Orientations in *Chhi! Tumi Naaki...*

Kaustav Chakraborty

Equality is not only about becoming equal citizens and participants in social life, but also about a right to be heard and to have our interests taken seriously.

Steven Seidman, "From Outsider to Citizen"

Introduction

"Minority discourse" is an emerging field which marks a significant departure from traditional socio-literary criticisms that have often treated minority experience as supplements, in its attempt to formulate a theory that is centered round the socio-political experiences of minority themselves. By focusing our attention on lesbians as an oppressed group, the words *homophobia*, *heterosexism* (or '*compulsory heterosexualiy*' as popularised by Adrienne Rich) and *heterocentrism* tend to spotlight the ways in which these differently oriented people constitute a political minority. In the context of *Exclusionary neglect* of the minorities, be it racial, ethno-cultural, gender etc., Amartya Sen (2009) comments:

> 'There is clearly an important issue in the neglect of the interests and perspectives of those who are not parties to the social contract of a polity but who bear some of the consequences of decisions taken in that particular polity'.

By *Exclusionary neglect*, Sen hints at the implied impartiality that excludes the voice of marginalised people who do not belong to the focal group, but whose lives are affected by decisions of that group (Sen, 2009). As an alternative to utility-based or resource-based lines of thinking, Sen refers to the capability approach where individual advantage is judged by the 'person's capability to do things that s/he has reason to value'. The capability approach, by its focus on human life and not on objects of convenience, recommends contemplating on the *actual opportunities* of living as preferred by the individual rather than mere analysis of the *means of* living like utility or wealth:

> 'The focus of the capability approach is thus not just on what a person actually ends up doing, but also on what she is in fact able to do...' (Sen, 2009).

This division finally reveals that an individual's essential identity lies in not what she does, but rather what she is able of doing, i.e., what she intends to do. The narrations of the women of alternative sexual orientation, scripted in *Chhi! Tumi Naaki...*, highlight the struggle of the excluded lesbians, against the social compulsion that obligates them to repress their actual intention/ capability with regulated act, they are forced to enact.

In *Preface-2* the editors-cum-founders of 'Sappho for Equality', Akanksha, Sumita and Rajosree Mukhopadhyay write:

> It is undeniable that treating these narratives as tales would have provided further comfort. We could have kept ourselves away from responsibilities, with eyes tightly shut and face plunged into grappling pillow,

> relishing the cocooned coziness. But we have commitments for unambiguous elucidation of the issue. Firstly, these narratives are indeed accurate confessions of each and every individual. However, they have refused to reveal their actual identities and we have valued their refutation. The incidents have got hundred percent authenticity for they are depicted in the very way they have been experienced. Secondly, ...apart from being personal statements of an individual subject, these incidents expose the reality of a group of people. These are autobiographical acknowledgments of a particular entity—yet they reveal the overall scenario of the lesbian female in general (Mukhopadhyay and Akanksha, 2005).

Recounting of the Exclusion: 1

The Junior's Chronicle—let this be the caption of the untitled first narrative of the anthology—is about the lesbian youngest daughter in the household of two-daughters residing with their parents. The first-person narrator recollects her childhood when she was an upcoming athlete. Then, like a bolt from the blue, she was made to realise that she is different. It was alarming. Filled with remorse, fear, she stated leading an isolated life. Constantly, someone seemed to make her conscious: "You are odd, pervert". She became an adult, yet, she could not come out of her closet, neither before her kith and kin, nor before her pals. Suddenly, the acute suffocation dragged her to Sappho. For the first time, through 'Sappho', she recognised that she is normal. The narrating woman admits that if there was no 'Sappho', she would have committed suicide. Then comes the episode when she got disclosed before her family members, followed by multiple questions, innumerable accusations—Are you a lesbian? How can you be? Do you have any mate? Where do you do all these? What filthy act do you carry out? "What will be your identity", her elder sister screamed, "unless, having got married, you get the name of a husband? How will people designate you? Didn't you feel embarrassed while choosing this sort of life? No revulsion?" (Mukhopadhyay and Akanksha, 2005). Her mother declared: "Now onwards, we cease every connection with junior" (Mukhopadhyay and Akanksha, 2005). The saga of exclusion is not only miserable but rather inhuman:

> Then commenced dreary days, myself cast out as untouchable. Segregating me from every object of the house was made to apprehend that no more I have right over this place, called home... By stopping me to use the comb of my pet dog, they made me feel that I am even lesser a creature than a dog. Constant psychological-cum-physical torture continued. I have never dreamt that my own elder sister, father, my mother could do this to me. Straight away they distanced themselves.
>
> My family members looked as if they were involved in a dangerous game of demolishing my independent existence. In front of me, they threw a challenge which was also a threatening: "We'll see how you can survive!" I was working in a private company as a marketing agent ...my parents informed my boss of my orientation. Boss summoned me to proclaim that my case ensures 'total abnormality' and since there were other female employees in the office, he was worried about them. Without directly terminating me, I was plainly suggested that I was a misfit. "Ok, fine", I bade them goodbye since I was compelled to resign from the post. Shedding lots of sweat, I got another job... however, same thing got repeated. My people intimated the office of my 'identity'. I had to give that up.
>
> I attempted to convince them a lot. Each time was a failure. I demonstrated many paper-cuttings related to this issue. They remained stubborn. For them, I was a sex-maniac, pervert, insane character. ... To get rid of my 'distortion', they tried many way-outs. Once all the sisters of my mom were called upon along with an uncle who was close to our family. Among my three aunts, one is a psychological counsellor. I was wearing a new-port red shirt, too dear to me for being gifted by my partner. While discussing with me, she got furious; holding my collar she shrieked: "Thoroughly spoilt! Going to hell! Stepping outside the house, she'll invite

> more hazards. Better keep her under lock and key". Spitting at my face, she continued—"If I had this kind of a daughter, I would have categorically hanged myself".... (Mukhopadhyay and Akanksha, 2005).

Recounting of the Exclusion: 2

The next case which is from the 4th chapter of the narratives is again that of a lesbian girl, abandoned by her family members. It is narrated in an epistolary manner, where the letter-writing-daughter is addressing her mother. From her letter we come to know, how having got married in 1977 her mother started prating for a girl child who was finally born in 1978. Since there was hardly any educational facility in the remote village where her father was posted, she was sent to her grandmother's house in Calcutta. Her mother kept herself busy with her second child—a boy. While studying at a higher class, by the time when her mother too returned back to Calcutta, she fell in love with her female class-mate. While proposing the beloved, she got scandalized: "Are you sick?" For five years, the affair continued together with her struggle against her inner conflicts. In order to prove herself 'sane', she involved herself with a boy, but the effort in no time turned futile; it was more claustrophobic. As a saving grace, she came into contact with Sappho, the lesbian support group:

> I started overcoming the pollution complex. From new-found-confidence, I gathered courage to share with you ma, about Sappho, about myself, my new found love. You refused to listen to me, pushing me away from you. You made me understand that you can never accept me, you do not even want me... after completion of the higher secondary exams, baba has opened a cyber café in my name. One day, you asked me to sign a paper and later I learnt that you got its ownership transferred to your name so that even brother can have an equal share in it. Why ma? Would I have cheated bhai? My sexual orientation even disoriented my relationship with you?

The guardians proposed her to visit mother's native home where her maternal uncle could fetch her with a job. A sense of responsibility towards her parents prompted her to accept the proposal and she left for Assam on 14th November, 2002. Slowly she realised that, in Assam, arrangements got started, more for marriage than for her employment. 17th June, 2002 was another murky day when, in the darkness of the night, the drunkard brother of her ma, entered into her room and raped her. Next day, while she was complaining about that to her parents, weeping constantly, they hardly believed her:

> You all didn't believe me...could not trust me, or you thought, that was a fair penalty for a fallen girl. You only aimed at wedding me off. Why couldn't you realise that along with me, a boy's life too would have been ruined, without any of his faults. You felt, I am crazy for sex, marriage is the suitable solution...(43)

The letter then depicts how she succeeded to flee from that hell and reached Kolkata, where with Sappho's assistance she got refuge in a home, run by an NGO. Being contacted by the NGO, her father said that he would come to receive her. Seven-eight days passed, yet none came to see her:

> ....I could not help myself from giving you a call. Baba informed me that none of you wanted to maintain any relation with me. You have been taking layer's advice to disown me legally. I failed to respond. My nearest ones are disclaiming me. From that moment, I am dead for my entire family. Ma, you have another child, hence it was easier for you—since I never had another ma—baba—bhai, till now I am not been able to overcome the void. (43)

She ends her letter by asking her mother questions that, she knows, will remain unanswered:

> How is your family? I really do not have any clue. What about you ma? Hope you are keeping yourself satisfied with your happy surrounding. Only one question keeps on haunting me—what sin has imposed this affliction that I have to suffer every moment?...Why am I an outcast? Only my aspiration to live the desired life—is this my unforgivable flaw? (44)

Conventional Exclusionary Ideology-cum-Instruments

If we consider Bengali fairy tales from *Thakumaar/ Thakurdaar Jhuli* ('grandma's/grandpa's stock'), then we can perceive that in most of the tales, a beautiful girl is rescued (implying that she is incapable to self-defense) from a dire situation by a dashing and daring young man who carries her off to marry and they live happily ever after.. The plot thus implies that marriage to the protective man is a guarantee of happiness and proper reward for a right-minded young woman. In all these tales, the female characters are stereotyped as either an included 'good girl' or an excluded 'bad girl'—the witches who are either 'ugly' (obviously from male gaze) or threatening (for they are more powerful than the conventional notion of 'a delicate fair sex' or 'a woman in distress') accordingly get stigmatized as 'bad'. If woman accepts her traditional gender role and obeys the patriarchal rules, she is 'good' and if she does not, she's 'bad'—the narrations of the lesbians in *Chhi Tumi Naaki...* reinforce this (Delphy, 1984).

The exclusion of lesbians can find its epistemological analysis in Guillaumin who argued that the primary form of women's oppression, which also reveals their function as property, is 'appropriation'. Women are oppressed by what Guillaumin calls "direct physical appropriation", by which she means, "the reduction of women to the state of material objects" (Guillaumin, 1996). Guillaumin calls this appropriation, *sexage*. *Sexage* occurs in four main forms:

1. Appropriation of women's time (the marriage contract puts no limit on the time the wife needs to work).
2. Appropriation of the products of women's bodies (number of children is a decision, taken by the male).
3. Women's sexual obligation (has to bed any time on demand and can never even feel concerned for any other male without the consent of the husband).
4. Women's obligation to care for whichever members of the family can't care for themselves (e.g., the rigorous religious ritual (*broto*) and austere customs (*upvas*) that are exclusively prescribed for women for the welfare of the family).

Since the lesbians/alternately oriented women form a major challenge/resistance before the patriarchal 'appropriation' through the above mentioned mechanisms, they become the worst victims of patriarchal rage.

The question "What is a lesbian?" is problematised by the fact that can a lesbian be defined as a woman who has sex with another woman? What activity constitutes sex? If the 'act' is the only signifier of sexuality then a heterosexual virgin who thinks herself as heterosexual cannot call her so unless she performs the act with a man. Perhaps, the better way to define a lesbian, then, is to say that she is a woman whose sexual desire is directed towards woman. The advantage of this sort of definition is that, it allows us to recognise lesbian existence even within the confines of heterosexual marriage. In *Chhi Tumi Naaki*...chapters 2, 7 and 9 narrate the accounts of women who discovered their lesbian self even after years of heterosexual married life. The female narrator of chapter 2 describes the turmoil that has resulted from her bisexual inclination:

> Who am I? One who loved Sujan and married him or the one who is now longing for Srimoyee?.... heterosexuality is perfectly fine; homosexuality is hardly tolerable; but what is bisexuality?—even while performing a bisexual, I failed to apprehend it fully... Problem no. 1—This is homosexuality. Problem no. 2—This is extra-marital. Problem no. 3—What will I do with this kind of life? (33)

In chapter 7, the female narrator is a mother of two children. After ten years of her marital life, she falls in love with the female-tailor, elopes with her, returns back for the sake of her children, however, as a transformed personality:

> Then who had left and the one who returned back, they are no long the same person. My husband, in-laws, neighbours, everyone are aware of this. ...They make out, I am a part of Sappho. I am a lesbian. (59)

The Counter-Exclusionary Discourses

1. Some lesbian theorists suggest that heterosexual identity itself is partial and lesbian is an all-inclusive identity, so

far a woman is concerned; for, lesbian identity is not restricted to sexual domain but consists of directing the bulk of one's attention and emotional energy to other woman, having other woman as one's primary source of emotional sustenance and psychological support. That is, a lesbian like any woman is a 'woman-identified woman'. Adrienne Rich (1980) makes use of this idea when she argues for a *lesbian continuum*, which "includes a range through each woman's life and throughout history—of woman identified experience, not simply the fact that a woman has had or consciously desired genital sexual experience with another woman." Woman-identified experience includes, for example, emotional bonding through shared work or play, receiving mental support or shared experience of joy in any form. Hence, from this standpoint, all woman are woman-identified woman since they experience compulsive lesbian continuum right from mother (here, it is important to note that, unlike male who is first exposed to heterosexuality by his preliminary intimacy with the mother, the very first exposure of a female is the homosexual world where she comes in primary touch, for the very first time with her mother) to female colleague, while heterosexual identity is a selective identity that can be excluded, if desired by a female.

2. Another 'exclusionary' practiced propagated by some lesbians is the separatist theory that dissociate woman from all men, including gay men and excludes heterosexual women as well. By rejecting all forms of male-dominated institutions, along with male themselves, they advocate women sufficiency. As Marilyn Frye (1978) argues:

   Access is the faces of power... It is always the privilege of the master to enter the slave's hut. The slave who derides to exclude the master from her hut is declaring herself not a slave.

Lesbian Inclusion in Indian Tradition

Various regional and cultural (Vaishnava, Shaiva and Shakta) interactions along with the existing *Vedas*, *Puranas* and epics like *Ramayana* and *Mahabharata* have resulted in the celebration of multifaceted sexual orientations in Hindu tradition. Details of these can be found in Giti Thadani's *Sakhiyani: Lesbian Desire in Ancient and Modern India* (New York: Cassell, 1996) and *Same-Sex Love in India: Readings from Literature and History* (Macmillan India: 2001) edited by Ruth Vanita and Saleem Kidwai. Here, let me provide one instance for each of these Lesbian, Gay, Bisexual and Transsexual categories.

Lesbian appears in the *Kama Sutra* translation of Danielou as the rendition of the term *svairini*. Lesbian family occurs in the Bengali *Ramayana*, written by the fourteenth-century poet Krittivasa, who assigns the birth of Bhagiratha to the divinely sanctified sexual intercourse between two women. The story as illustrated in the *Adi Kanda* of *Sachitra Krittivasi Saptakanda Ramayan*,(cited by Vanita and Kidwai 2001) informs that with the death of Dilipa, the king of Ayodhya, the gods in the heaven have become worried as how would Vishnu be born in the family of the sun if the very lineage comes to the end. As per the unanimous decision taken by the gods, Shiva riding on his bull, comes to Dilipa's two widowed queens and forecasts that one of them will be blessed with the ability to give birth to a son. The widows automatically are astonished. Mahadev then asks them to have intercourse with one another. The two wives, having taken their bath, start making love and one of them conceives consequently.

The British colonizers, taught with the orthodox Christian notion that heterosexual reproductive sex is exclusively the 'natural' and 'normal' one, along with their inherent hypermasculine syndrome which made them perceive the less-aggressive, timid Indian male in totality as passive and effeminate, got motivated in banishing all sorts of deviant sexual practice. The present day criminal law in India that penalises the queer is the residue of the British law that was grafted into the Indian legal system during the colonial regime. Indian scholars like Partha Chatterjee (1989) Ashis Nandy (1983), Mrinalini Sinha (1995) and Indira Chowdhury (2001) have rightly pointed out what Gayatri Reddy (2006) has brilliantly summarised:

As several scholars have noted with respect to the politics of European colonial rule, sexual prescriptions along the lines of race, class and gender have often been the linchpin of colonial ideologies...with regard to British imperial ideology, the concepts of 'private' and 'public', moral and scandalous have hinged...decisively on questions of sexuality.

Consequently to equip the natives with ethical form of conduct, which has obviously resulted from their orthodox Christian faith, the section 377 of the Indian Penal Code got introduced in 1861 to stop "carnal intercourse against the order of nature with any man, woman" with their aim at the regulated manufacturing of, what Foucault (1995) calls, "docile bodies".

Conclusion

Chhi Tumi Naaki... deserves critical acclaim for its significant *thick description* (Geertz,1973), which, according to the new historical and cultural criticism should be a prominent feature of marginalised narratives. *Thick description* focuses on the personal side of history—the history of family dynamics, of profession, sexual practices—as much or more than on such traditional historical topics as war or passing of laws. *Chhi Tumi Naaki...*, by its confessional scripting of personal history of these marginalized women, excluded as the sexual 'other' of the mainstream, serves to illustrate the motif of *thick description*, that is, history is not only a matter of dominant facts, but also of interpretations of the concealed private domain of the marginalized, tactfully ignored/regulated by the patriarchy.

References

Danielou, Alain. (1994). *The Complete Kama Sutra*, Rochester, Vermont: Park Street Press.

Delphy, Christine (1984). *Close to Home: A Materialist Analysis of Women's Oppression*, London: Hutchinson.

Foucault, Michel (1995). *Discipline and Punish: The Birth of the Prison*, New York: Vintage Books.

Frye, Marilyn (1978). "Some Reflections on Separation and Power?" *Sinister Wisdom*, Vol 6.

Geertz, Clifford (1973). *The Interpretation of Cultures: Selected Essays by Clifford Geertz*, New York: Basic Books.

Guillaumin, Colette (1996). "The Practice of Power and Belief in Nature" in Diana Leonard and Lisa Adkins (ed.) *Sex in Question: French Materialist Feminism*, London: Taylor and Francis.

Mukhopaduyay, Rjosree, Sumita and Akanksha (2005). *Chhi Tumi Naaki...: Ekti Sappho Shankolon*, Kolkata: Saptarshi Prokashan.

Reddy, Gayatri (2006). *With Respect to Sex: Negotiating Hijra Identity in South India*. New Delhi: Yoda Press.

Rich, Adrienne (1980). "Compulsory Heterosexuality and Lesbian Existence", *Signs*, 5(4).

Sen, Amartya (2009). *The Idea of Justice*, London: Penguin Books.

Vanita, Ruth and Saleem Kidwai (2001). *Same-Sex Love in India: Readings from Literature and History*, Macmillan: India.

10

Portrayal of Women in Recent Mainstream Hindi Films: A Case Study

Pallav Mukhopadhyaya

Introduction

Patriarchy refers to the social, cultural and material structures by which a male, heterosexual way of being is privileged. In a patriarchal society, women are predestined to play a fixed number of roles. Mainstream Hindi films cannot present women revolting against patriarchal society because of what Noam Chomsky describes as the function of media in manufacturing consent. Popular film is a consensus between the filmmaker and audience expectation, it is an agreement between people who finance a film and their expectation of recovering that money by entertaining an audience without offending their 'sensibilities'. This includes their individual understanding of the position held by women in families and extended social groupings.

The 'feminisation' of mass culture has been shown to be a feature of cultural theory in the Modern West (Huyssen, 1986).[1] Thus, the gendered polarisation of culture into a masculine sphere of autonomous modernist works of art and a feminine sphere of heteronomous and formally diffused mass culture has led to an affirmation of melodrama as a feminine form and its pleasures as the denigrated but real and valued pleasures of female audiences. On the other hand, a study of Indian film melodrama shows that in its most fragmented, patchwork texture, its most 'feminised' appearance going by Huyssen's argument, it addressed to a wide, undifferentiated audience. Thus, women's melodrama appears to be a specific branching off from a popular form but the question of the conditions of possibility of melodrama remains unresolved.[2]

Indian actresses represent a nexus, an intersection of different discourses like issues of sexuality, desire and portrayal. The recent mainstream Hindi films have portrayed the Indian film actress's presence-the lifestyle of the woman character, the clothes she wears, the choreography of the dances, the settings for the dances, the music, etc. The first decade of 21st century has witnessed liberalisation, privatisation and globalisation. In this neo-liberal era, mainstream Hindi film actresses are expected to portray globalised images of a liberated female sexuality, but are still circumscribed by shifting yet narrow definition of 'Indian' femininity. The contemporary films rather than expand the subject positions for actresses, regulates and disciplines them within limited definitions of selfhood and sexuality. The distinction between 'admirable' and 'trashy' roles is coded by representations of female sexuality that reiterate an existing hierarchy among Bollywood actresses. As a result, success for the Bollywood film actress is contingent upon strategic negotiations and presentations of her sexual self. The contemporary mainstream Hindi films portrayal practices repeatedly fetishise these women as 'feminised' bodies, subjecting them to a voyeuristic male gase – their sexual and gendered selves continued to be circumscribed.[3] Caught between these competing subject positions, contemporary Hindi film actresses have very little room for maneuvering. A new nomenclature has originated 'item girls'. The actresses who portray the item girls in the film have their star status hinging on their sexualised persona. This public display of sexuality also binds their careers with in the 'item' roles. Strategies for resistance or subverting hegemonic norms of Indian womanhood through the mainstream Hindi films, consequently, are very limited. In Sudhir Mishra's "Hazaaron Kwaishein Aisi" (2003), a woman like Geeta Rao (Chitarangada Singh) is too miraculously free-thinking to exist in the Naxalite-inspired Delhi University coffee houses of the 1970s. Sujoy Ghosh's 'Kahaani' is a thriller about a woman in search of her husband in Kolkata, who finds herself struggling in an environment that is completely alien to her. "Kahaani revolves around the plight of a woman played by Vidya Balan," he says.

Characters tell their own stories and the gender is incidental, says author Advaita Kala of 'Almost Single', who wrote the story for 'Kahaani'. Now when was the last time you saw a Bollywood film dissecting female sexuality without being apologetic about it? Can't remember, can you? Bollywood has mostly turned its back to the sensual woman as a protagonist. Typically, there have been just two ways mainstream cinema has viewed female eroticism. By and large, the Indian film heroine is represented as a romantic, albeit asexual creature. The rest is straight-jacketed into the whore and vamp category.

Aims and Objectives

This essay has tried to investigate the portrayal of women in recent mainstream Bollywood Hindi films. Earlier, the good heroines catered to our pious aspirations and the wicked vamps stoked our carnal fires; but now the wife and the whore were mixed up together in a cocktail and this whetted the male appetite for more. This essay is also an attempt to enquire the status of women in recent mainstream Hindi films in the first decade of the 21st century.

Methodology

The present study follows the Historical Method. It tries to focus on the representative films of the first decade of 21st century. It tries to interpret the relationship between women characters, state, society, family, times, events and narratives. The essay mainly depends on the articles, books, magazines and also critical appreciation of the films. The essay has analysed the films, documents and records and has drawn inferences. The primary sources of data and information lie on articles, newspapers, magazines, books, and such other sources. To follow this method, author has tried to maintain the genuineness of the sources and the admissibility of data as evidence and has attempted to find out the meaning of the assertions contained in the sources and the truthfulness of such assertions. It has offered explanations based on thorough analysis of films.

Besides, the present study also follows the Method of Content Analysis. It has been done to study diverse kinds of problems and crisis faced by the women in mainstream Hindi films. In this essay, author has tried to analyse the messages, causes and antecedents of messages and the effects of such messages in the films discussed and have identified 2001-2010 as its time span of discussion and selected purposefully certain films as sample of study which represents the decade.

Nature of Heroines/Actresses

The gaze mobilised by the popular film is a national gaze which reads the woman-in-public as a 'public woman' and thus denies her subjectivity. It is a rule in mainstream Hindi films, in particular, and Indian mainstream films, in general, that the heroine will be both good-looking and sexy. Why does Indian film deal in beautiful women? It could be that since the audience for popular film is disproportionately made up of young, desperate, thwarted men, the heroine's looks and sex appeal matter. Indian film favours good-looking women because its audiences consist of good-looking women. If we cast our eyes over mixed gatherings in classrooms, offices, weddings, literary festivals, fairs, cultural programmes etc. Indian women are routinely better-looking. Before marriage, the heroine usually sports salwaar-kameez, after marriage, saris... as a mark of her status as both "womanly and "adult" (Dwyer 2000).[4] A mainstream heroine today has to come from the ramp. She has to come from consumer India. She must either be a Miss Universe or Miss World like Aishwarya Rai, Sushmita Sen, Priyanka Chopra and Lara Dutta, or a model like Priety Zinta, Amrita Arora, Neha Dhupia, Bipasha Basu, et al. In other words, she has to be a film star by consensus, not by talent. Aishwarya Rai is testimony to the market's persistence in keeping faith with the most reliable 'consumer durable'. So how can an actress in mainstream film act convincingly as a woman struggling against patriarchy? It is paradoxical that despite being adored by millions, Indian actresses aren't considered strong enough to carry a film on their shoulders.

It's been decades since we had a Mother India or an Umrao Jaan. But the contemporary time notices a slew of women-centric Bollywood films like Onir's 'I Am', Prakash Jha Productions' 'Turning 30', Sujoy Ghosh's 'Kahaani', etc. Though trade analysts would love to argue that men will always rule the box office, it hasn't stopped talented directors like Rajkumar Gupta from making 'No One Killed Jessica', or Vishal Bhardwaj doing a 'Saat Khoon Maaf' and Madhur Bhandarkar roping in Kareena Kapoor for 'Heroine'. The themes are all different, but the common thread that binds them all is the filmmakers' belief in the power of a woman's story.

Housewives in Mainstream Bollywood Hindi Films

Majority of the housewives of mainstream Hindi films are decked up to their teeth in saris and jewellery that might total up to the annual income of many lower middle class families. All they do is backstabbing each other and manipulate relationships and property. These women do not believe in housework either. Their kitchens are like the ultimate in advertisements for modular kitchens. Their palms are soft, manicured revealing their complete indifference to the kitchen and to housework and all that goes along. The mainstream Hindi films represent women in a flawless complexion, an unwrinkled face, fair skin, slim, lissome and tall figure wrapped alluringly and teasingly in a sari or salwar and shapely figure that have become the metaphor for female success because attaining these symbols of female achievement requires a great deal of sacrifice, hard work and control.[5] The impact is huge. The business of beauty parlours shoots up. Gold facials, fruit and herbal facials, facials to tighten the skin find their way into middle class Indian homes. In fact, all these films perform the dual duty of entertaining and advertising at the same time. Their eyebrows are plucked, their make-up and lipstick in bed are intact, suggesting that the men in their lives either probably believe in the celibate state of life. Critics argue that majority of these mainstream Bollywood Hindi films have marginalised the space for intelligent entertainment.[6]

'Mother' in Mainstream Bollywood Hindi Films

By and large, our mainstream Hindi filmmakers have steered clear of all cultural and symbolic references and have stuck to the straight and narrow while portraying the mother figure as a weepy woman in white with a halo riding her shoulders. In Bollywood, she is typically the widowed or abandoned woman who weathers many storms to keep the family together and bring up her children. In return, she expects them to be forever obedient and loyal. Bollywood has witnessed a transformation from Maa to Mata-ji to Mummy to today's Mom. There are screen mothers with several poster mothers lining the way in the last decade of mainstream Hindi films. They include Jaya Bachchan, Farida Jalal, Rekha, Reema Lagoo, Kiran Kher, Rohini Hattangadi, Roti Agnihotri, Supriya Karnik and many others. Their endless puja rituals and soft hullabies, the pain-filled eyes and quiet dignity with which they conducted themselves rekindled memories of a bygone era. In between, there have been the occasional treacherous or manipulative mothers, but more often than not, the mother has stood out as a doting, almost divine being, incapable of doing any wrong. Mothers slaving for their children have been a recurrent theme of Bollywood tearjerkers for a long, long time. At times, she is separated from one son. At other times, she loses them all, only to be reunited in the film's climax scene amidst fisticuffs and fireworks. The reel mother started getting changed. She now looks happy, even fun-loving, dances with her husband and family members at wedding reception. The 'new age' mother appears as a friend of her children. She dresses smart and offers smarter advice in crucial matters like making career opportunities and finding love in life. These mothers do not like to appear as an epitome of goddess and is rarely seen in crumpled white saris. Jaya Bachchan, as the regular NRI mother, is often seen bedecked in gorgeous silk saris and gold jewellery.[7] To many, these exaggerated representations have totally destroyed the halo accompanying the mother figure, reducing her to a caricature of her defied predecessors on screen. On the other hand, a section of the critics find nothing wrong in such women who have freed themselves from the shackles of stereotyped femininity while continuing to be power centres in the family as mother, nurturer and often as bread-earner keeping her inner strength, sense of values and virtues intact. The screen mothers are the master chefs. They are so adorably huggable, full of human kindness, their foreheads are coloured with worry lines. Mothers were once dominating figures in Bollywood films. Screen mothers taught the viewers to obey traditional rules, sacrifice herself for the larger good and to combat every sort of calamity, be it in the time of any disease, or clashes between family members.

The following actresses have achieved popularity for portrayal of their 'mother' characters in recent mainstream Bollywood Hindi films:

Rakhee

As Amitabh Bachchan's mother in 'Shakti', Rakhee had a sensational start of screen mother which have had an inordinately high quota of melodrama. As a mother, her popular films include 'Khalnayak', 'Ram Lakhan', 'Baazigar', 'Karan Arjun', etc.

Jaya Bachchan

Bachchan acquired the tag of 'new age' mother with films like 'Fiza', 'Kabhi Khushi Kabhie Gham', 'Kal Ho Na Ho', etc.

Farida Jalal

Jalal has appeared on screen as an adorable mother. She can make the absurd come across as plausible. Her popular films include 'Henna', 'Raja Hindustani', Dilwale Dulhania Le Jayenge', etc.

Representation of Women in Films – Women Director's Views

Though Bollywood has traditionally been a male dominated industry, women have always managed to make their presence felt. From Kalpana Lazmi to Tanuja Chandra and Farah Khan, female film directors have been breaking new barriers and creating a niche for themselves. Farah says the audience has become more urbane. "The audience has opened up to smart, clever and intelligent films. They aren't biased towards directors of any gender." Filmmaker Zoya Akhtar seconds the thought of Farah being a woman with the eyes of a man. "It makes no difference whether the director is a male or a female. Farah gives her film womanly touches when she feels the need to do so. Another Director Alankrita Srivastava comments, "As a director, I will always make women-centric films because I am here to explore women and delve into their lives and minds. So when I start writing a script, it's naturally about women."[8] Though women-related themes comprise only a small percentage of the subjects that filmmakers prefer, the gender doesn't matter for writer-director Aparna Sen. She explains, one can't generalise that women-oriented subjects don't get viewers' acceptance."

Filmmaker Alankrita Shrivastava, who previously assisted Prakash Jha in films like 'Rajneeti', 'Apaharan', 'Gangaajal' and 'Dil Dosti', etc. is busy giving her directorial debut 'Turning 30' the finishing touch. "It is not that all women-oriented films flop. The key is interesting stories and good execution," she says.

Jha himself has 'Mrityudand', a strong women-centric film, to his credit. Shrivastava adds, "I'm going to make a woman-centric film."

Industry insiders agree that content is the king, but they still insist that there are other factors that need to be addressed to keep the cash registers ringing. They reveal that our society has its own limitations and women here are not seen as powerful entities.

Film and admaker Pradeep Sarkar says that in the ad world, women call the shots and we are also seeing a surge of women directors coming to the fore and delivering meaningful cinema, yet Bollywood is largely hero-struck.

Case Studies

Chandni Bar (2001)

Mumtaz (Tabu) is a young village woman whose family is killed in communal riots. She moves to Mumbai with her uncle, the only family member she has left. They are desperately poor and her uncle persuades her to become a bar girl at Chandni Bar. This is merely temporary, he promises, until he gets a job.

Mumtaz is shy and loathes the work, but she forces herself to dance and flirt. However, the uncle doesn't keep his promise; he lives on her earnings, drinking them away, and never gets a job. He adds one final, unforgivable crime to the list when he gets drunk and rapes her. By this time, she has caught the eye of a gangster called Potiya Sawant (Atul Kulkarni). When she tells Potiya what her uncle did to her, Potiya decides to "defend her honour." Potiya kills the uncle and marries her. She lives with him for several years and gives birth to a son, Abhay, and daughter, Payal. She wants Abhay and Payal to be educated and stay far away from her world of dancing girls and Potiya's gangsters. Potiya gets in the bad books of other gangsters, loses his connections, becomes a target for the police, and is killed in a planned "encounter," leaving Mumtaz to return back to dancing at the Chandni Bar. Years pass and Abhay and Payal are in their teens and attending school. Mumtaz still works at Chandni Bar, not as a dancer, but as a waitress. Then the unexpected happens — Abhay is arrested by the police for extortion and held in a juvenile home for the crime he had not committed. At the home, Abhay gets sodomised by a couple of other inmates. Mumtaz attempts to talk to the police, but to no avail. She then meets with some influential people, who agree to help her out for a price, which she must bring to them in less than two days. Mumtaz hustles and sells her body to obtain the money but is still short. Seeing her mother's plight, Payal takes up dancing at Chandni Bar and brings the rest of the money to her troubled mother. With the money turned over to release Abhay, the family heaves a sigh of relief — until Mumtaz notices that it is not the same Abhay she had known two days earlier. This one is cold, ruthless, and has only purpose in life: vengeance. Abhay takes his revenge and shoots the inmates that raped him. It looks like Payal is going in her mother's footsteps, and Abhay is set to be another Potiya.

Daman (2001)

Set in the backdrop of Assam, a state in the north eastern part of India, the film portrays the conservative pan Indian socio-cultural life where the women are subject to domestic violence. The Saikia family is extremely wealthy. The two sons of the family are Sanjay (Sayaji Shinde) and Sunil Saikia (Sanjay Suri). The latter being the kinder of the two whilst the former is very hot-tempered and has occasional mood swings. The parents decide to get him married to Durga (Raveena Tandon), a lower caste girl from a poor family, thinking she will be able to cope with Sanjay's temper. Sanjay initially refuses to marry Durga, but when his mother threatens to cut him off from the family will, he relents. Thus, Durga marries Sanjay and looks forward to her new life. From day one, Durga is subjected to physical and mental harm by her husband. To add insult to injury, he spends their wedding night with a prostitute called Chameli. Durga continues to be tortured by her husband and after a drunken night, he rapes her. Soon Durga is pregnant, but Sanjay is convinced the child is not his but Sunil's. Durga gives birth to a girl, named Deepa, but this only disappoints Sanjay and he shuns the child. Sanjay decides to get Deepa, now twelve years old, married to a much older man. When Durga protests, he viciously beats her. Durga's only companion Sunil is killed by Sanjay after he suspects that he and Durga were having an affair. Durga is devastated by Sunil's death and decides that enough is enough. She runs away with Deepa and decides to cut all ties with Sanjay. Sanjay files a police complaint but is unsuccessful in finding the two. Durga carries on with her life but it's not long before Sanjay finds the two. Finally, Durga learns to stick up for herself and she kills her evil husband.

Zubeidaa (2001)

Zubeidaa is the story of Riyaz's (Rajit Kapoor) search to understand his mother, who is not known to him, as he was brought up by his grandmother in the absence of his mother. His mother's name was Zubeidaa (Karisma Kapoor) and she was the only daughter of a filmmaker named Suleman Seth (Amrish Puri). Zubeidaa acts in films secretly, but when her father finds out, he forbids her to carry on and quickly arranges her marriage to Mehboob Alam. Things look happy for her when she gives birth to Riyaz. However, a misunderstanding arises between Suleman Seth and Mehboob's parents, and Mehboob divorces Zubeidaa few days after she gives birth. Zubeidaa then meets Maharaja Vijayendra Singh of Fatehpur (Manoj Bajpai). Vijayendra is already married to Maharani Mandira Devi (Rekha) and is the father of two children. Nevertheless, he falls in love with Zubeidaa and they get married, but there is continuous turmoil in their relationship. Riyaz learns through Zubeidaa's journal that though she loved Vijayendra dearly, she was unable to follow the mainly Hindu customs and traditions of the palace, being a Muslim. She was also uncomfortable because of her brother-in-law Uday Singh's sexual advances towards her, and his demands of her to have an extra-marital affair with him. Away from her own family, she was unable to enjoy the beautiful surroundings of the palace. Riyaz travels to Fatehpur and asks many people about his mother. However, all except Mandira, whom Zubeidaa called "Mandy Didi" deny that his mother ever existed, or say that she was a horrible woman who seduced their king and caused his death in a mysterious accident. On reading the journal, Riyaz finds out that Vijayendra had become a politician and was about to go to Delhi for an important meeting. Zubeidaa felt frustrated that whenever her husband needed help, he looked to Mandira for support, and at the last minute, she insisted that only she will go for the meeting. They never make it, however, as they die in a plane crash. In the end, Riyaz and his grandmother watches a tape of one of his mother's films with his family. Though he loves his mother very much, Riyaz never succeeds in deciphering the mystery behind his mother's demise.

Tehzeeb (2003)

Anwar (Rishi Kapoor) and Rukhsana (Shabana Azmi) had been married for years. After the birth of their daughters Tehzeeb and Nazeen, Anwar gets into a deep depression and commits suicide. Rukhsana is a famous, ambitious and popular singer. After her husband's mysterious death, her elder daughter Tehzeeb (Urmila Matondkar) suspected her to be the cause of his departure. Despite the court declaring Rukhsana innocent, Tehzeeb still bears a grudge against her and accuses her of deserting her and Naazeen (Dia Mirza). Years later, Tehzeeb has grown up and has married Salim (Arjun Rampal) against her mother's wishes. Nazeen is mentally challenged, and

Tehzeeb takes her under her custody. Tehzeeb lives happily with her husband and Nazeen, until Rukhsana decides to visit them and renew ties after five years. Both mother and daughter are happy about the upcoming visit, but the tension between them turns up eventually.

Chameli (2003)

Chameli is the story of a prostitute played by Kareena Kapoor. Aman Kapoor (Rahul Bose) an investment banker, lost his pregnant wife, Neha (Rinke Khanna) in a car accident on a rainy night. The accident left him depressed and lonely. He drowned his grief with alcohol and smoking. Chameli (Kareena Kapoor) is a prostitute who was sold to a brothel by her uncle when she was young. She is now a tough, street-smart woman. On one rainy night, Aman and Chameli, two strangers, meet each other in South Mumbai. The movie starts with Aman narrating, in a party he is throwing but is reluctant to attend. He gets in his car after it starts raining to go home, but at the gate of his residence, he decides to go elsewhere. On the way, his car breaks down, and his cell phone battery discharges and he takes refuge in an alleyway where he meets Chameli. She is plying her trade, and offers him a match for his cigarette. He is initially repulsed by her, but when he scares off a potential customer, he offers to pay for her missed wages. At this point, a young boy comes selling coffee and cigarettes. Chameli is familiar with him and pays his school fees. He promises to come back with a mechanic to fix Aman's stalled vehicle. Next to appear is Raja, who is in love with Haseena, and has made off with Rs 50,000 from his father's safe. Chameli consoles him and takes him away, when Haseena makes an appearance. She is a eunuch, and when Chameli returns, she advises Haseena to run away with Raju to another city with the money. Raju's father and his henchmen turn up looking for them but leave soon afterwards. Chameli's pimp, Usman, has rented her out to Naik, which she isn't very keen on. She avoids Naik's men, and Aman and she goes to Sweety bar to meet Usman. There, Aman offers to pay off the rest of the amount that Chameli owes in exchange for not having to entertain Naik. Usman agrees, but at the ATM kiosk, he pulls a knife demanding more money, and gets hurt.

Then, Aman and Chameli are picked up by the police, when he makes a phone call that brings the Assistant Commissioner of Police K.P. Singh to the station. They troop to the hospital where Usman is recovering and with a gun to his groin, he phones Naik. Singh convinces Naik to back off Chameli. When Aman finally gets back home, he is a changed man, altered by Chameli's philosophy on life. He reconnects with his father-in-law whom he had avoided since his wife's demise. He then returns to see Chameli, and they meet again, as they did when they first met.

Aitraaz (2004)

Aitraaz is a film about Raj Malhotra (Akshay Kumar), Priya Malhotra née Saxena (Kareena Kapoor), and Sonia Roy (Priyanka Chopra). Raj and Priya accidentally meet each other and fall in love. One day Priya gets pregnant and the couple is very happy. Raj even buys a bungalow for the couple. They are very happy with their new lives. Raj is expecting a promotion to C.E.O. on the annual company day. The chairman (Amrish Puri) arrives with his new wife, Sonia Roy. Sonia Roy sees Raj and goes to the stage. She discusses something with the chairman and then announces the promotions. The post that Raj was expecting was given to his friend Rakesh (Vivek Shauq). To Raj's surprise, he was included in the list of Board of Directors. They had a party that night and Priya also comes with Raj and they all enjoy. Sonia starts flirting with Raj even in front of Priya. Priya doesn't like Sonia's behavior and warns Raj to watch out for her. Raj agrees. The next day, Rakesh tells Raj that they have a defect in their new mobile handsets and its production needs to stop. The defect is that the call goes to two people at once, the one we are trying to call, and another in the phone book contact list. He needs the permission of Sonia to do this work. Raj thus goes to Sonia's home. Sonia there tells that she has got a chance to meet him after long years and thus she is very aroused. She hugs him from the back all of a sudden while he was talking to his friend in Bangkok. She tries to seduce him but Raj denies her and goes home. Sonia is angry with Raj and tells her husband, Mr. Roy that he tried to rape her and exploit her. Roy becomes angry and gives Raj his resignation notice. Raj decides to fight against Sonia. Raj requests his lawyer friend, Barrister Ram Chauthrani (Annu Kapoor) fight his case and he agrees. In the meantime, Sonia and Mr. Roy have hired Lawyer Patel (Paresh Rawal). They fight a lot but Lawyer Patel discloses that Raj was the one who raped her. When it looks like there is no hope, Raj's friend who was in Bangkok returns and hands him over a tape in which their talk in Sonia's house was recorded. He gives it to the lawyer and the lawyer tests it in a forensic lab and concludes that it is real, but he is run over while returning by a person deployed by Sonia. At the moment, his assistant takes the cassette and puts a destroyed cassette in its place and hands it over to the person who ran over his senior. It is handed over to Sonia. Priya asks Raj why he called the bank manager at Sonia's house, and Raj realises he didn't call the manager, but Rakesh, and the defect in the mobile connected the line to the bank manager, as well. Priya, who is also a lawyer, now fights the case due to the accident of Raj's previous lawyer, Mr. Chauthrani. Priya uses Rakesh's mobile as evidence against Sonia along with the fact that Sonia met Raj in South Africa eight years ago. Their infatuation for each other led to Sonia being pregnant with Raj's child. However, Sonia and Raj split as Sonia wanted to abort their child, for she lusted for money, status, luxury and power. The baby was a wall between her dreams of becoming rich. After Raj left her, Sonia aborted their child and bumped into Roy. Seeing her chance, Sonia hit the jackpot, and married Roy, who was much older than her. However, Roy wasn't able to give Sonia any sexual pleasure, so Sonia tried to seduce Raj, but being the loyal husband, Raj rejected her sexual advances. As a result, Priya wins the case and Roy leaves Sonia. Feeling humialiated and guilty, Sonia is unable to bear the shame and commits suicide by jumping from the top of a building. The film ends with a song, showing that Raj and Priya have a baby boy and live together happily ever after. Sexual harassment as a theme is bold by Bollywood standards. The female protagonist is not the victim here. Rather, Raj Malhotra finds himself faced with false molestation charges levelled by Sonia Roy after he has spurned her advances.

Paap (2004)

The story is about a young girl, Kaya (Udita Goswami), living in the beautifully serene valley of Spiti, waiting to join a Buddhist monastery, an idea which has been fed to her all her life by her father (Mohan Agashe) and one which she has never questioned. When Lama Norbu, a senior lama from the monastery has a dream that the Buddhist teacher, the Rinpoche has been reborn as a young child, he sends Kaya to Delhi on a mission to bring him back to the monastery. Kaya goes to Delhi and manages to get the child, but just when they are about to return home, the child witnesses the murder of a Police Officer in a hotel. The investigations are taken over by another Police Officer, Shiven (John Abraham) and he prohibits Kaya (Udita Goswami) and the young boy from returning home. During this time, the boy identifies (Gulshan Grover) as the Junior Police Officer, Manali turns out to be the Commissioner of Police, and soon Shiven (John Abraham) finds himself caught in a web of intrigue and deceit where he can trust no one. He is forced to make an escape to Spiti along with Kaya and the young boy who he is now determined to protect. Shiven has however seriously been injured and upon reaching Spiti has to undergo treatment at Kaya's home. While nursing him back to health, Kaya begins to find herself attracted to Shiven, an exciting feeling she has never experienced before. Shiven too finds himself drawn to Kaya, a girl unlike any he has ever known. Kaya is caught in a dilemma for she has too long subdued her natural instincts and desires in her search for the 'ultimate truth'. A sexual attraction is one that her conditioned mind sees as a sin (paap), but one which she cannot deny. Shiven sees this dilemma and tries to show Kaya that there is a life out there which she has a full right to live. In the meantime, Kaya's father (Mohan Agashe) finds out about what has been going on under his roof and is furious with Shiven. He sees Shiven as a polluting influence upon his peaceful life, a man who has brought defiling things like pistols into their home. At this juncture, Shiven's past catches up with them and Manali's men are close on his heels.

Matrubhoomi : A Nation Without Women (2005)

Director Manish Jha gives a face to a shocking statistics (a UNESCO report states that nearly 50 million women are missing in India due to gender discrimination). That is Kalki (Tulip Joshi) – the voice of a woman, who faces the brutality of a medieval society that is apparent in most parts of the Hindi heartland. If the girl child forfeits the right to live, man will have to resort to beastly acts to satiate his underbelly. In such a scenario, investing in daughters would be a lucrative proposition.

Page 3 (2005)

Madhavi Sharma (Konkona Sen Sharma) arrives in Mumbai and soon lands into a journalist job. Her boss Deepak Suri (Boman Irani) gives her the task of reporting celebrity news. She begins her journey in the glitzy and glamorous world of celebrity lifestyle working on Page 3. Her roommate Pearl Sequiera (Sandhya Mridul) is an air hostess and wants to marry for money. Gayatri Sachdeva (Tara Sharma) later joins them. She is an aspiring actress and gets involved with a leading actor Rohit Kumar (Bikram Saluja). When she tells him that she is pregnant, he suggests she have an abortion. Depressed and shattered, she unsuccessfully tries to commit suicide and in the process loses her unborn child. Meanwhile, Pearl marries a wealthy old man and moves to the United States. Madhavi plans to expose Rohit (by writing an article on his relationship with Gayatri), but her editor kills the article and she is forced to apologise to Rohit. Madhavi finds out that her boyfriend is gay when she finds him in bed with her best friend Abhijeet (Rehaan Engineer). As soon as Madhavi begins to get disillusioned with her job, she declares that "the party is over" for her. She soon realises that the glamorous world of celebrity life is not as glamorous as it seems. Gayatri, who supposedly returned to Delhi, sleeps with a director and gets cast in a movie.

Salaam Namaste (2005)

The film's hero Nick (Saif) loves the idea of romancing his heroine Ambar (Preity). But unlike Bollywood's prototype romantic 'hero', he is not ready to commit by way of marriage. Not even when the girl is pregnant. Love for Bollywood's new age lover boy hero (who dons a rather unconventional garb at work – the chef's cap – despite being a qualified architect) is defined by fun and fun alone. It is not about the labour of responsibility. New-age whiff is also inherent in Ambar's persona – hates marriage, prefers live-together, does not mind pre-marital sex. She is a single, independent youngster who works part time as a radio jockey while studying to become a surgeon. Yet, when it comes to abortion, Ambar draws the line. She had rather be an unwed mother.

Chingaari (2006)

The story is about Basanti, the prostitute with a nothing-scares-me attitude, who lashes out at the village priest warning him not to come in the way of her dream – of protecting her family, of getting her daughter out of danger. The film based on Dr. Bhupen Hazarika's book, 'The Postman and The Prostitute' is about double standards, love, archaic values, religious fanaticism, frustration and a dream. It is Basanti's story through her director Kalpana Lajmi tries to highlight the ills committed in the name of religion.

Corporate (2006)

Corporate centers around the power games between two industrialists, The Sehgal Group of Industries (SGI) owned by Vinay Sehgal (Rajat Kapoor) and the Marwah Group of Industries owned by Dharmesh Marwah (Raj Babbar). The two companies are traditional rivals in the food products business. Bipasha Basu plays Nishigandha Dasgupta aka Nishi, vice president of SGI, while Vinay Sehgal's brother-in-law Ritesh (Kay Kay Menon) joins in later as senior vice-president. Ashwini, a politician backed by Sehgal, become the Union Finance Minister, which helps the Sehgal Group to enter a lucrative partnership with international food products giants Friscon. In a CII meeting, the state Finance Minister Gulabrao declares that a public sector unit (PSU) is for sale. Both the companies pounce into the competition using every tactic they have to outperform each other. But last-minute politicking by Marwah with Gulabrao leads to the PSU going to the Marwah Group, leaving Sehgal disappointed. However, Nishi charms Marwah Group's CEO Pervez, and is then able to steal critical information from his laptop computer: she finds out that Marwah had been misleading the media that they were planning to manufacture mineral water in the plant, whereas in reality they were planning to manufacture a mint-based soft drink. The Sehgal Group publicly announces that they will be launching their own mint-based soft drink, which they've named "Just Chill", pre-empting the Marwah Group's planned launch. Marwah traces the leak to Pervez and fires him. Ten days before the launch of the drink, Sehgal learns that the FDA has found the presence of a large amount of pesticides in the drink. But Sehgal, cold-heartedly, decides to launch the product by bribing the FDA agents. However CEO Naveen resigns from the SGI. The drink is a great success. However, another of SGI's executive is unhappy that Ritesh is being made the CEO, and he gives Marwah the information that SGI's product contains pesticides. Marwah along with Gulabrao blow up the issue in the media, leading to a raid on the SGI plants and filing of a court case on the Sehgals. Sehgal decides that the only solution is for an employee of SGI who is not a member of the Sehgal family to take the blame for the blunder. Nishi is chosen for that role. Ritesh is hesitant but Nishi agrees and is convicted. Meanwhile, Friscon chief Steve meets with Ashwini and threatens to withdraw all investments from India. Ashwini contacts Gulabrao and both the politicians convince both the business giants to compromise and the ban on the soft drink is lifted. Sehgal had promised Ritesh that Nishi will be out of the Enquiry Commission soon; but after the compromise, he abandons her. Ritesh, angry about it, threatens to expose Sehgal in front of the media if Nishi is not released within 48 hours. The next day he is found dead, having fallen from the terrace of his apartment building. It is assumed to be suicide but some think otherwise. A few days later, SGI's product is back on the market. In the new elections, Gulabrao becomes the Chief Minister. The movie ends with Nishi shown as fighting the case. She also has a daughter sired by Ritesh.

Teesri Aankh : The Hidden Camera (2006)

Sudama Pandey (Mukesh Rishi) is a notorious criminal who runs a global operation of capturing women on camera. He operates out of London and is assisted by his two partners in crime (Mukesh Tiwari and Murli Sharma). Be it a honeymoon bedroom, changing rooms, girls hostels, none of these places miss the third eye. The eye of a camera! First they capture girls on films and then abuse them, both physically and mentally. One such girl who gets trapped by them is Sapna (Neha Dhupia). She is a lovely girl who had dreams in her eyes and wanted to make it big in her career. She was happy to have found love in her life through her fiancé. But her life was to be short-lived. She is murdered by Sudama's gang and a lovely personality came to an end. As luck would have it, the murder is witnessed by Ammu (Amisha Patel) who tries to rescue Sapna but her effort goes in vain. Ammu is terrorised by the events around her. But this was not an end to her ordeal as now she is being chased by Sapna's murderers. Meanwhile, her sister Aarti (Aarti Chabaria) and her partner Rahul (Aashish Chaudhary) too are in lookout for her as she has gone missing. Soon, enters the scene Sapna's fiancé Arjun Singh (Sunny Deol) who turns out to be none other than an A.C.P. in Mumbai. As a part of his assignment, he had been on lookout for Sudama that leads him to London. And in London, he has only one clue that could take him to his destination - Ammu! Unfortunately, the clue herself is gone missing. He makes all possible attempts to find her but reaches a dead end. He can't find Ammu...and he doesn't have anyone else for help. He has to do everything all alone. The war is on and the world would see the good win over evil. Because Arjun just doesn't have to mere fight criminals, he also has to fight technology. The film talks about how innocent Indian girls are duped and exploited by porn filmmakers who sell their products in the international market.

Vivah (2006)

Poonam (Amrita Rao) lost her parents, when she was very young. She was brought up by her uncle Krishna Kant (Alok Nath) and her aunt Rama (Seema Biswas). However, Rama is jealous of her niece and dislikes her, since Poonam is more beautiful than her own daughter Rajni (Amrita Prakash). Poonam grows up to be a soft-spoken, traditional and beautiful girl. Her only wish is to get a mother's love from her aunt Rama. Bhagat-ji (Manoj Joshi), a jeweller and a friend of Krishna Kant's, likes Poonam and her beautiful nature. He decides to match-make for her with Prem (Shahid Kapoor), son of Mr. Harishchandra (Anupam Kher). Mr. Harishchandra, a rich businessman, tells Prem about the proposed marriage. He believes Prem is of proper age to marry. Prem's brother, Sunil (Samir Soni), had also married Bhavna (Lata Sabharwal) at the same age. Prem, however, is hesitant to marry, since he feels himself to be very young and wants to focus on his career first. Harishchandra convinces Prem to meet Poonam before deciding anything. They visit Krishna Kant's family and let Prem and Poonam get acquainted with each other. Though their first conversation is awkward, Prem and Poonam agree to get married, as they are instantly attracted to each other. The marriage date is set after six months and the two families plan a short vacation at Krishna Kant's summer residence in Som Sarovar as an opportunity to know each other better. Poonam and Prem blissfully enjoy their time together at Som Sarovar. After several carefree days, Harishchandra and his family returns home to attend to its business, which leaves Poonam and Prem the choice to communicate via telephone, internet or letter. Despite the distance between them, they grow closer and Prem, before going on a business trip to Japan, calls her for support. Poonam tells him on the phone that she loves him. When Prem calls Poonam from the airport in Japan, he confesses his love for her as well. Soon after, Prem comes back from Japan and is pleasantly surprised to find Poonam with the rest of his family. She spends some time at his house and finally returns to her own family to prepare for the wedding. Both families get busy in preparing for the wedding. Rama becomes very irritated and angry with Krishna Kant for spending lavishly on Poonam's wedding, as she fears there will be no money left for Rajni's marriage. As a result, Rama acts colder than usual to Poonam and wants nothing to do for the wedding. This hurts Poonam. The night before the main wedding ceremony, a fire emerges at Krishna Kant's house. Though Poonam runs out of the house in time, she realises that Rajni is still inside and goes back to save her. In this attempt, Poonam gets severely burnt. She is immediately taken to the hospital, where the family is told that the burns on her body are extremely grave, but luckily, her face is untouched. The fact that Poonam risked her own skin to save Rajni changes Rama's view about her. Prem and his family, occupied with their own wedding preparations, are informed of Poonam's accident and rush to the hospital. Poonam is now very unsure if Prem will marry her because she has been scarred and the marks will take months to fade away. The doctor (Mohnish Behl) informs the family that Poonam will take much time to recover. Harishchandra arranges for burn specialists to be flown in from Delhi for Poonam's operation. Prem is determined to marry Poonam and, when she tells him to take a look at her deep scars, he refuses, saying that his love does not deserve this test. He says that he will always love her no matter what and puts sindoor (vermilion) on her hairline, marking her as his wife. The operation is successful. Finally, Prem and Poonam get married, to begin their life together as husband and wife. Prem asks Poonam to see her at a nearby teela in that small town. Poonam agrees. But passing through the corner of the house, Prem sees a beautiful terrace. He asks her why she did not tell him they have a beautiful meeting point even inside the house? Poonam says since he wanted to go to the teela, she didnot want to state her wish to stay at home. It annoys Prem. Why it is only the boy who should take a decision, he questions her.

Namastey London (2007)

Indian-born Manmohan Malhotra (Rishi Kapoor) re-located to London, England, established himself, returned to India, got married to Bebo (Nina Wadia), and after four years got a visa for her so that she could live with him. Shortly thereafter, she gave birth to Jasmeet (Katrina Kaif). Manmohan was always embarrassed by Bebo as she was fat and could not speak English. As a result, he always left her out of important occasions, while he socialised. Bebo did not want Jasmeet to end up like her, so she got her educated in an English school, encouraged to mingle with British friends, and Jasmeet was transformed in to Jazz — a beautiful young woman, modern in looks, talk, habits, and heart. Her father had set her to meet a young lad, Bobby Bedi (Ritesh Deshmukh), though the date turns out to be a disaster and Bobby rejects her. Manmohan thinks that it is impossible to get him a Indian son-in-law, although his friend, Parvez Khan

(Javed Sheikh), is in a similar situation with his son, Imran (Upen Patel), who has a blonde girlfriend, Susan (Tiffany Mulheron). Manmohan takes his family for a tour in India and forces Jasmeet to marry Arjun Singh (Akshay Kumar). On their return to London, Jasmeet announces that she is getting married to Charlie Brown (Clive Standen), who is well educated and has good friends and connections, even with Prince Charles. She refuses to recognise her marriage with Arjun as there is no proof of the wedding. When Jasmeet is introduced to the friends of the Brown family, she is subjected to considerable racist abuse (snake charmers, Indian rope tricks, tandoori chicken) as well as a quote from Winston Churchill: 'When we leave India, the country will be in the hands of goons'. On the other hand, Imran is asked by Susan's parents to leave Islam, become a Christian, change his name to Emmanuel or Ian, as well as provide a written proof that his family is not associated with terrorists. The film ends on a happy note with Imran and Susan being accepted with Imran's family; Jazz runs away from her wedding to Charlie Brown and goes with Arjun back to India where they are seen riding Arjun's motorcycle. Jasmeet replete with all the perceived ills of girls born and brought up in the U.K., so she drinks vodka, wears minis, dances in discotheques, quarrels with parents and wants to run away from any mention of an arranged marriage with an Indian guy. How the NRI girl realises Arjun's goodness, her mistakes and of the uplifting Indian culture that makes the storyline get momentum.

Nishabd (2007)

The film opens with young Ritu (Shradha Arya) bringing her friend Jia (Jiah Khan) to spend the holidays with her at her home in Kerala. Ritu's parents Vijay (Amitabh Bachchan) and Amrita (Revathi) have a beautiful home surrounded by picture-perfect surroundings. Vijay is a photographer and Amrita is a homemaker. Jia's mother lives alone in Australia (Jia's parents are divorced), and she studies in India. She is a free-spirited teenager with no attachments and no worries. She professes some affinity to Vijay, but it doesn't go much further than that. But Vijay's world is turned upside down when he takes pictures of Jia watering herself down with the garden hose. Something innocent grows into something bigger, and something bigger grows into something beyond control. Jia's world collides with Vijay's causing three casualties. Ritu witnesses an intimate moment between Vijay and Jia and tries to get Jia out of the house without revealing the truth to her mother but fails. Around this time, Amrita's brother Shridhar (Nassar) visits them. Through a sequence of events, he uncovers the disturbing truth about Jia and Vijay. Shridhar questions Vijay and realises that things are serious between Jia and him. Vijay confesses his love for Jia to Amrita, leaving her shattered. Rishi (Aftab Shivdasani), the unrequited lover of Jia, visits to surprise her on her birthday. Shridhar tells Vijay to objectively look at things and decide if he is right for Jia. Vijay realises that the relationship with Jia is not the best for her and tells her to leave. Jia is heartbroken, calls him a hypocrite, and leaves with Rishi. The family is still in pieces after Jia's departure: Ritu leaves for America, and Amrita is unable to forgive her husband. Vijay relives his moments with Jia all the time. He drives for hours and finally stands on top of rocks ready to jump. But then he remembers his moments with Jia and returns home. Shridhar asks Vijay where he had gone and Vijay tells him he had gone to commit suicide. The film ends with his conversation with Vijay saying that he is not scared of death. He says he has nothing left to live for, no wife, no daughter, no Jia. But he came back as he wants to live for a while with Jia's memory; that's all. It is about a man in love with a girl who happens to be all of 18. Vijay does not lust for her. He is not going through any mid-life crisis. He is definitely not a paedophile. Like all lovers, he does not even know when Cupid struck or why. Critics argue that such sexual distractions are not in consonance with Indian values. Director Ram Gopal Verma sanitises the film completely of all sexual overtones which would necessarily be a part of such a cross-generational attraction. It is not physical sexual. Jia, a product of a broken home, with a step dad, succumbs to Oedipus. Destroying the idols of custom, breaking the shackles of tradition Jia is free in her own way, free for an uninhibited expression of sinful pleasure.

Chak De India (2007)

Shimit Amin's "Chak De India" (2007), a film ostensibly about hockey, is the most unconventional film about women. All the hockey players are characters with opinions; they express themselves openly, are more articulate, more real, and have bigger roles than any conventional heroine in recent years. The oppression in their homes is shown by their struggle to play the game against all odds of parents, boyfriends and harassment on the streets (the restaurant scene where the women beat up men who tease the girls from the North East). It is even implied that one or two of the players have survived domestic violence. Indeed, it may be the most progressive film about Indian women in recent times. The interesting thing is that, if we examine the career graphs of the girls who have worked in "Chake De India", not one of them has got significant work since. They acted well, have got terrific exposure through a 'hit' film, but are unemployable. This is because they come from the wrong side of the tracks. The officials sneer at the women's sports, the sponsors shy away. And the girls have no encouragement. The girls first learn to talk to each other rather than talking at each other. Then they learn to live with each other, before finally realising they have to live for each other to win at the international level.

Fashion (2008)

Aspiring model Meghna Mathur (Priyanka Chopra) expresses her wish to go to Mumbai and pursue her dream of becoming a supermodel. Against her dad's wishes, Meghna leaves her house with dreams in her eyes to strike it big in the modeling world. She experiences some major difficulties in her initial days auditioning several times but being rejected. But she gets a good helping hand with an old acquaintance, Rohit (Ashwin Mushran), an aspiring gay designer who assists big shot designer Vinay Khosla (Harsh Chhaya). She keeps bumping into another struggling model, Maanav (Arjan Bajwa) while making the rounds of modeling agencies for auditions. She visits Rahul Arora's fashion show where she comes face-to-face with reality of the major people in the industry including the reigning supermodel Shonali Gujral (Kangana Ranaut). She is mocked by the show choreographer Christine and is advised to visit hotshot photographer Kartik (Rohit Roy) for her portfolio. To pay Kartik's high fee, she attends functions and even shoots for a lingerie advertisement, all the while mentored by another smalltime model Janet (Mugdha Godse). Subsequently, Meghana's lingerie pictures appear on the cover of a magazine found by her relatives. Meghna becomes good friends with Maanav and even starts sharing his apartment after she faces accommodation problems. Meghna is noticed by a top official Anisha Roy (Kitu Gidwani) of a major modeling agency Panache who brings her to her boss, Abhijit Sarin's (Arbaaz Khan) notice. Abhijit is impressed by her ambitious nature and go-getter attitude. Panache's face is Shonali but though very successful, her drug abuse starts becoming a problem for her and subsequently for Panache. Just as Abhijit decide's to put Meghna for a fashion show organised by Vinay Khosla, a misunderstanding happens which leaves Meghna being replaced in that fashion show. She is left emotional and comforted by Abhijit. Abhijit then decides to terminate Shonali's contract and ropes in Meghna as Panache's new face. Shonali warns Meghna that she will lose herself just as she did. Meghna becomes an overnight success which nips the budding relationship between her and Maanav. She also starts having an affair with Abhijit. Meanwhile, Janet grabs an opportunity of being designer Rahul Arora's (Samir Soni) showstopper. Rahul gets worried as his mother becomes increasingly doubtful of his sexual orientation and asks Janet to marry him though he tells her that his relation with his boyfriend will be compromised to some extent. Shonali, on other hand, has a wardrobe malfunction and her career ends. Her drug abuse gets worse and she lands up at a rehab centre. Meanwhile, Meghna becomes pregnant with Abhijit's child and reluctantly has an abortion due to the conditions in the contract. She tells about their relationship to Abhijit's wife and Abhijit terminates Meghna's contract with Panache. An angered Meghna, unable to believe what happened, resorts to alcohol to relieve herself. She gets into a verbal fight with Janet and on the same night attends a rave party where under the influence of cocaine, she unknowingly ends up in bed with a black man. When she comes to her senses, she feels guilty of her act and realises how low she had fallen. She returns to her parents in Chandigarh. Broken and depressed, Meghna lives in Chandigarh for more than a year but she has lost all taste for life including her self-confidence. However, encouraged by her father, she goes back to Mumbai. There she befriends Janet again and models for Rohit's show. However, she freezes on stage and gets negative reviews from the whole industry and media. She visits Maanav to ask forgiveness and learns that he is engaged. Shonali is shown on TV as a highly disturbed alcoholic on the streets. Meghna brings her home and takes it as a challenge to rehabilitate Shonali. She also gets an offer from Rahul to be his showstopper and accepts. One day before the show, Shonali goes missing from Meghna's home. Just before Meghna is to walk the ramp, she gets a call from the police that Shonali has been found dead apparently from a drug overdose. Meghna becomes frigid with sadness, but overcomes the grief and walks on the ramp, which not only revives her career but also heals her self-esteem. She ultimately acknowledges that her ensuing success is not due to her own efforts to revamp herself, but due to Shonali and Shonali alone, for she was the one who instilled once again her newly found self-confidence and gave her a self-recognition in this so-called glamorous world of fashion. Meghna, hence, gives up her drinking and smoking habits. The movie ends with Meghna walking the ramp in Paris.

Love Sex or Dhoka (2010)

The movie begins with three exciting "stories", which are the inter-connected episodes of the film:

Love: Rahul, a 20-something infatuated with the candy-gloss of Bollywood romances, is a wannabe director who decides to shoot a small budget film to enter a contest hoping to meet his idol, Bollywood director Aditya Barjatya. During auditions, he falls in love with the young woman he picks to be the leading actress, Shruti. She belongs to an orthodox, nouveau riche New Delhi family, and her father is a real estate magnate who is lampooned for his philistinism. The two bond become closer, and define their relationship by confessing their love for each other. However, Shruti's overprotective and aggressive brother overhears their telephone conversation and vandalises the movie set to find out the identity of the guy who loves Shruti but to no avail. Shruti and Rahul elope. From their honeymoon suite, they call Shruti's family for their love and acceptance. Shruti's father and brother are initially furious, but then relent and tell them they will be sending a car to pick them up from the hotel. During the car ride, the couple is ambushed by Shruti's brother and his hired goons, who beat them up in a graphic scene with hockey sticks, and then brutally cut their bodies using an axe, burying the dismembered parts under a railway culvert. The episode ends with the murderers casually sharing booze and joking with the accomplice saddled with the task of digging.

Sex: Shruti's friend Rashmi works night shifts in a local supermarket to support her family. Adarsh is a 20-something supermarket supervisor who has obtained the job due to his family connections with the store's owner and has outstanding debts to settle with the local committee. He makes a pact with one of his friends to make a sex tape with one of the employees to sell for a large amount of money to the media. Adarsh sets his sights on Rashmi, ultimately resulting in him developing genuine feelings for her. He decides to back out of the MMS plan, but his feelings for Rashmi are suppressed by his greed. Rashmi receives news regarding Shruti and Rahul's horrible death and is deeply saddened. Taking advantage of her vulnerability, he has sex with her and records it on the local shop camera.

Dhokha: Prabhat, an investigative reporter who uses spy camera to establish sting operations is in desperate need of a groundbreaking story to get a bonus from the news company which employs him. He saves Naina (short for Mrignaina), an aspiring dancer, from drowning when she jumps from a bridge. Naina, who is initially furious at Prabhat, plans a sting operation with him to exact revenge on Loki Local, a music icon who asked her to trade sex for the position of leading dancer in his upcoming music video. The duo bring the sting footage to the media, who provoke them to plan another sting: Naina will supposedly blackmail Loki by threatening to reveal the initial footage in an attempt to catch him red-handed as he tries to bribe her—to render false any accusations by Loki of fabrication of footage. Naina meets Loki in the supermarket where Rashmi works to carry out the sting, while Prabhat watches closely.

The plan goes awry when Loki tries to steal the camera and shoots Prabhat, who is immediately admitted into the hospital. Naina comes to meet Prabhat to hand over the footage so that he can get the bonus, but he decides to protect Naina's dignity and refuses to give his superiors the footage and resigns. However, it is revealed that Naina shockingly betrayed Prabhat by accepting the role as dancer in Loki's new music video, "Love, Sex Aur Dhokha," which is a parody on the events of the sting operation.

Hello Darling (2010)

Hello Darling is the plight of three glamorous looking and intelligent women who have to bear a lewd and lecherous boss at the office. It is all about the plight of working women who have to bear the brunt at their offices. Three glamorous girls who share a house—Candy, Mansi and Satvari (Celina Jatily, Gul Panag and Eesha Koppikhar)—belong to different strata of society and work at a posh designing office in Mumbai. They have to face their playboy boss Hardik (Javed Jaffrey) who has an innocent Gujarati housewife Purvi who speaks in Gujarati most of the times. He has the habit of addressing the girls in the office as "hello darling". Hardik keeps making passes at the girls in the office and offers them a promotion only if they please him in bed. Hardik has a secretary (Aswari Joshi) who keeps him informed about the goings on in the office. The three girls decided to outsmart their boss in some way or the other and teach him a lesson in life. The trio hatch a plan to bring Hardik down. So one night, on the pretext of pleasing him in bed, they kidnap him and chain him in their house. They seize control of his company and bring about changes. In the meantime, Hardik's wife Purvi contacts the Nari Sanghatana who runs a pati sudhar samiti to tame down her lecherous husband.

Life Express (2010)

Tanvi (Rituparna Sengupta), a career minded woman with a yuppie husband (Kiran Jhanjhani), were planning their first child after three years of wedded bliss. Since society has not one example to offer of a successful working mother, poor Tanvi is caught in a dilemma of keeping either her career or her baby. An abortion later, the couple hits upon a unique solution – why not have another woman go through the rigours of pregnancy and deliver them one bonny child? Their distress is expressed by Tanvi's husband in a drunken state. The future surrogate mother Gouri (Divya Duta) lives in a village with her husband Mohan (Yashpal Sharma) whose traditional clay artefacts find no takers. Gouri is going to 'rent out' her womb to save her family from economic privation. Tanvi awaits in the city and we have plenty of poignant interactions between the two women on the joys of motherhood and the hollow nature of professional success.

Mirch (2010)

Vinay Shukla upholds four tales where the woman seeks out sexual satisfaction on her own terms. Having earlier made 'Godmother', another woman-oriented film, the director does seem to have an adequate understanding of the female psyche. All his four stories have a delightful and cheeky charm to them. Two of the stories feature Raima Sen as the protagonist as she enjoys a bit on the side, first as a carpenter's (Raghubir Yadav) wife and then as a modern woman who finds a lover, just to spite her suspicious husband (Shreyas Talpade). The other two focus on Konkona Sen Sharma's naughty escapades, first as an unsatiated young queen of yore and then as a shrewd wife of a philandering husband (Boman Irani). Added to this, is the turbulent romance between the scriptwriter and his girlfriend (Shahana Goswami). The garbled end and the misconstrued tenor of the film do act as a deterrent. Even as the women seem to be enjoying themselves with their unbridled expression of their sexual needs, the film tends to view them as the traditional not-to-be-trusted temptress. Overlook that and we can enter a world where women indeed are full-bodied flesh and blood characters.

Observation and Findings

Portray of Female Sexuality

There are new issues like the diaspora, sexuality, the growing role of women, the changing ideas of sexuality that dominate contemporary mainstream Hindi films. Women need freedom of a different kind. Marriage and family do not resolve everything. *'Anjaana Anjaani'* is a good example of a film which is inarticulate about the diaspora. Munni or Sheila upholds the questions at a populist level between two forms of Bollywood dance, where sexuality is formulated twice.

Sandra Bartky extends Michel Foucault's understanding and analysis of power to offer a gendered view, one that contends that women in patriarchal societies internalise disciplinary procedures and self regulate their bodies and sexuality.[9] In patriarchal societies, there is no need for external surveillance mechanisms to control women. We extend these insights to the realm of the Indian media industry to underscore the mechanisms through which representations of virtuous and wanton female sexuality help discipline women but also the modalities through which women participate in limiting female subject positions.[10]

In the Indian public sphere, actresses have to locate themselves strategically within a limited rubric of sexual identities – the vamp, the virgin, or some blurring of the two. Although the meanings and content associated with these identity categories are constantly shifting, the necessity of having a label of sexual identification for actresses remains unquestioned in the Bollywood hierarchy.[11]

This problem of representation of female sexuality is compounded by process of globalisation because of the increasingly public and easily commodified nature of their personas; actresses must find a satisfactory convergence between the characters they play on screen and their 'real' personalities through various media outlets. Their presentations on-screen are either altered to match their personalities off-screen, or vice-versa, but both of these strategies are ultimately representative of the same patriarchy that disciplines and regulates women's sexuality.[12] Indian actresses quest to create a seamless persona between their reel and real sexualities.

The main female lead in Hindi films has often been represented as an idealised woman, and historically, her body language, appearance and behaviour as a character defined her status as a heroine within the film. Throughout most of Hindi film history, the heroine could be identified by her dress,[13] her chastity, and her character's inevitable marriage. Traditionally, the virgin's love songs were often filmed as fantasy or dream sequences, where the heroine was 'imagined' to be dancing in erotic poses with the hero. As Jyotika Virdi writes, "the song and dance sequences stand in for sex scenes. The focus is particularly on the heroine, the fetishised female sexualised through close attention to her costumes, graceful body movements, and carefully angled shots that heighten scopic pleasure...[she feigns] an unawareness of [her] sexualised body and the camera's voyeuristic gaze" (Virdi, 2003).[14] Thus, the virgin could be (and often was) cast in an eroticised light, but it was rare that the actress directly communicated the sexuality of the character to the audience.

Unlike the virgin, the vamp is a trope in Hindi films that occupies a more complex and difficult discursive location, both within the diegetic space of the narrative and the culture at large. As with the virgin, key markers in dress, status, and behaviour code for her position, however, she was often the only female character with the sole and exclusive right to exhibit physical pleasure and desire directly to the audience.[15, 16] She was rarely a heroine, or even a secondary character, and usually appeared in the film for one or two of what were (and are still) euphemistically referred to as "item", or cabaret songs. Helen, the best-known vamp of the 1960s, typified these sexual markers: "not so much the 'wicked' woman as the 'naughty', sexually alluring, immodest one, coded by her erotic and nimbly performed dance numbers...Located in the public sphere, in the world of men, she [was] somehow bereft of a man of her own. Desired by all, yet loved by none...within the pleasures and dangers of a liminal but exciting nightlife, the role enacted...is that of the 'bad', undomesticated woman" (Virdi, 2003).[17]

However, Karen Gabriel observes the gradual disappearance of the vamp as a separate character from Hindi films. The coding of the vamp/virgin binary has not disappeared entirely from Bollywood films; rather, aspects of the vamp have been incorporated in the presentation of the character of the heroine. Today, women who play vamps in Bollywood films must more actively negotiate the nexus between their film roles and the presentation of their personal lives."[18]

Resistance versus Transformation

Srimati Basu (2001) acutely observes, "Transgression may be negated through speaking – by bringing certain forms of sexual behaviour into discourse, one may render them 'docile' by defining and regulating them, incorporating them into the ideologies of dominant discourse".[19]

A section of critics argue that the actresses portraying the item girl or vamp do not represent an informed, complex understanding of the power relations at work in commodifying female sexuality.

Using/Being used by the Gaze

Actresses in the Bollywood internalise and make organic the panoptic gaze of the industry they inhabit, and as a result, must draw together the strands of various contradictory and hybrid sexual expectations.[20] In this new globalised Bollywood, women are expected to 'move' the film product through selling a fetishised, eroticised packaging of female heterosexual desire, but must also demonstrate a coy disavowal of this desire and its implications in order to advance to the ranks of top-tier actresses.

Filmic demonstrations of sexual desire, public declarations of sexual self-acceptance – is subverted in order to advance or protect the actress's celebrity status.

The rapidity of the changes in the Bollywood film industry place all women in the odd position of both highlighting and denying their own sexuality, but without the private sphere that allowed Indian women celebrities room for negotiations and transgressive behaviour. When the gaze is directed inward, the field for boundary events and transformative agency is narrowed and the public discourse surrounding women's sexuality is circumscribed as well.

Although the fetishisation of the female body in Bollywood films may partially represent loss as Mulvey describes it, it also seems to me that on the part of the audience, there is also a kind of pleasure in these films that cuts deeper than a mere substitution for "real sex" – the act of viewership itself is enjoyable. There are several authors who criticise Mulvey's construction of the "male gaze" for being overly simplistic and ignoring the ways in which women themselves consume and absorb sexualised media inages.[21, 22]

It is possible to understand this as a disappearance of 'safe spaces' for actresses in which to make autonomous or at least semi-autonomous decisions in experiencing sex and relationships.

Foucault has analysed in the context of modern women's practices of embodying femininity through regulating their bodies and sexual behaviour, such as wearing make-up, dieting, and choice of clothing.[23]

Sue Scott and Stevi Jackson (1996) elaborate : "Although Foucault himself pays little attention to gender and regards the regulation of women's sexuality as only one form among many, feminists have found much in his work useful. In particular, it allows us to see female sexuality as constructed and reconstructed in complex and often contradictory ways, rather than as simply being repressed".[24]

This refers to "exposure" the term given to the showing of flesh or wearing of skimpy costumes in Bollywood films; "a specific code of clothes, body, and body language" (Dwyer, 2001).[25]

Asha Kasbekar (2001) describes this phenomenon as such: "[Any] erotic voyeurism on the part of the film spectator is disavowed by the deliberate mediation of the diegetic spectator, who is determined as the true owner of the voyeuristic gaze...it allows erotic contemplation of the female body but simultaneously disavows any prurient intention".[26]

Male Appeal

The Indian audience is undoubtedly partial to its heroes. Bollywood, for some reason, has not managed to shed its gender bias. Female-oriented films generally fall within the bracket of art house film which commands a niche audience; while men play the leads in comedies, thrillers and action films which have a wider appeal. "That is why films with saleable heroes get great initials but if a film has a big and saleable heroine teamed up with a lesser hero, there are strong chances the film may open to poor houses. We live in a male-dominated society and that reflects in our film preferences too," says trade analyst Komal Nahta.

Jagmohan Mundhra, who has critically acclaimed women-centric films 'Provoked' and 'Bawandar' to his credit, adds, "Big difference now is that sellable male actors are not willing to work in female-centric movies and distributors are not willing to finance a film without a sellable male name in the cast."

Onir, director of 'I Am' believes that in the '70s and '80s there were many mainstream films in which female protagonists played important roles. "With multiplexes and high ticket prices, family movie outings became selective and with that the demand for wholesome entertainers soared high. But now, with women earning independently, the scenario has to change. This is why space is being created in a male-dominated industry. Women must change the way cinema portrays them by saying yes to strong portrayals of women and no to regressive films," says Onir.[27]

Scope of the Script

"This is a mystery to me. I find it much more interesting to make a film through female protagonists. They understand the idea of loss better and are not afraid of showing their weaker side. They are as capable of betrayal as their male counterparts, but in the end, are perhaps more there when it comes to the crunch. The Indian heroine is capable of shouldering the burden, perhaps the fault is in the scripts and the fact that they are sketched in a one-dimensional, flat sort of way," says filmmaker Sudhir Mishra, who has delivered a gem like 'Hazaaron Khwaishein Aisi'. He directed 'Yeh Saali Zindagi' with his muse Chitrangada Singh playing a strong-headedwoman.

Scriptwriter Manisha Lakhe thinks women-centric films end up being box office poison as one tends to stereotype them as films with hard-hitting messages. 'Lajja' had a strong script but it made a martyr of women and that bored audience to tears, she explains, adding, "A strong script will pull in not only women to theatres, but it will drag in the men folk too."

Actor Rani Mukerji in an interview was quoted as saying, "Women-centric roles have been there right from the beginning."[28]

Budget Boost

Tanuja Chandra is one of the few radical women directors in Bollywood, whose female characters are fiery and path-breakers. Director Madhur Bhandarkar, whose success chart is marked with hits like 'Chandni Bar', 'Satta', 'Page 3' and 'Fashion', which got Priyanka Chopra and Kangana Ranaut their first National Award for convincingly portraying the dilemma of fashion models, has made his ambitious project 'Heroine'.[29]

Future Scenario

Will we ever see female heroes driving their films to the "success point"? Chandra seconds, "The Indian heroine has always been ready to shoulder a film, and can do it masterfully at any time. The question here should be—when will the business of entertainment be ready to shoulder heroine-oriented films?" Advaita adds that if we are going to work towards successful female-centric movies, then it will have to be a collaborative shift, involving filmmakers, actors, writers and most importantly viewers.[30]

Conclusion

What strikes about Indian mainstream Hindi films is the ocean that separates the portrayal of women from their immediate reality. Mainstream Bollywood Hindi films are male dominated over decades after decades starting from 1950s. The women characters were looked down upon. The birth of a female child has been regarded as a disaster in the Hindi films especially in family melodrama. There is also the disgusting practice of dowry in majority of the family films. The decade of 1990s exhibit some progress in women's education. The female protagonists of the urban-oriented narratives of the films of 21st century are educated. The films of this period exhibits that women are doing a variety of professions even. However, in many other respects the representation of women is as bad as it was before. The films exhibit that most women characters do not have real freedom. In many cases, the female characters are guided by superstitions. The male dominated narratives cast women driven by remnants of feudal and medieval practices and mentality.

The mainstream Bollywood Hindi films need a complete revolution in its thinking and attitude towards women. Bollywood, as a means of popular entertainment and mass culture, must strive and contribute to this goal. There is need for much greater gender equality and sexual liberalisation. Women, utilizing every opportunity to advance their rights, resisting all attacks on them – this type of characters should get priority in mainstream Hindi films. Bollywood should desist from objectifying women for its commercial outlook. Mainstream Bollywood Hindi films should uphold the rights of the oppressed and exploited sections of women in our society.

References

1. Huyssen, Andreas (1986). *After the Great Divide*, Bloomington: Indiana University Press.
2. Prasad, M. Madhava (1998). *Ideology of the Hindi Film: A Historical Construction*, New Delhi: Oxford University Press.
3. Ghosh, S. (2005). "Looking in Horror and Fascination: Sex, Violence, and Spectatorship in India." in G. Mishra and R. Chandiramani (eds) *Sexuality, Gender and Rights: Exploring Theory and Practice in South and Southeast Asia,*. Thousand Oaks, Calif: Sage, 29-46.
4. Dwyer, R. (2000). "Bombay Ishtyle" In S. Bruzzi and G. P. Church (ed) *Fashion Cultures: Theories, Explorations and Analysis.* New York: Routledge.
5. Chatterjee, Shoma A. (2006). "Picture perfect unreality." *The Statesman,* 2nd December, 2006.
6. *Ibid.*
7. Bose, Derek (2010). "Mother figure in Bollywood" *The Statesman,* 4th October, 2010.
8. Bhagat, Shama (2011). "Bollywood's got its women on top." *The Asian Age,* 26th January, 2011.
9. Bartky, S. (1988), "Foucault Femininity and the Modernisation of Patriarchal Power" in I. Diamond and L. Quinby (ed) *Feminism and Foucault: Reflections on Resistance*Boston: Northeastern University Press, 61-86.
10. Scott, S. and S. Jackson (1996). "Sexual Skirmishes and Feminist Factions: Twenty-five Years of Debate on Women and

Sexuality" in S. Scott and S. Jackson (ed.) *Feminism and Sexuality* New York: Columbia University Press, 1-34.

11. Dwyer, R. (2001). "Shooting Stars: The Indian Film Magazine, Stardust" in C. Penny and R. Dwyer (ed.) *Pleasure and the Nation: The History, Politics, and Consumption of Public Culture in India*New Delhi: Oxford University Press, 247-285.
12. Virdi, J. (2003). *The Cinematic Imagination: Indian Popular Films as Social History*, New Brunswick, N.J.: Rutgers University Press.
13. Dwyer, R. (2000). "Bombay Ishtyle" in S. Bruzzi and G.P. Church (ed.) *Fashion Cultures: Theories, Explorations and Analysis* New York: Routledge, 185.
14. Virdi, J. (2003). *The Cinematic Imagination: Indian Popular Films as Social History*, New Brunswick, N.J.: Rutgers University Press.
15. Mehta, S. (2004). *Maximum City: Bombay Lost and Found*, New York: Alfred A. Knopf.
16. Moorti, S. (2003). "Desperately Seeking an Identity: Diasporic Cinema and the Articulation of Transnational Kinship." *International Journal of Cultural Studies 6 (3)*: 355-376.
17. Virdi, J. (2003). *The Cinematic Imagination: Indian Popular Films as Social History*, New Brunswick, N.J.: Rutgers University Press.
18. Frank, K. (2002). *G-Strings and Sympathy: Strip Club Regulars and Male Desire*. Durham, N. C.: Duke University Press.
19. Basu, S. (2001). "The Blunt Cutting-Edge: The Construction of Sexuality in the Bengali 'Feminist' Magazine Sananda." *Feminist Media Studies,* 1 (2): 178-196.
20. Appadurai, A. and C. Breckenridge (1995). "Public Modernity in India" in C. Breckenridge (ed) *Consuming Modernity*Delhi: Oxford University Press, 1-17.
21. Mulvey, L. (1999). "Cosmetics and Abjection: Cindy Sherman, 1977-1987" in M. Schiach (ed) *Feminism and Cultural Studies*New York: Oxford University Press, 319-332.
22. Ghosh, S. (2005). "Looking in Horror and Fascination: Sex, Violence, and Spectatorship in India" in G. Mishra and R. Chandiramani (ed.) *Sexuality, Gender and Rights: Exploring Theory and Practice in South and Southeast Asia* Thousand Oaks, Calif: Sage, 34.

23. Bartky, S. (1988). "Foucault, Femininity, and the Modernisation of Patriarchal Power." in I. Diamond and L. Quinby (ed) *Feminism and Foucault: Reflections on Resistance* Boston: Northeastern University Press, 61-86.
24. Scott, S. and S. Jacksonn (1996). "Sexual Skirmishes and Feminist Factions: Twenty-five Years of Debate on Women and Sexuality" in S. Scott and S. Jackson (ed.) *Feminism and Sexuality* New York: Columbia University Press, 9.
25. Dwyer, R. (2001). "Shooting Stars: The Indian Film Magazine, Stardust" in C. Penny and R. Dwyer (ed.) *Pleasure and the Nation: The History, Politics, and Consumption of Public Culture in India* New Delhi: Oxford University Press, 267.
26. Kasbekar, A. (2001). "Hidden Pleasures: Negotiating the Myth of the Female Ideal in Popular Hindi Cinema" in C. Penny and R. Dwyer (ed) Pleasure and the Nation: The History, Politics, and Consumption of Public Culture in India New Delhi: Oxford University Press, 286-308.
27. Sethi, Nidhi (2010). "Hall of Femme" *The Asian Age,* 7th November, 2010. Print.
28. *Ibid.*
29. *Ibid.*
30. *Ibid.*

11

Social Inclusion of Women and Decentralisation Reforms: Evidence from India

Durga P. Chhetri

Introduction

Women have been marginalised from the political sphere throughout the past centuries. Most countries in the world have failed to give due space and representation to women in political institutions. Even in societies where women exercise relatively more freedom in day-to-day living, they remain politically marginalised and excluded. The public sphere is still been considered predominantly a male domain and thus dominated by men. Hence, women are underrepresented in political leadership positions throughout the world. In September 2013, women comprised only 21.4 per cent of all parliament members in the world, up from 18 per cent in 2008. Compared to economic opportunities, education and legal rights, political representation is the area in which the gap between men and women has narrowed the least between 1995 and 2000 (Norris and Inglehart, 2000). This gender gap in political representation coexists with a well established gender gap in political views: women and men have different policy preferences with women more likely to support liberal policies, in particular, spending on child care and other child related expenses (Lott and Kenny, 1999; Edlund and Pande, 2001; Edlund, Haider and Pande, 2003). Recognising this fact, many governments are taking active steps for gender mainstreaming and social inclusion notably by establishing quotas for women in parliaments or in local governments and through decentralised and participatory governance. Gender quotas are a type of equal opportunity measure that aims to ensure women's inclusion in electoral politics by recommending, mandating, and/or reserving a certain number or percentage of positions within candidate lists or parliamentary seats for women (Dahlerup, 2002; 2006; Phillips, 1995). Applied at the various stages of the electoral process, quotas work to ensure the nomination or selection of a minimum number of women for political positions (Dahlerup, 2006). Globally, more than one hundred countries, most within the last two decades, have adopted the provisions of quotas for the increased representation of women (Krook, 2009).

Recently, considerable progress has gradually been achieved in gender mainstreaming and inclusion, beginning with women obtaining the right to vote, followed by achieving the legal right to run for public office. Furthermore, increasing number of women have gained entry into the arena of representative politics in recent times. These great achievements have been realised by nations throughout the world over a wide range of time. Today, the United Nations, UNDP, donor agencies and women's movements are primarily concerned with increasing the representation of women in the political arena so as to create a more just society and to better represent the interests of women nationally. This apart, a plethora of new democratic spaces have been created - whether through the promotion of 'civil society organisations' or the institutionalisation of participatory governance mechanisms - to redress the issue of gendered inequities and inequalities. It is a logical step in the general progression of gender equality to increase the presence of women in public office as well as in other primarily male-dominated domains.

Defining Social Inclusion and Decentralisation

The concept of social inclusion is linked to that of social exclusion. Both are concerned with access to societal resources (be they tangible, such as financial resources or intangible, such as decision-making power). However "where exclusion is viewed as the problem, inclusion is seen as the solution" (Cushing, 2003). The concept of inclusion means the encompassing of the entire population in the performances of the individual function systems. On the one hand, this concerns access to these benefits and, on the other, dependence of individual modes of living on them. To the extent that inclusion is achieved, groups disappear that do not or only marginally participate in social living (Luhman, 1990; 1998). The social inclusion literature states that a fundamental goal of society is to enable its members to participate fully as valued, respected and contributing members (see Toye and Infante, 2004; Laidlaw Foundation, 2002; European Union, 2001). European Commission defines social inclusion as "a process which ensures that those at risk of poverty and social exclusion gain the opportunities and resources necessary to participate fully in economic, social and cultural life and to enjoy a standard of living and well-being that is considered normal in the society in which they live. It ensures that they have a greater participation in decision-making which affects their lives and access to their fundamental rights" (European Commission, 2005). Social inclusion, in Collin's view, means selectively re-privileging in the name of justice those groups that have been traditionally, customarily, or even routinely excluded (Collin, 2005).

Decentralisation

Decentralisation is usually referred to as the transfer of powers from central government to lower levels in a political-administrative and territorial hierarchy (Crook and Manor, 1998; Agrawal and Ribot, 1999). Decentralisation, in its simplest definition, is a form of governance that transfers authority and responsibility from central to intermediate and local governments (ODI, 2002). Mawhood (1983) and Smith (1985) defines decentralisation as any act by which central government formally cedes powers to actors and institutions at lower levels in a political administrative and territorial hierarchy. Decentralisation, to Hans Bjorn Oslen (2007), is the transfer of authority and responsibility for public functions from the central government to intermediate and local governments or quasi-independent government organisations and/or the private sector. Falleti (2008) defines decentralisation as 'a process of state reform composed by a set of public policies that transfer responsibilities, resources, or authority from higher to lower levels of government in the context of a specific type of state'.

The definition by Rondinelli and Cheema (1984) is one of the best general definitions of decentralisation. According to them, decentralisation 'is a transfer of responsibilities for planning, management, and resource raising and allocation from central government and its agencies to: (a) field units of central government ministers or agencies; (b) subordinate units or levels of government; (c) semi-autonomous public authorities or co-operation; (d) area circle, regional or functional authorities, or (e) non-governmental private or voluntary organisations'. Decentralisation is understood as the restructuring of authority so that there is a system of co-responsibility between institutions of governance at the central, regional, and local levels according to the principles of subsidiarity thus increasing the overall quality and effectiveness of the system of governance, while increasing the authority and capabilities of sub-national levels.

Decentralisation Reforms and Social Inclusion

In the discourse of governments and international aid agencies, decentralisation appears as a solution to several core problems: efficiency deficits, fiscal crises, governance failures, government legitimacy, or even inequity (World Bank, 1997; Bresser Pereira, 1998; World Bank, 2000). Further, the institutional reforms through decentralisation have contributed to greater inclusion of historically excluded groups, minority and poor within the nation-state by increasing their number in the institutions of local self-government. Social exclusion is the concern of every government since it involves the denial of access to social spaces, ownership, and control over resources, denial of opportunities and basic needs, denial of right to representation and participation in social, economic, and political participation. The way forward to social exclusion should be the inclusion of disadvantaged and marginalised groups in all the development aspects. The process of decentralisation, in this connection, is viewed as one of the most important projects for reorganisation of the life of the society. Decentralisation aims to enable the citizens, either directly or indirectly, to be more involved in the decision-making process. The implementation of the reforms regarding decentralisation process is essentially changing the basic social relations and the place of the citizen in the governing of the community. Therefore, decentralisation in most of the countries including India, especially in the arena of social policies, was therefore, driven by the idea of reducing social inequalities and correcting allocative distortions. Hence, high centralisation, bureau-cratism, low accountability and lack of the inclusion and participation of society in the public policy-making were the elements attacked by the decentralisation strategist in a democratic context. Advocates of decentralisation extol its many virtues, including the inclusive growth. Supporters project that decentralisation will lead to more efficient policymaking (Tiebout, 1956) and other including Crook and Manor (1998) argue that decentralisation plays an important role in the democratisation and people participation, public service performance, poverty alleviation and political and macro-economic stability. Decentralisation theorists and policy makers evoke developmentalist arguments contending that the increased efficiency, equity and inclusion that should arise from decentralisation results in better and more sustainable management (Larson and Ribot, 2004). Decentralisation reform therefore tries to address the different causes of social exclusion like social inequalities, poverty, corruption, ineffectiveness and poor governance as most of the local benefits from decentralisation are believed to come from increased popular participation, which in turn, leads to increase in democracy, efficiency and equity (Agarwal and Ribot, 1999; Ribot, 2002). The positive outcomes of decentralisation include greater participation and inclusion. Hence, decentralisation reforms initiated by governments of various countries have opened space for civil society and empowerment, giving citizens opportunities to better participate in the planning and decision–making processes. The ethnic minorities and other social groups who were otherwise previously marginalised and excluded are started getting involved in community affairs and have got a better opportunity to influence local development under this reform policy. Brady, Schlozman and Verba (1999) also opine that since the government is nearby and more accessible, citizens will feel like they can make a difference and have an impact on decisions process, leading to greater political efficacy and trust. More decentralisation would lead to creation of inclusive, responsible and accountable governance which in turns lead to empowerment and inclusion of disadvantaged sections of society including women (see Fig.1). One can conclude from the above analysis that there is a causal relationship between decentralisation and social inclusion. Decentralisation reforms, if implemented properly, encourage the citizens who are on the margins of society to participate effectively in the local decision-making and power structures. This leads to the important policy conclusion that decentralisation reforms should go together with the implementation of other policies and be part of a larger plan to empower the excluded and reduce disparities in society.

Decentralisation, Social Inclusion and Women

Many people believe that decentralisation increases popular participation in decision-making because it brings government closer to people which is not possible in the centralised governance. Through people's participation in decision-making, planning, implementation and monitoring and backed by appropriate institutions and resources, it can go a long way in improving the quality of life, particularly of the poorer and marginalised segments of population. Decentralisation reforms in India, particularly after enactment of 73rd and 74th Amendment Acts, served as an important mechanism for social inclusion through enhancing the participation of the disadvantaged groups in local governance. It seeks to promote greater participation of marginalised groups within political processes, through addressing inequalities associated with gender, class, race, ethnicity, caste, disability and sexuality, among other variables, and greater accountability of governments towards those who have traditionally been excluded from political action. This new democratic variant of decentralisation introduced in early 1990s in the country

Decentralisation
POLITICAL , ADMINSTRATIVE &
FISCAL,
INCLUSIVE, RESPONSIBLE & ACCOUNTABLE
INSTITUTIONS
INCLUSION & EMPOWERMENT OF
SOCIALLY EXCLUDED GROUPS & WOMEN

Fig. 10.1

increases participation, accountability and transparency and efficiency in local governance, along with empowerment for previously marginal groups. According to the logic of current decentralisation, efficiency is linked to local enfranchisement or the broad-based inclusion of local people in public decision-making. Recent theorists of decentralisation assert that "underlying most of the purported benefits of decentralisation is the existence of democratic mechanisms that allow local governments to discern the needs and preferences of their constituents, as well as provide a way for these constituents to hold local governments accountable to them" (Smoke, 1999). The more accountable local authorities are to the population, the more inclusive their decisions are likely to be. Adablah (2003) and Mani (2003) argued that local authorities tend to act more in line with local preferences and conditions, and their response to local needs is more expeditious. Decentralisation provides opportunities to marginalised segments, such as women, minorities, etc., to participate at the local level, enabling a more sensitive approach to policy formulation and implementation. It is quite obvious that decentralisation provides opportunities for more people, including the underrepresented groups (like women, poor, minorities) to participate in decisions that affect their lives. An effective decentralisation creates inclusive, accountable, responsive and participatory local institutions which can help the target group to come out of social exclusion. The greater the degree of decentralisation, more inclusive and responsive is the governance and hence greater the degree of empowerment and social inclusion of marginalised sections of population (see Fig. 10.1). Fig. 10.1 shows that there is a significant relationship between decentralisation (political, administrative and fiscal) and social inclusion.

Among the different dimensions of decentralisation, the political decentralisation is the most important one which aims to give citizens and their elected representatives more power in decision-making. It is concerned with transfer of political power and authority from national to sub-national levels of government. Devolution, which involves full transfer of responsibility, decision-making, resources, and revenue generation to an independent and autonomous local-level public agency, is considered a form of political decentralisation. The main aim of political decentralisation is to give citizens or their elected representatives more power in decision-making and to support the process of democratisation by giving citizens and their representatives, more influence in the formulation and implementation of public policies. This is particularly important in a country like ours, where broad segments of the poor have been marginalised and excluded with respect to political decision-making. From this perspective, decentralisation is a tool to improve the legitimacy of the democratic system (Larson and Ribot, 2004). Although democracy is not a necessary part of decentralisation, its presence can have a significant influence on the perceived legitimacy of decentralised systems. The democratic decentralisation process enlarged the democratic potential of local governments, empowered them and helped to emerge as true self-governing institutions. It facilitates the process of political participation and arouses the confidence of people of all social sections including the minorities and socially excluded communities in local democracy and development. Decentralisation strengthens citizen participation by bringing governments closer to the people they are intended to serve (Shah, 1998). Advocates of political decentralisation contend that decisions made with greater participation will be better informed and more relevant to diverse interests in the society than those made solely by national political authorities. Political dimensions of decentralisation are therefore, generally, concerned with increasing public participation through citizens being actively engaged in public institutions.

Democratic decentralisation provided space for the deprived and marginalised social sections for their collective bargain and to get their due share in local governance and development process. Decentralisation and democratisation process helps to protect the interests of the most excluded social groups like scheduled castes, scheduled tribes and women. The provisions like Gram Sabha (Art. 243A), direct election {(Art. 243B (2)}, reservation of seats (Art. 243D) for SCs, STs and women, etc. encourage the poor and marginalised citizens to participate in the development process and hence is central in social inclusion of deprived classes. The 73rd Amendment mandated that seats be reserved for SCs, STs, and women as a means of partially correcting long-standing, social inequalities. A minimum of 1/3rd of all seats in local bodies are to be reserved for women. Seats are to be reserved for SC/STs in proportion to their population in each constituency—one third of these must be reserved for women. The election of representatives from local electoral jurisdictions allows citizens to know better their political representatives and allow elected officials to know better the needs and desires of their constituents. Elected local governments may also be more accountable to the community and inclusive of the poor in decision and policy-making. In India, for example, an astonishing two million rural women have held office on the local and regional level since 1993. This has been made possible by a constitutional mandate that reserves one-third of all local seats in the panchayati raj system of governance. The reservation of seats in the local bodies also increases the number of SCs and STs representatives. The reservation has improved the physical/numerical presence of women and SC/STs in elected bodies and has been successful in ensuring that they have an equal voice in PRI deliberations, in particular at the village level. Hence, the overall increase in opportunities brought about by the decentralisation reforms for participation in the democratic processes of society and the policy of reservations, in particular, has created an enabling environment for the underprivileged and historically excluded groups of society. Reservations in the legislature, panchayats and municipalities have provided a space for SCs and STs in the executive and the decision-making process. The formal reservation policy in the government sector has also contributed to an improvement in the human development of SCs and STs. The political decentralisation thus play a important role in addressing the issues of social exclusion through increased participation of historically excluded groups in local government to influence policy and decisions regarding pro-poor programmes, and improved services for the poor and marginalised. It is believed that participatory local governments are in a better position to assess needs at the local level, monitor and control development of local communities, and provide more responsive services.

Of the three dimensions of decentralisation, the political decentralisation is found to have a huge positive impact on social inclusion by virtue of the involvement of marginalised and poor people in decision-making, planning, implementation and basic service delivery. More specifically, political decentralisation seeks to promote greater participation of marginalised groups within political processes through addressing inequalities associated with caste, ethnicity and gender. The poor and the disadvantaged groups in the country are experiencing benefits. The administrative and fiscal decentralisation too has provided a structural arrangement for popular or community participation in governance and development. Decentralisation of specific services such as health and education has been attempted in the country through administrative decentralisation.

Concluding Observations

Decentralisation raises expectations for increased participation in decision-making by women. The Government of India has made use of decentralised governance as a tool for social inclusion through enhancing the participation of the disadvantaged groups, including women, in formal decision-making processes. With the introduction of the decentralised democracy, several systems are in place for their empowerment and inclusion. The decentralisation reforms and reservation has increased the number of women in the village councils. Many of the studies reveal that women representatives have become empowered through their involvement in local government (Hust, 2004; Nandal, 2003; Isaac, 2005). Women representatives gain knowledge of politics, status and political visibility in their community. The decentralisation reforms coupled with gender reservation policy, particularly in the post 73rd Amendment period, has resulted in the increased participation of women in the political life at the grass root level, growing political awareness among the women, enhancement in the self-esteem and prestige of women, better political orientation of the women. Through decentralisation, the vast majority of civic bodies, hitherto excluded from the development planning and implementation process, would become actively engaged with formal governmental institutions. Hence, democratic decentralisation, when well structured, provides institutional infrastructure - representation and meaningful powers - for sustained inclusion. The inclusion of disadvantaged sections has, in principle, ensured equality of political opportunities. The creation of institutions like Gram Sabha, accountability mechanisms, people's planning, and the like lead to establishment of inclusive self-governance. And the main goal of inclusive governance is to include those who have traditionally been excluded from political action, and thus, to reduce disparities in society. The success of democratic decentralisation depends largely on the achievement to include former marginalised groups in local decision-making and power structures effectively. Previously, many people on the basis of their social positioning - whether according to caste, ethnicity or gender - were excluded from certain social, economic and political opportunities. However, the decentralisation efforts in the country since early 1990s created an opportunities to all and enabled all disenfranchised and disadvantages groups to emerge as empowered participants in local democratic processes. Decentralisation, through the process of democratisation, created an enabling environment and act as a tool for social inclusion through enhancing the participation of the disadvantaged groups in local governance.

References

Adablah, Cornelius (2003). 'The Role of Civil Society in Decentralised Governance for Poverty Alleviation: The Experience of West Africa', presented in the workshop on Decentralisation and Poverty Reduction, Dakar, Senegal.

Agarwal, A and Ribot, J.C. (1999). Accountability in Decentralisation: A Framework with South Asian and West African Environmental Cases, *The Journal of Developing Areas,* Vol. 33: 473-502.

Brady, Henry, Schlozman, Kay and Verba, Sidney (1999). Prospecting for Participants: Rational Expectations and the Recruitment of Political Activists, *American Political Science Review*, Vol. 93 (1): 153-168.

Collins, Hugh (2005). *Social Inclusion: A Better Approach to Equality Issues?* 14 Translat'L L. & Contemp. Probs. 897, 900 (2005).

Crook, R.C. & Manor, J. (1998). *Democracy and Decentralisation in South Asia and West Africa: Participation, Accountability and Performance*, Cambridge: Cambridge University Press.

Cushing, P. (2003). *Policy Approaches to Framing Social Inclusion and Social Exclusion: An Overview*, Toronto: Roeher Institute.

Dahlerup, D. (2002). Using quotas to increase women's political representation, in *Women in Parliament: Beyond numbers* (revised edition), Available at http://www.onlinewomenin politics.org/ beijing12/Chapter4_ Dahlerup.pdf

______. (2006). Introduction, in D. Dahlerup (Ed.), *Women Quotas and Politics* New York, NY: Routledge, 3-31.

Edlund, L. and Pande, R. (2001). 'Why Have Women Become Left-Wing? The Political Gender Gap and the Decline in Marriage', *Quarterly Journal of Economics*, Vol. 117: 917-961.

Edlund, L., Haider, L.and Pande, R. (2003). 'Unmarried Parenthood and Redistributive Politics', *Journal of European Economic Association,* Vol. 3(1): 95-119.

European Commission (2005). *Report on Social Inclusion 2005: An Analysis of the National Action Plans on Social Inclusion (2004-2006)* submitted by the 10 New Member States.

European Union Social Protection Committee (2001). *Report on Indicators in the field of Poverty and Social Exclusion*.

Falleti, Tulia (2008). *Decentralization and Sub-national Politics in Latin America*, Cambridge: Cambridge University Press.

Hust, Evelin (2004). *Women's Political Representation and Empowerment in India: A Million Indiras Now?* New Delhi: Manohar.

Isaac, T. M. Thomas (2005). Women Elected Representatives in Kerala (1995-2000): From Symbolism to Empowerment in L.C. Jain (ed.) *Decentralisation and Local Governance*, New Delhi: Orient Longman, 366-416.

Krook, Mona L. (2009). *Quotas for Women in Politics: Gender and Candidate Selection Reform Worldwide,* New York: Oxford University Press.

Laidlaw Foundation (2002). *The Laidlaw Foundation's Perspective on Social Inclusion*. Toronto: The Laidlaw Foundation, http://www. laidlawfdn. org/ files/children/summaries_dec2002.pdf.

Larson, A.M. and J.C. Ribot (2004). Democratic decentralisation through a natural resource lens: An Introduction, *European Journal of Development Research,* Vol. 16(1): 1-25.

Lott and Kenny (1999). 'Did Women's Suffrage Change the Size and Scope of Government?' *Journal of Political Economy*, Vol.107: 77-95.

Luhman, Niklas (1990). *Political Theory in the Welfare State,* Berlin, New York: Walter de Gruyter.

Luhman, Niklas (1998). *Observations on Modernity,* Stanford: Stanford University Press.

Mani, Devyani (2003). 'Human Security and Decentralised Planning: The Training Experience of UNCRD' presented in the workshop on Decentralization and Poverty Reduction" Dakar, Senegal.

Mawhood, P. (1983). *Local Government in the Third World*, Chichster: John Wiley.

Nandal, Santosh (2003). Reflections on new partnerships between women and local self-government in India: a rural revolution? *Journal of International Women's Studies* Vol. 5(1): 122-131, Retrieved on November 27, 2007 from Infotrac.

Norris, P. and Inglehart, R. (2000). 'Cultural barriers to women's leadership: A worldwide comparison', IPSA 2000 paper.

Olsen, Hans Bjorn (2007). *Decentralisation and Local Governance*, SDC.

Overseas Development Institute (2002). 'Decentralisation and Governance', Key Sheet for Sustainable Livelihoods No. 11 for DFID and DGIS, available at www.odi.org.uk.keysheet

Phillips, A. (1995). *The Politics of Presence*, Oxford: Clarendon Press.

Ribot, J.C. (2002). African Decentralisation: Local Actors, Power and Accountability, Democracy, *Governance and Human Rights Working Paper No.8*, Geneva, UNRISD and IDRC

Rondinelli, Dennis A. and Cheema, Shabbir G (1984). Decentralisation in Developing Countries: A Review of Recent Experience, Washington DC: World Bank.

Shah, A. (1998). 'Balance, Accountability, and Responsiveness: Lessons about Decentralisation', Washington D.C.: World Bank.

Smith, B.C. (1985). Decentralisation: The Territorial Dimension of the State, London: George Allen.

Smoke, P. (1999). Decentralisation and Health in the Philippines and Indonesia: An Interim Report, available from http://www.sti.ch/pdfs/swap243.pdf, Retrieved in March 2011).

Teibout, Charles (1956). A Pure Theory of Local Expenditures, *Journal of Political Economy*, Vol. 64: 416-424.

Toye, M. and Infanti, J. (2004). *Social Inclusion and Community Economic Development Literature Review,* Ottawa, The Canadian CED Network.

World Bank (1997). *World Development Report,* New York: Oxford University Press.

World Bank (2000). *Entering the 21st Century, World Development Report 1999/2000,* Oxford: Oxford University Press.

12

Social Exclusion of Religious Minorities in India

Pawan Gurung

Social exclusion refers to process and outcome of keeping some social groups outside the power centre and resources as long as those social groups remain silent and there is no conflict, but as soon as they articulate their exclusion and demand their constitutional and human rights, then those who have subjected them to exclusion unleash reign of terror. It's a powerful source of discriminatory practice. Social exclusion has a broad concept; in this essay I have taken the realm of religion to discuss the extent of social exclusion in India. By the religion related exclusion, I mean to cover the exclusion of people from the domain of religious freedom and equality. A religion-based exclusion occurs when a person's religion or religious identity is seen to be sufficient ground for excluding him/her from the legal, economic and political benefits/rights available generally. Religious exclusion can be of two kinds. First, when a religious group excludes its own members from the domain of religious liberty and equality. A religious group may exclude its own members from many of its important practices. In medieval Christendom, ordinary, lay persons had access to God only via the Clergy. Even potentially, salvation was not, therefore, available to everyone. For centuries in India, a religious sanction has been granted to the horrendous practice of untouchability that excludes Dalits from, say, entry into Hindu temples. This is an instance of internal religious exclusion. In case of the external religious exclusion, the religion of a group is misrecognised, denigrated, deliberately falsified, marginalised or suppressed by the State or by the dominant group in society. Any denial of religious liberty and equality by members of one religious group to another religious group is external religious exclusion. So, the practice of external religious exclusion is rampant wherever there is persecution of religious minorities. Historically, Jews have been victims of religious external exclusion in most Christian societies. In India, it's the Muslims and Christians who have been the victims of the religious exclusion.

Despite minorities' rights that have been prescribed by the Constitution of India, the constant intensified discrimination and exclusion of religious minorities in social, political and religious realm is still a constant character and has threatened the secular fabric of the Indian democracy. Can we claim ourselves as a plural democratic citizen of a multicultural race and religion? Does the notion like Hindutva has any significance in multicultural religious place like ours? Is this way, we are going to tackle the challenges of communalism which has threatened the religious and cultural rights of the minorities.

Hindu Nationalists favoured democracy before independence not only because of the prestige they could draw from the claim that India has been a democracy since its antiquity; they also espoused it as early as the 1930s because this regime relied on the notion of majority rule.[1] Savarkar was favorably inclined towards democratic principles, because they guarantee the domination of the overwhelming majority, that is, the Hindus – a logic which would enable Hindi to become the national language. The universalistic discourse of democracy was evidently hijacked in order to promote deep communal interests.[2] This discourse has been a present - day propaganda of the RSS and its offshoots in favour of the disbanding of the Minorities Commission. Even though this Commission was established by the Janata Party, of which the former Jana Sangh was a component, the Hindu nationalist movement quickly criticized it as an institution responsible for the division of the nation. The aim was to remove some of the protections granted to the minorities because of their vulnerability and, in effect, to assert the strength of the Hindu majority.[3] The Fundamentalist organisation like RSS (*Rashtriya Swaymshevak Sangh*), VHP (*Vishwa Hindu Parishad), Bajrang Dal (Army of God Hanuman)* and BJP (*Bharatiya Janata Party*) leaders continues to question status of religious minorities mostly the Christians and Muslims. Sometimes, they accuse the secular parties for appeasing the minorities and sometimes they question their loyalty to the nation and often blame them as foreigners or invaders. Hindu Nationalist Organizations that includes the political branch, the Bharatiya Janata Party and the cultural wing, the Vishwa Hindu Parishad, the long – term aim of this organization is the spread of Hindutva, or Hinduness, and the transformation of Hindu culture into an undifferentiated, unified whole, for the purpose of achieving 'one nation, one people', one culture'[4]. This kind of singular Hinduism assumes that India has always been 'fundamentally Hindu', a community united by geographical origin, racial connection and religious beliefs.[5] Their coercive intention to apply *Hindutva (a mix of fundamentalism and fascism) or* (Hinduness) as a plan to unify the nation in one cultural skeleton refuses to recognise the minority status and their distinct socio-cultural status. The cultural nationalism of RSS highlights religious exclusivity, not inclusivity. No secular democracy will succeed without the acceptance of plural character in the field of religion. Its ideology of *cultural nationalism* is not only simplistic but also harmful for India's diversity. For RSS, diversity is weakness, but for democracy, it is vital for its existence. Hindu Rasthra is not a Hindu state; it is a modern phenomenon to impose pre-social hierarchies on all sections of society. It is the goal of certain sections of society which is the most beneficiary of current social privileges – the section of society which has gained in the process of development of last few decades (zamindars and Brahmins). The Hindu Rasthra which is trying to engulf the society since the last two decades is the battle cry of a section who again happen to be the upholders of the *status quo* vis-a-vis the social position of women, workers, Dalits and Adivasis. On the other hand, Indian nationalism is a positive concept, incorporating different religions, ethnicities and cultures and is an integral part of the term global village. The apparent target of the Sangh Parivar is Muslims. On the one hand, they have been so much battered by Hindutva fanatic forces that they cannot afford to lie quiet any longer. Second, unlike the Dalits, they lie in a sub – critical zone of backwardness where they find it difficult to come out of the grip of their own religious leaders—the Muslim obscurantist-claiming to be speaking on behalf of their own community. Thus, they face dual attack from Hindu fascism and Muslim fundamentalism. There is a limit to the legitimate interference of collective opinion with individual independence, and to find that limit and sustain against encroachment, is as indispensable to good condition of human life. As Mill in his *"Essay on Liberty"*, writes, *"If all mankind minus one were of opinion and only one person were of the contrary opinion, mankind would be no more justified in silencing that one person that he, if he had the power, would be justified in silencing mankind"*. The agencies and the personnel of the State were openly involved in the 1984 riots against the Sikh community, and the secular credentials of the Indian State were compromised irremediably in 1992 when the Babri Masjid was brought down and consequently riots swept the country. It is not surprising that religious minorities continue to feel disadvantaged. On the other hand, critics of secularism accuse the state of practicing pseudo – secularism, and pampering the minorities. The Shah Bano case in a profound sense bears on two issues for India as a polity made up of plural religious and cultural communities: (a) Should there be, and is there a necessity for, a uniform civil law code applicable to all citizens of India or should the customary 'personal laws' of different religio—cultural communities be permitted to be observed even though they manifest substantive differences in matters such as gender roles and rights, marriage, divorce, inheritance, property rights, etc., (b) If different system of personal laws are recognized as legitimate, how is the issue to be faced if there is a conflict or contradiction between the personal laws of different religio—cultural communities and provisions that are considered fundamental rights applicable to all citizens.[6] Shah Bano, a 62 year old Muslim woman and mother of five from Indore, Madhya Pradesh, was divorced by her husband in 1978. The Muslim family law and a few other civil laws are under the purview of personal laws in India. They are different for Christians, Muslims and Hindus and allow the husband to do this and not the wife. Shah Bano having no means to support the five children approached the court for securing maintenance from her husband. The Supreme Court felt for the need of remedy in the matter under section 125 of code of criminal procedure, which applies to everyone regardless of caste, creed, or religion. It ruled that Shah Bano be given maintenance of more, similar to alimony.[7]

The debate over the uniform civil code arises from the tension between two notions of rights in the fundamental rights section (chapter III) of the Indian Constitution.[8] It is the common tension found to be in the liberal democratic societies between the individual rights to equality and freedom, and the rights of religious minorities regarding religious, cultural and education autonomy. This tension has become most apparent in the personal laws which govern religious communities in matter of marriage, inheritance and legal guardianship over children, while the personal laws of religious communities have been considered instrumental for protecting the rights of religious minorities, they have also often discriminated against the fundamental rights of women as individual citizen.[9]

Some hardcore Muslims felt threatened by it. They had formed an organisation known as All India Muslim Personal Law devoted for upholding Muslim personal law. In 1986, the secular party which had an absolute majority in parliament passed an act the Muslim Women Protection of Rights on Divorce. That nullifies the Supreme Court's judgment in the Shah Bano's case.

In order to secure the support of influential Muslim power-brokers across north India, late Prime Minister Rajiv Gandhi disregarded the secular foundations of the State that had been fought for by his grandfather, and trampled on a political philosophy that had, according to conventional wisdom, afforded Muslims a measure of freedom and protection in country dominated by non- Muslims.[10]

As the Shah Bano case demonstrated, successive governments have failed to enact a uniform civil code as regards to marriages, and in this case, the dissolution thereof. A significant observation from this case was that despite a direct ruling from the Supreme Court of India, the Rajiv Gandhi government, in pandering to the Minority vote bank not only failed to protect the interests of a divorced female in a secular and even handed manner (Shah Bano was 62 and a mother five when her husband divorced her), the Muslim Women (Protection of Rights on Divorce) Act, 1986 was enacted.[11] The government's decision (the government in question here being that of Rajiv Gandhi associated with the Indian National Congress as the ruling party) to allow Muslim Personal Law to prevail in reversal of the Apex Court decision is one of the conspicuous grievances voiced by the leaders of the various components units of the Hindu Nationalist Movement (Sangh Parivar). It is constantly led forth by them as a case of the Congress's favouritism towards the Muslim minority at the expense of the sentiments and the interests of the Hindu majority. Shah Bano herself, under pressure from the mullahs, withdrew her claim. However, the earlier court decision is still on record, and there is a powerful drive among some court judges not to treat Muslims as a category excluded from the provision that are viewed as national in scope and applicable to all citizens.[12]

The major problem for the secular state, undoubtedly, the most serious problem, is that of communalism. It is tenacious loyalty to caste and community which tends to undermine the secular state at every turn. Communal loyalties easily lead to communal rivalries; any of these tendencies is greatly accentuated by underdeveloped economy in which there is never enough of anything to go around. Even after, the secular approach of the constitutional makers, it could not stop the happening of the multiple communal riots in India.[13]

The 2002 Gujarat violence depicts another shameful outcome of the communal hatred in India; it describes one of the severest blows to the notion of Indian secularism after the shameful act of demolition of the Babri Masjid in Ayodhya by the Hindu fundamentalists supported by the leaders of BJP implicitly. The incident started with the Godhra train burning and resulting communal riots between Hindus and Muslims.

The Godhra riot was all pre-planned makeshift from some fundamentalist organization from both the communities but most of the victims after the post-Godhra riots were 750 Muslims and 254 Hindus who were ultimately killed and 223 more people reported missing. Now my question is who is to blame for such a heinous crime? To the fundamentalist organisations who don't have even a fraction of humanism in their actions or the government who claims to be the represented of public security. It is quite often in the government who has interfered in multiple communal riots. I would rather see it as a place of majoritarianism cultural domination over the minority groups because the minority groups lack the number which is required in government jobs, private institutions, education political parties, etc. Majoritarianism is understood here as a political idiom in which secularism is subordinated to the interests of the majority community.[14] There is a great necessity for a uniform civil law code which is applicable to all citizens of India. Recognising different system of personal laws as legitimate, will lead to conflict or contradiction between the personal laws of different religions. The question of minorities is important in considering the prospects for the secular state in India. The presence of sizable religious minorities, effectively well organized and articulate, will be an important factor in the development of the secular state.[15]

References

1. Christophe, J. (2000). Hindu Nationalism and Democracy, in Francine R. Frankel, Zoya Hasan, Rajeev Bhargava and Balveer Arora (ed.) Transforming India: Social and Political Dynamics of Democracy, New Delhi: Oxford University Press, 361.
2. *Ibid.* 361.
3. *Ibid.* pp. 362.
4. Khilnani, S. (1997). The idea of India, London: Penguin Books, 151.
5. Froerer, P. (2007). Religious Division and Social Conflict, The Emergence of Hindu Nationalism in Rural India, New Delhi: Social Science Press, 3-4.
6. Stanley, T. J. (1998). The crisis of secularism in Indiain Rajeev Bhargava (ed) Secularism and its Critics, New Delhi: Oxford University Press, 427.

7. *Ibid.*, 428.
8. Bose, A. (2009). Hindutva and Politicization of Religious Identity in India, *Journal of Peace, Conflict and Development,* Issue 13, February, 18:1-30.
9. *Ibid.*, 18-19.
10. Corbridge, Stuart and Harriss, John (2000). Drifting towards Catastrophe: The Powerlessness of Congress – (I) in S. Corbridge and J. Harriss (ed.) Reinventing India Liberalisation, Hindu Nationalism and Popular Democracy, Cambridge: Blackwell Publishers, 115.
11. Tambiah, J Stanley (1998). The crisis of Secularism in India in Rajeev Bhargava (ed.) Secularism and its Critics, New Delhi: Oxford University Press, 430-431.
12. See open Letter to Muslims, Iquilab, 13 Nov. 1985, and rpt. in Ashgar Ali Engineer (ed.) The Shah Bano Controversy (Orient Longman: Hyderabad, 1987), 211.
13. Smith, D.E. (1998). India as a secular state, in Rajeev Bhargava (ed.) Secularism and its critics, New Delhi: Oxford University Press, 225.
14. Upadhyaya, P.C. (1992). The Politics of Indian Secularism, *Modern Asian Studies,* 26(4): 815-853.
15. Smith, D.E. (1998). India as a Secular State, in Rajeev Bhargava (ed.), Secularism and its critics, New Delhi: Oxford University Press, 189.

13

Empowerment of Women and Inclusive Governance in India

Anil Rajak

Introduction

In ancient India, women played a very important role in being a part of political and cultural activities. In early Vedic period, women enjoyed equal status with men. Rig veda and Upnishads mention several names of women sages and seers notably Gargi and Maitrey (Prema, 2012). But as time passed by, their activities became limited to their home and the male members became sole important persons in the family, thus giving rise to a strong patriarchal society. In modern India, women played important role in Indian freedom struggle and have contributed at par with their male counterparts in overthrowing the Britishers from India. The initiative, bravery, guts and headship that the women have showed in the freedom movement for the country's independence from colonial rule have given them widespread name, fame and significance in the Indian society. The names of Maharani Ahilyabai Holkar and the famous Lakshmi Bai of Jhansi had become iconic figures in the Indian political arena (Mukherjee and Panikkar, 1989).

Since then, our women have come a long way crossing tough hurdles, fighting for their survival and rights. It's very ironical that we worship different goddesses and also refer to one of them as '*Adisakti* (Jha, 2003) but when it comes to women in our societies, we tend to forget all these and look at them with prejudice. Women have always played important role in the past and are doing the same at present given the opportunities and favorable environment. "The extent to which the women are free to make decisions affecting their lives may be the key to the future, not only of the poor countries but rich ones too. As mother, producers or suppliers of food, fuel and water, traders and manufacturers, political and community leader, women are at the center of the process of change.... The most effective route to smaller families is to provide women with the means of social and economic self-determination; full rights in the family and society, excess in income and career development, education and health care, and real say in the decisions that their lives-of which one of the most important is family size" (UNESCO, 1991).

Operational Definitions

Empowerment

Empowerment has been defined as "increased well being, community development and self-sufficiency, expansion of individual choices and capabilities for self-reliance and transformation of power relations throughout the society (International Network of Alternative Financial Institution, 2004). Kabeer (2001) define empowerment as "The expansion in people's ability to make strategic life choices in a context where this ability was previously denied to them".

Women's empowerment is a new phrase in the vocabulary of gender literature. The phrase is used in two broad senses that are general and specific. In a general sense, it refers to empowering women to be self-dependent by providing them access to all the freedoms and opportunities, which they were denied in the past only because of their being 'women'. In a specific sense, women empowerment refers to enhancing their position in the power structure of the society (Bhuyan, 2006).

Keller and Mbwewe (1991, as cited in Rowlands, 1995) describe it as "a process whereby women become able to organize themselves to increase their own self-reliance, to assert their independent rights to make choices and to control resources which will assist in challenging and eliminating their own subordination".

Inclusion

The term 'exclusion' and 'inclusion' are two terms mostly used by politicians, social scientists and the public in the recent years. The term social inclusion first originated in French social policy in the year 1970s. It was given more emphasis during economic crisis of 1980s when state-sponsored republican tradition of solidarity was in vogue (Bhalla and Lapeyre, 1997).

The concept of inclusion means the encompassing of the entire population in the performances of the individual function systems. On the one hand, this concerns access to these benefits and, on the other, dependence of individual modes of living on them. To the extent that inclusion is achieved, groups disappear that do not or only marginally participate in social living (Luhman, 1990). Later, the term was theorised by the scholars like Bourdieu and Luhmann (Sonowal, 2008). The United Nations concept on social inclusion speaks as follows: "An inclusive society must be based in respect for all human rights and fundamental freedom, cultural and religious diversity, social justice and the special needs of vulnerable and disadvantaged groups, democratic participation and the rule of the law" (Sonowal, 2008). Social inclusion is based on subjective understanding of what 'right' or 'fair' is but this notion or understanding differs across countries, societies and individuals.

Exclusion

Exclusion is the denial of control over natural resources; the denial of opportunities for healthcare, education, housing; the denial of the right to participation in social, economic, political and cultural life; the denial of human rights and human dignity (Sayed and Balgopalan, 2007).

As a definition, "social exclusion reflects the multiple and overlapping nature of the disadvantaged experienced by certain groups and categories of the population, with social identity as the central axis of their exclusion" (Kabeer, 2006). According to Valencia, 2001 "Exclusion is not only segregation and marginalisation; it is a type of social relationship that does not recognize the other's right of existing." UK Department for

International Development (DFID) (2005) 'describes social exclusion a process by which certain groups are systematically disadvantaged because they are discriminated against on the basis of their ethnicity, race, religion, sexual orientation, caste, descent, gender, age, disability, HIV status, migrant status or where they live. Discrimination occurs in public institutions, such as the legal systems or education and health services, as well as social institutions like the household.

Constitutional Provisions and Empowerment of Women

Development and empowerment of socially disadvantaged groups is a commitment enshrined in the Constitution of India. The framers of the Constitution have made various provisions for empowering the women which are placed under Fundamental Rights and Directive Principles of State Policies. Some of them are hereunder:

Article 14 - Men and women to have equal rights and opportunities in the political, economic and social spheres.

Article 15(1) - Prohibits discrimination against any citizen on the grounds of religion, race, caste, sex, place of birth, etc.

Article 15(3) - Special provision enabling the State to make affirmative discriminations in favor of women.

Article 16 - Equality of opportunities in matter of public appointments for all citizens.

Article 39(a) - The State shall direct its policy towards securing all citizens men and women, equally, the right to means of livelihood.

Article 39(d) – Equal pay for equal work for both men and women.

Article 42 - The State to make provision for ensuring just and humane conditions of work and maternity relief.

Article 51A (e) - To renounce the practices derogatory to the dignity of women (Basu, 2001).

The Government also has enacted several women-specific and women-related legislations to protect women against social discrimination, violence and atrocities and also to prevent social evils.

1. The Equal Remuneration Act of 1976 provides for equal pay to men and women for equal work.

2. Hindu Marriage Act of 1955, amended in 1976, provides the right for girls to repudiate a child marriage before attaining maturity whether the marriage has been consummated or not.
3. The Marriage Act, 2001 amended the Hindu Marriage Act, Special Marriage Act, Parsi Marriage and Divorce Act, the Code of Criminal Procedure providing for speedy disposal of applications for maintenance; the ceiling limit for claiming maintenance has been deleted and a wide discretion has been given to the Magistrate to award appropriate maintenance.
4. The Immoral Traffic (Prevention) Act of 1956 as amended and renamed in 1986 makes the sexual exploitation of male or female, a cognizable offence. It is being amended to decriminalise the prostitutes and make the laws more stringent against traffickers.
5. Also a new criminal offence of 'Dowry Death' has been incorporated in the Indian Penal Code. An amendment brought in 1984 to the Dowry Prohibition Act of 1961 made women's subjection to cruelty a cognizable offence. The second amendment brought in 1986 makes the husband or in-laws punishable, if a woman commits suicide within seven years of her marriage and if it has been proved that she has been subjected to cruelty.
6. Child Marriage Restraint Act of 1976 raises the age for marriage of a girl to 18 years from 15 years and that of a boy to 21 years and makes offences under this Act cognizable.
7. Medical Termination Pregnancy Act of 1971 legalizes abortion by qualified professional on humanitarian or medical grounds. The Act has further been amended specifying the place and persons authorised to perform abortion and provide for penal actions against the unauthorised persons performing abortions.
8. Indecent Representation of Women (Prohibition) Act of 1986 and the Commission of Sati (Prevention) Act, 1987 has been enacted to protect the dignity of women and prevent violence against them as well as their exploitation.

9. The Protection of Women from Domestic Violence Act, 2005 provides for more effective protection of the rights of women guaranteed under the Constitution who are victims of violence of any kind occurring within the family and for matters connected therewith or incidental thereto. It provides for immediate and emergent relief to women in situations of violence of any kind in the home.

The Government of India has taken initiative to create National Commission for Women that would look in the matter of women and their welfare. In January 1992, the Government set-up this statutory body with a specific mandate to study and monitor all matters relating to the constitutional and legal safeguards provided for women, review the existing legislation to suggest amendments wherever necessary, etc. The National Plan of Action for the Girl Child (1991-2000) was launched in 1991. The Plan of Action is to ensure survival, protection and development of the girl child with the ultimate objective of building up a better future for the girl child. The Department of Women and Child Development in the Ministry of Human Resource Development has prepared a "National Policy for the Empowerment of Women" in the year 2001. The goal of this policy is to bring about the advancement, development and empowerment of women. Very recently the Lok Sabha passed the Sexual Harassment of Women at work place (Prevention, Prohibition, and Redresal) Bill 2010. The proposed Bill, if enacted, will ensure that women are protected against sexual harassment at all the work places, be it in public or private. This will contribute to realisation of their right to gender equality, life and liberty and equality in working conditions everywhere. The sense of security at the workplace will improve women's participation in work, resulting in their economic empowerment and inclusive growth.

Developmental Programmes for Women

Since independence, the Government of India, in the different Five Year Plans, has launched a various developmental programmes for the advancement and empowerment of women. Some of these programmes help to combat the poverty and exclusion of women, in general and rural women, in particular. The programmes which are women-specific and meant for their development and empowerment are as follows:

(a) Swarnajayanti Gram Swarozgar Yojana [SGSY] launched on 1999 a self-employed programme [credit-cum-subsidy] that aims to bring the assisted family above the poverty line in three years.

(b) The Rural Women's Development and Employment Project [SWA-SHAKTI] was launched in October 1998 as a centrally sponsored programme. It aims at establishing self-help groups [SHG's] which will improve their access to and control over resources (Vijayanthi, 2002).

(c) In order to meet the credit needs of poor women in the informal sector, the Rashtriya Mahila Kosh [RMK] was set up on March 1993. Its main objective is to facilitate credit support or micro-finance to poor women, as an instrument of socio-economic change and development.

(d) To improve the skills of the employment opportunities for women below poverty line in sectors of agriculture, small animal husbandry, handlooms etc., a programme called Supporting to Training and Employment for Women [STEP] was started in 1987.

(e) A Women's Economic Programme [WEP] was launched in 1982-83 for extending financial assistance to women's development corporations, autonomous bodies, and public sector corporations, etc., to train poor women in non-traditional trade.

(f) Socio-Economic Programme [SEP] was established to provide work and wages to needy women such as destitutes, widows, etc.

(g) Besides expanding the ongoing programmes, the government has evolved innovative schemes such as "STREE-SHAKTI" for empowerment of women and "SANTHWANA" for providing assistance to victims of various atrocities in the society. Stree Shakti was launched during 2000-01 with an objective to empower rural women and make them self-reliant by inculcating the habit of savings and proper utilisation of financial resources. Santhwana was launched during 2001-02 with a view to console and rehabilitate the women who are victims of various atrocities such as dowry, rape, sexual harassment, domestic violence, and such others (Panda, 2012).

(h) MahilaYojana (1996) — rechristened as Swayamsidha (2000-01), a centrally sponsored scheme — was launched for development and empowerment of rural women.

(i) 33 per cent of the seats in Panchayat have been reserved for women in order to improve their participation in the political decision-making process.

(d) For improving the literacy standard of women, Mahila Samakhya Programme was launched in 1989.

(e) In order to encourage institutions to undertake research projects in the area of women studies, the University Grants Commission [UGC] provides funds and grants.

(f) Health improvement measures to improve the health status of women, particularly expectant and nursing mothers, an Integrated Child Development Service [ICDS] programs was started in 1975 -76 which is still operating.

The Mahatma Gandhi National Rural Employment Guarantee Scheme (MGNREGS) is an example of a programme that explicitly seeks to provide paid work to poor women. The scheme mandates that at least one-third of workers should be women and makes several provisions to enhance the participation of women (for example, the provision of crèches at worksites for working mothers and a guarantee of equal wages among men and women).

Political Participation and Representation of Women

Women in India raised the issue of representation in politics first in 1917. At that time, it was basically a demand for universal adult franchise and political participation. By 1930, women had gained the Right to Vote, which initially benefited women from elite families. Women's involvement in struggles for political and civil rights in India were however sought to be linked to nationalist movements in alliance with males against the common foreign enemy. In any case, women's involvement in nationalist struggles changed their lives; in that event, though they were denied equal opportunities to shape the new state. They gained constitutional and legal rights but even after the right to vote became a reality for all women, their representation in the parliament, political parties and other decision-making bodies remained low even after independence, and after the Indian Constitution came into force in 1950 (Kaushik, 2004). A few women, no doubt, have attained positions as members of parliament and state legislatures and as leaders of opposition, and the like, but they are mostly through family dynasties or through male political patronage. However, the percentage of women in legislatures and decision-making positions always remained low. Women do not share the power of decision-making and are not involved in policy making in Indian democracy in proportion to their numerical strength. Thus, there is a gap between the formal idea of women's participation and their meaningful use of power (Kaushik, 1993). The quest for greater political representation of women is, therefore, still relevant.

Rural (inclusive) Governance and Empowerment

The notions of rural governance and inclusive growth are often paired in discussions of fiscal and political reforms in India and around the world. The rural governance and decentralisation, more generally, may be a critical element in ensuring that the benefits of national economic growth are shared broadly across the economy, both between rural and urban areas, and among different groups within rural areas. But, while there appears to be some level of consensus about what increasing rural governance means in the context of India, it is less clear what is meant by inclusive growth. This distinction is important because different elements of inclusive growth may be differentially served by increased democratisation of rural governance and by fiscal decentralisation (Mkhinze, Meenaksh is undaram and Nagarajan, 2012). Good governance creates a good environment for women's participation and empowerment of the poor especially those who are marginalised; it also improves development outcomes. 'Governance' is defined as the norms, traditions and institutions through which the country exercises authority of common good (Sinha, Singh and Bajpai, 2002). India follows mixed governance with centralised and decentralised mode of polity which is also complex. The Constitution of India formalised a part of Mahatma Gandhi's ideal villages of self-governing bodies in its Article 40. The Article states that the state shall take a step to organise village Panchyat and endow them such powers and authority as may be necessary to enable them to function as units of self-government. There have been many committees to look into the working of the Panchayati Raj Institutions (PRIs) right from Balwantrai (1957) to Singhvi committee (1986) but not much progress was made until 1992 when 73rd Amendment Act was passed. The PRIs were given constitutional status and women were given reservations at all levels, a landmark in the history of decentralised planning and inclusive governance. The Panchyati Raj system became applicable all over the country and gave vision of village level democratic governance and paved the way for rural development on both basis—participatory and community. The application of decentralisation in PRIs has meant administration and financial devolution of power from top to bottom through a three-tier structure.

73rd Amendment Act and its Impact on Women

It was Balwantrai Mehta Committee in 1957 that recommended inclusion of women in panchayats to carry out specific programmes for women and children. Later, they were nominated rather than elected in the panchayati raj system (Singh, 2008). This was just the starting of women empowerment in rural India which culminated in 1992 by bringing out 73rd Amendment Act. This Amendment added a new Part namely Part IX "The Panchayats" and a new schedule (the XI Schedule) to the Constitution listing the powers, authorities and responsibilities of the panchayats. Articles 243 to 243(O) were inserted in the Constitution dealing with the establishment and other matters relating to the panchayats in detail. The Act, *inter alia*, incorporates the following provisions to ensure the political participation of women in local government (Chhetri, 2010):

(a) Reservation of one-third of the total number of seats to women in all the levels of panchayat on rotation basis;
(b) Reservation of one-third of seats for women of SCs and STs from the total number of seats reserved for SCs and STs in all tiers;

(c) Reservation of one-third of offices of chairpersons of panchayat at all levels for women, including, women from SCs and STs.

With the reservation of seats for women, it has politically empowered the women in the rural India and given them confidence and sense of responsibilities towards families and societies as whole. The women have also got some freedom from their male dominant society and are capable of providing leadership to the people if they are given time, support, resource, training and freedom from men. Women are slowly becoming politically aware and assertive in their own rights. They are playing important role in taking decisions on day-to-day activities. The Table 12.1 indicates the total number of elected members and women representatives at decision-making levels in different tiers of panchayats in India.

Table 12.1
Composition of Panchayats in India

Panchayat Level	*Number*	*ER (Total)*	*Women (%)*	*SC (%)*	*ST (%)*
G.P	234676	2073715	41	18	11
I.P	6097	110070	43	22	13
Z.P	602	11825	40	16	11

(*Source: Chhetri, 2010*).

It clearly shows that India provides the most pronounced example of formal inclusion of excluded groups including the women in local self-governance. The Constitution guarantees reserved seats at all levels of local government for women (one-third) and for "Scheduled Castes" and "Scheduled Tribes" (based on their proportion of the total population). It also guarantees to women one-third of the leadership (chief) positions in the village councils. State governments have adopted legislation to enforce these provisions, with some states having made up to a 50 per cent reservation for women. The 73rd Amendments of the Constitution have impacted nearly 600 million Indian people in 500,000 villages. Interestingly, the percentage of women at various levels of political activity has risen from 4-5 per cent to 25-40 per cent.

Constraints in Women Empowerment

Both nationally, as well as at the state and local levels, women in elected bodies have been very few and even those who have been elected, when observed from closer quarters, present a complex picture. The money and muscle associated with the electoral process inhibits a large number of women from joining politics. Restriction on mobility, lack of control over resources and low literacy rates are well known obstacles but recent panchayat elections have evidenced a phenomenally large number of elected leaders much beyond reserved 33 per cent seats. Inclusion of the lower strata in Constitution should be followed up by granting them the opportunities to be represented in political parties and parliament.

It is very clear now that there are many provisions in the Constitution as well as laws enforced by the government from time to time for empowering women. But the situation has not changed as it should have been. There can be many reasons to it but the most important ones are:

- Lack of awareness
- Lack of social and economic empowerment
- Lack of political will
- Feebleness of accountability mechanisms
- Lack of enforcement by the police forces
- Lack of gender culture

Concluding Remarks

Even after 65 years of our independence, our women have not tasted the fruits of democracy. The government has been trying to mainstream gender issues through economic, political and social programmes. It can be argued among those, the most empowering policy has been 33 per cent seat reservation for women in panchayats through 73rd Amendment Act. As result of this Act, there has been process of institutionalising grassroots democracy and new elite has emerged with responsibility of supervising, as well as implementing the programmes, related to health, education, employment, shelter and anti-poverty schemes. The elected women representatives are engendering the development process at the grassroots level, with enabling support and capacity building by civil society agencies and women's groups. Despite deep-rooted systemic, cultural and political resistance, the above assessment shows that women have demonstrated the potential of challenging the iniquitous power relations in the public domain. The representation of more than one million women in the PRIs, directly and indirectly, has given an impetus to the processes of social mobilisation, and women are reinventing gender roles in private and public spaces. Interestingly, due to their increased visibility the gender-based distinction between the private and public space is becoming blurred.

References

Basu, D.D. (2001). *Introduction to the Constitution of India*, 19th ed, Nagpur: Wadhwa Publishers.

Bhuyan, D. (2006). 'Empowerment of Indian Women: A Challenge of 21st Century', *Orissa Review,* January, 60-63.

Chandra, B, Mukherjee, M., Mukherjee, A., Panikkar, K.N. and Mahajan, S. (1989). *India's Struggle for Independence*, 3rd ed., New Delhi: Penguin Book.

Chhetri, Durga P. (2010). Political Empowerment of Women through Panchayats in Sikkim, *Journal of Women's Studies*, Vol. 1: 39-45.

Bhalla Ajit, Lapeyre Frédéric (1997). Social Exclusion: Towards an Analytical and Operational Framework, *Development and Change*, 28: 413-433.

Department for International Development (DFID) (2005). Reducing poverty by tackling social exclusion, A policy paper.

Jha, D.N. (2003). *Ancient India in Historical Outline,* New Delhi: Manohar Publishers.

Kabeer, Naila (2006). "Social Exclusion and the MDGs: The Challenge of 'Durable Inequalities' in the Asian Context", Institute of Development Studies, paper presented at the Asia 2015 Conference.

Kabeer, Naila (2001). "Reflections on the measurement of women's empowerment" in Discussing Women's Empowerment - Theory and Practice, Sida Studies No. 3. Novum Grafiska AB: Stockholm.

Kaushik S. (2004). *Voice of Women in Panchayati Raj,* New Delhi: Friedrich-Ebert-Stiftung.

Kaushik, S. (1993). *Women's Participation in Politics,* New Delhi: Vikas Publishing House.

Luhman Niklas (1990). *Political Theory in the Welfare State*, Berlin, New York: Walter de Gruyter.

Mkinze, Hans P, Meenakshisundaram, SS and Nagarajan Hari K. (2012). *Decentralization and Empowerment for Rural Development: A Case Study of India,* Cambridge: Cambridge University Press.

Pandey, S. (2006). *Coercion versus empowerment: Perspective from People's Tribunal on India's coercive Population Policies and Two-child Norm*, New Delhi: Human Rights Law Network.

Panda, B.M. (2012). 'Financial Sustenance for Women's Empowerment – A Measure Towards Inclusive Growth', February-March, *Odisha Review:* 28-30.

Prema, A. (2012). 'Women's Status in India', *Indian Streams Research Journal*, Vol. 2(1): 1-4.

Rowlands, J. (1995). "Empowerment examined", Development in Practice, 5(2):101-107.

Sonowal, C. J. (2008). 'Indian Tribes and Issue of Social Inclusion and Exclusion', *Studies of Tribes and Tribal*, Vol. 6(2): 123-134.

Sayed, Y. and Balgopalan, S. (2007). *Education Enclusion and Inclusion: Policy and Implementation in South Africa and India,* DFID, London.

Sinha, R. Singh, A and Bajpai, P. (2002). 'Women's Participation in Panchayati Raj for Improving Health Status: A Case for Uttar Pradesh', *The Journal of Family Welfare*, Vol. 48 Special Issue, 77-91.

Singh, D. P. (2008). 'Impact of 73rd Amendment Act on Women's Leadership in Punjab', *International Journal of Rural Studies*, Vol. 15(1): 1-9.

UNESCO (1991). *Women Population and Development*, UNESCO, Bangkok.

Vijayanthi N. K. (2002). "Empowerment of Women through Self Help Groups: A Participatory Approach", *Indian Journal of Gender Studies,* Vol. 9(2): 263-274.

Index

E

F

I

J

K

L

P

Q

R